David —
With best regards,
Laura

May, 2003

D1609569

THE IDEA OF PROPERTY
ITS MEANING AND POWER

The Idea of Property:
Its Meaning and Power

LAURA S. UNDERKUFFLER

OXFORD
UNIVERSITY PRESS

OXFORD
UNIVERSITY PRESS

Great Clarendon Street, Oxford OX2 6DP

Oxford University Press is a department of the University of Oxford.
It furthers the University's objective of excellence in research, scholarship,
and education by publishing worldwide in

Oxford New York

Auckland Bangkok Buenos Aires Cape Town Chennai
Dar es Salaam Delhi Hong Kong Istanbul Karachi Kolkata
Kuala Lumpur Madrid Melbourne Mexico City Mumbai Nairobi
São Paulo Shanghai Taipei Tokyo Toronto

Oxford is a registered trade mark of Oxford University Press
in the UK and in certain other countries

Published in the United States
by Oxford University Press Inc., New York

British Library Cataloguing in Publication Data
Data available

Library of Congress Cataloging in Publication Data
Data available
ISBN 0–19–925418–4

1 3 5 7 9 10 8 6 4 2

Typeset by Hope Services (Abingdon) Ltd.
Printed in Great Britain
on acid-free paper by
T. J. International Ltd., Padstow, Cornwall

To
Thatcher, Katharine, and Anna

Preface

Although I had been thinking and writing about the nature of property for quite a while before, the impetus for the creation of this book can be traced to a letter that I received from Professor André van der Walt, then of the University of South Africa, in the summer of 1994. Through that letter, and extensive contacts with Professor van der Walt and others that followed, I was forced to focus on the questions that I had previously considered with sharper critical judgement and intensity. The story that Professor van der Walt told can be summarized as follows.

In the process of drafting a final constitution for the new, democratically elected government of South Africa, a particularly contentious issue was whether property should be protected by an entrenched, constitutional guarantee. On this question, the drafters faced profoundly conflicting needs. On the one hand, the inclusion of a property clause seemed advisable as a way to underline a commitment to social stability and foreign investment. On the other hand, there was widespread recognition that the simple entrenchment of existing property holdings would protect the fruits of past injustice and inhibit the accomplishment of critically needed reforms.

In their consideration of this question, South African drafters debated all of the possibilities: the simple exclusion of a property clause; the simple inclusion of a property clause, which would protect existing holdings without further elaboration; and the adoption of a property clause which would incorporate—through its understanding of 'property' or its subordination to other, 'specific' or 'general' constitutional limitations—the idea of both protection and change. In the end, a complex provision was chosen, which attempts to achieve—through internal understandings and external textual elaborations—some parts of each objective.[1]

The fundamental question of whether—or to what degree—property should protect was certainly not new. Indeed, it bedevils every constitutional or other legal system which attempts to address the question. The starkness of the conflicting needs in the South African context precluded, however, the glib or murky answers that property theorists such as myself had previously been inclined to offer. In particular, prior to my involvement in this debate—along with parallel efforts by other colleagues in the United States—I had worked on the development of a conception of property which incorporated, as an *internal* matter, the idea of collective change. Work on such conceptions—in which the

---

[1] For an excellent discussion of the South African debate and its underlying theoretical issues, in both South African and comparative contexts, see A. J. van der Walt, *The Constitutional Property Clause: A Comparative Analysis of Section 25 of the South African Constitution of 1996* (Kenwyn: Juta and Company, Ltd., 1997).

idea of property itself does not necessarily privilege individual interests—was largely a reaction to the seemingly ubiquitous assumption in American law that the protective force of property is its defining characteristic. Indeed, it was my work in the development of this alternative conception of property that first led the South African drafters to contact me. My exposure to the struggle in South Africa, however, led me to completely rethink this approach.

Although I still believe that a 'non-protective' conception of property has a vital place in critical analysis and law, the South African debate made me realize that neither the protective nor the non-protective conception of property was the answer to the property dilemma. Whether one considers the South African setting or our own, to see property rights in invariably powerful or impotent terms fails to capture either our own intuitive notions about property or its role in law. If we are completely honest, we must acknowledge that we sometimes want property rights to protect individual interests—and sometimes not.

Even more importantly, I came to realize that the way in which property theorists (including myself) had previously framed the question was itself part of the problem. Perhaps influenced by the general failure of property theory to advance the definition of property beyond a descriptive cast—property as incidents of ownership, or rights, or other privileges or powers, as applied to things, and so on—property theorists have assumed that the question was the choice of a protective or non-protective model, with the consequences that property has as a legal concept flowing from that choice. The limitations of this analysis, however, quickly become apparent when one attempts to design a constitutional system's guarantees. First, neither the protective nor the non-protective conception of property is satisfactory across the board. Moreover, if we acknowledge that we conceive of property in different ways in different settings, the simple availability of competing conceptions of property gives us no coherent reason *why* property—in particular cases—should be seen in protective or non-protective terms.

Indeed, we seem—at this juncture—to have stumbled upon a fundamental problem: whether property is, in fact, a coherent idea in law. As scholar after scholar has ultimately observed, it seems to be impossible to define or understand the idea of property in a way that identifies those rights that we believe to be 'property' or explains their relative power. Whether one embraces what J. W. Harris has called a 'full-blooded', protective conception of property or something less, why a particular conception of property rights is chosen, and how—if at all—the different conceptions of property found in law are unified, have remained remarkably obscure.

The focus of this book is whether *the idea of property, itself*, provides any answers to these questions. There is, I shall argue, a deeper analytical structure to the idea of property that we can uncover and—as a result of that discovery—deeper reasons that we can find for property's variable power. Using these insights, we can explain and justify, on new grounds, why some property claims are traditionally powerful and others not. We can also determine how claimed property rights in controversial or emerging areas *should* be treated—such as those involving the body as property, personal information as property, cultural property, and state redistributive claims.

The arguments of this book have, I believe, far-reaching implications. The book establishes, for instance, that a deeper analytical structure of the idea of property exists, and must be identified if the operation of this idea is to be understood. It establishes that the conventional belief in the choice of property as either protective or non-protective in nature is a false one—property can be either, and properly so. It establishes why the right to protection of property is, in fact, *necessarily* different from freedom of speech, freedom of religion, due process of law, and other rights—a question which is addressed, in the constitutional context, in the final chapters of the book.

A confluence of events in the past decade has moved questions about the nature and power of property into the centre of heated debate in academic, political, and legal circles. The need to sort out conflicting property claims in the aftermath of radical regime change in Africa, Eastern Europe, the former Soviet Union, and elsewhere, the emergence of 'new property' claims as the result of rapid technological advances (whether in information gathering, biotechnology, or other forms of intellectual property), the recognition of cultural property as an enforceable legal claim in domestic and international law, and the continuing controversy over government interference with land-use rights in the name of environmental and other public-policy objectives, have all worked to destabilize prior understandings of the nature of property and to push basic questions about the nature and protective power of property to the forefront of both popular culture and academic consciousness. So far, these developments have generated more questions than answers. It is the goal of this book to advance a new and (I hope) challenging way to understand this very powerful legal and social idea.

L. S. UNDERKUFFLER
Duke University
Durham, North Carolina
July 2002

Acknowledgements

Through the years, I have been the grateful beneficiary of conversations and critical review of portions of this work by persons too numerous to name. I am particularly grateful to Alon Harel, who first interested me in the subject of property and whose help was critical in the clarification of many ideas. I would also like particularly to thank Thatcher Freund, Judith Miller, Jeff Powell, Carol Rose, Pablo Ruiz-Tagle Vial, Joe Singer, and André van der Walt for their detailed review and invaluable criticism of many prior drafts; Kim Scheppele, for her invaluable comparative insights; colleagues at Yale University, Duke University, the University of Maine, Georgetown Law Center, and the University of Pennsylvania for ideas, comments, and other assistance in many aspects of this project over the years; and colleagues from throughout the United Kingdom, Europe, South America, and Africa, with whom I discussed these ideas at various conferences and the International Colloquium on Property Law and Theory held in Maastricht in 1995.

Some paragraphs in Chapters 2, 3, and 8 were originally published in IX *Canadian Journal of Law and Jurisprudence* 161 (1996), under the title 'Takings and the Nature of Property'; some paragraphs in Chapter 12 were originally published in 71 *Notre Dame Law Review* 1033 (1996), under the title 'Property: A Special Right'; and a few paragraphs in Chapters 5, 7, 8, and 9 were originally published as the Edward S. Godfrey Endowed Lecture, 52 *Maine Law Review* 312 (2000), under the title 'When Should Rights "Trump"? An Examination of Speech and Property'.

I am grateful to John Louth, my editor at Oxford University Press, for his excellent ideas and advice throughout this project. I am also indebted to Danielle Moon, Kate Elliott, Michelle Thompson, Sarah Nattrass, and Sandra Sinden for all of their invaluable help in the publication of this book.

Contents

Part III
PROPERTY AS A CONSTITUTIONAL RIGHT: NEW DIRECTIONS

Table of Cases

Table of Constitutions and Statutes

Table of International Treaties and Agreements

Introduction

> . . . In our time, property is the root of all evil and of the sufferings of men who possess
> it, or are without it, and of all the remorse of conscience of those who misuse it, and of
> the danger from the collision between those who have it and those who have it not.
>
> Property is the root of all evil; and, at the same time, property is that toward which all
> the activity of our modern society is directed, and that which directs the activity of the
> world. States and governments intrigue, make wars, for the sake of property. . . .
> Bankers, merchants, manufacturers, landowners, labor, use cunning, torment them-
> selves, torment others, for the sake of property; government functionaries, tradesmen,
> landlords, struggle, deceive, oppress, suffer, for the sake of property; courts of justice and
> police protect property; penal servitude, prisons, all the terrors of so-called punish-
> ments—all is done for the sake of property.
>
> Leo Tolstoy, *What Is to Be Done?*[1]

Since Leo Tolstoy penned those words more than a hundred years ago, not
much has changed. Property—as an idea and as a social and political institution—continues to be of tremendous importance in our lives. From the earliest
moments of childhood, we feel the urge to assert ourselves through the language
of possession against the real or imagined predations of others.[2] 'Property' as an
assertion of self and control of one's environment provides human beings with
a place of deep psychological refuge. With its concreteness and its unfailing
assurances, property promises to protect us from change and from our fear that
we will leave no evidence of our passage through this world. As Kevin Gray has
eloquently stated, '[o]ur lives are in every respect dominated by an intuitive
sense of property and belonging.'[3]

With this visceral power of property comes similarly visceral outrage when
property needs and claims—so obvious to those who assert them—are not honoured. For those who claim property, of whatever kind, the threat of collective
interference with this property is an emotionally charged issue. Whether property claims involve land, stock, ideas, body parts, personal information, or one's
cultural heritage, those claims are deeply held and fiercely defended. Property is
seen as a bulwark which protects material wealth, liberty, and autonomy; for the

---

[1] (New York: Thomas Y. Crowell and Company, 1899).

[2] The recognition of possessive relationships has been argued by some psychiatrists and social scientists to be an important part of the development of the human individuative sense. See Kevin Gray,
'Equitable Property' (1994) 47 (pt. 2) *Current Legal Problems* 157, 158 nn. 2 and 3 (citing studies). As
Gray writes, '[i]n this context we are still not far removed from the primitive, instinctive cries of identification which resound in the playgroup or playground: "That's not yours; it's *mine*".' *Ibid*. 159.

[3] *Ibid*. 158.

government to impair this bulwark—without recognizing that impairment—touches, on the deepest levels, the feelings of security of ordinary citizens.

Property's place in the vortex of contentious social and political issues is, of course, nothing new. In the United States, the role of government in the creation or abrogation of the rights of private property has been a source of recurrent social and political conflict. Revolutionary-era debtor relief laws,[4] early nineteenth-century legislative grants of private monopolistic and condemnatory powers,[5] the abolition of slavery at the end of the Civil War,[6] and other government acts generated bitter rhetorical and political debate about the nature, extent, and sanctity of claimed individual rights to private property.

The rapid rise of the regulatory state in more recent times has created new strains between private property's protective ideals and what can be seen as the exigencies of modern governance.[7] Although private property systems have recently triumphed—in a formal sense—over collective ones in Eastern Europe and elsewhere, the practical erosion of traditional property rights within the embrace of contemporary regulatory regimes continues apace. Private property may have won in the struggle for systemic supremacy, but the devil is in the details. The idea that property rights—particularly those involving land—are presumptively free from collective claims has been decisively abandoned, if ever it was true.[8] Environmental laws, zoning regulations, endangered-species laws,

---

[4] See James W. Ely, Jr., *The Guardian of Every Other Right: A Constitutional History of Property Rights* (New York: Oxford University Press, 1992), 37, 41.

[5] See Morton J. Horwitz, *The Transformation of American Law 1780–1860* (Cambridge, Mass.: Harvard University Press, 1977), 47–53, 122–139.

[6] See, e.g., Robert M. Cover, *Justice Accused: Antislavery and the Judicial Process* (New Haven, Conn.: Yale University Press, 1975).

[7] See Ely, n. 4 above, 101–134; Harold J. Berman, *Law and Revolution: The Formation of the Western Legal Tradition* (Cambridge, Mass.: Harvard University Press, 1983), 36–37.

[8] Indeed, property has long been understood to include ideas of trust and duties as well as rights. See, e.g., Carol M. Rose, 'Property as Wealth, Property as Propriety', in John W. Chapman (ed.), *Nomos XXXIII: Compensatory Justice* (New York: New York University Press, 1991), 223, 232–239; Laura S. Underkuffler, 'On Property: An Essay', originally published in (1990) 100 *Yale Law Journal* 127, reprinted in Elizabeth Mensch and Alan Freeman (eds.), *Property Law: International Library of Essays in Law and Legal Theory* (New York: New York University Press, 1992), bk. i, 403. Discussing eighteenth-century understandings of property in England, Robert Gordon has written:

> What strikes the backward-looking observer as curious is simply this: that in the midst of such a lush flowering of absolute dominion talk in theoretical and political discourse, English legal doctrines should contain so very few plausible instances of absolute dominion rights. . . . The real building-blocks of basic eighteenth-century social and economic institutions were . . . property rights fragmented and split among many holders; property rights held and managed collectively . . .; . . . property subject to arbitrary and discretionary direction or destruction . . .; property surrounded by restriction on use and alienation; property qualified and regulated for communal or state purposes. . . .

Robert W. Gordon, 'Paradoxical Property', in John Brewer and Susan Staves (eds.), *Early Modern Conceptions of Property* (London: Routledge, 1996), 95, 96. For an excellent discussion of competing ideas of property in American legal history see Gregory S. Alexander, *Commodity & Propriety: Competing Visions of Property in American Legal Thought 1776–1970* (Chicago, Ill.: University of Chicago Press, 1997).

historic-preservation statutes, cultural-property laws, and other collective restraints have overwhelmed traditional ideas about what property is and the extent to which it should be protected. As Kevin and Susan Gray have recently written, '[t]oday the concept of property in land may well denote no more than a temporarily licensed form of utility or user privilege which may be extended, varied, or withdrawn at the sole discretion of the state and on terms dictated by it.' 'So distant is this perception from the classic liberal image of property as a self-interested claim of unfettered power that some American commentators have now begun to predict a wholesale reconstruction . . . of property [in land] in terms of "socially derived" privileges of use.'[9]

The growing divergence between traditionally protective notions of property and the realities of the contemporary regulatory state has alarmed some observers. In particular, the courts' failure to protect what are seen as legally—indeed, constitutionally—cognizable property rights has drawn deep and abiding criticism. Property-rights activists have aggressively challenged the courts' inaction and have proposed a host of legislative initiatives on the national and state levels to roll back what they see as oppressive government interference with the rights of private property.[10] The courts' apparent failure to protect property rights has been decried by academic commentators as well. Richard Epstein, James Ely, Bernard Siegan, and others have argued that the courts' failure to protect property rights against the ordinary goals of government is a betrayal of the idea of property as a constitutionally protected or fundamental right.[11] Whether one thinks of zoning laws, historic-preservation laws, wetlands-protection laws, or laws that simply redistribute income or advance one person's commercial interests at the expense of another's, it is apparent, in the view of these writers, that the courts routinely—and, in their view, unjustifiedly—uphold government regulation that destroys or adversely affects recognized property interests.

One could conclude from current regulatory trends that we, as a society, have simply abandoned traditional notions of property-as-protection in favour of an

---

[9] Kevin Gray and Susan Francis Gray, 'The Idea of Property in Land', in Susan Bright and John Dewar (eds.), *Land Law: Themes and Perspectives* (Oxford: Oxford University Press, 1998), 15, 41, 43.

[10] See, e.g., Fla. Stat. Ann. § 70.001 (West Supp. 2002) (U.S.) (state cause of action for government regulation that 'inordinately' burdens real property); La. Rev. Stat. Ann. §§ 3:3602 (11) and 3:3610 (West Supp. 2002) (U.S.) (state statutory cause of action for diminution in value of agricultural land of 20% or more); Tex. Government Code Ann. § 2007.002 (5) (B) (ii) (West 2002) (U.S.) (state statutory taking if there is a market value reduction of 25% or more of the portion of the land affected by a government action). By the mid-1990s, all states had considered, and many had enacted, some kind of takings legislation. See Mark W. Cordes, 'Leapfrogging the Constitution: The Rise of State Takings Legislation' (1997) 24 *Ecology Law Quarterly* 187; Carol M. Rose, 'A Dozen Propositions on Private Property, Public Rights, and the New Takings Legislation' (1996) 53 *Washington and Lee Law Review* 265, 265–266 and n. 3.

[11] See, e.g., Richard A. Epstein, *Takings: Private Property and the Power of Eminent Domain* (Cambridge, Mass.: Harvard University Press, 1985); Richard A. Epstein, 'Property, Speech, and the Politics of Distrust' (1992) 59 *University of Chicago Law Review* 41; Ely, n. 4 above, 147–148; Bernard H. Siegan, *Property and Freedom: The Constitution, the Courts, and Land-Use Regulation* (New Brunswick, N.J.: Transaction Publishers, 1997).

idea of property that confers much greater collective control.[12] Although this may be true in part, the existing state of affairs seems much more complex. For although claimed property rights seem to enjoy little presumptive power in some settings, they retain tremendous presumptive power in others. For instance, property claims that involve patent rights, land titles, and 'autonomy' claims (such as the control of one's body as a property interest) enjoy tremendous presumptive power, as both an intuitive and a legal matter, even when opposed by compelling public interests.

We seem, in fact, to have multiple conceptions of the power of property in law—some of which strongly protect individual interests, in the way that rights are traditionally understood, and some of which do not. The impressions from existing literature are that such results are either aberrational and unprincipled exceptions to the power that property (as a right) should have, or—from the opposite view—that our insistence upon the presumptive power of property in some cases is simply evidence that the socially contingent nature of property has been, to date, incompletely recognized.

Is there any other way to make sense of this situation? Is there any other way to explain why title to one's land or the control of one's patented drug should have such presumptively powerful protection, while title to one's money (against redistributive taxation) or the use of one's land (in so many circumstances) should not? Is there a way to explain these and other results, other than the simple assertion that they reflect arbitrary normative judgements, which contradict the (supposedly) unifying idea of property?

It is the goal of this book to provide a theoretical structure which *explains, predicts, and justifies* the variable power of claimed individual property rights in law. There are, I shall argue, deep reasons for property's protective power, or lack of it, in these and other cases—reasons that are grounded in the nature of property, as an idea, and in the conflicts of that idea with competing public interests. I shall argue that the different conceptions of property that we can theoretically construct and—in fact—identify in law are not the products of random choice, but are the products of identifiable, understandable, and predictable power relations. It is not a random event that we use a protective conception of property when it comes to most disputes involving land titles, or patent claims, and a non-protective conception of property when it comes to environmental regulation or redistributive taxation. These results are driven—

[12] For instance, Eric Freyfogle has argued that we are witnessing the rise of 'a new property jurisprudence of human interdependence'. '[A]utonomous, secure property rights have largely given way to use entitlements that are interconnected and relative. . . . Property use entitlements will be phrased in terms of responsibilities and accommodations rather than rights and autonomy.' Eric Freyfogle, 'Context and Accommodation in Modern Property Law' (1989) 41 *Stanford Law Review* 1529, 1530–1531. See also Lynton K. Caldwell, 'Rights of Ownership or Rights of Use?— The Need for a New Conceptual Basis for Land Use Policy' (1974) 15 *William and Mary Law Review* 759, 766–775; Richard J. Lazarus, 'Changing Conceptions of Property and Sovereignty in Natural Resources: Questioning the Public Trust Doctrine' (1986) 71 *Iowa Law Review* 631, 632–633.

indeed, *predetermined*—by the nature of the individual claims, the nature of the collective claims, and the relations between them, that are involved in these cases.

Furthermore, I shall argue that although property is not unique among claimed rights in the sometimes failure of its protective power, it *is* unique among rights in the wide range of cases in which this treatment is justifiedly presented. Because of the particular nature of property, as an idea—and of the 'objects', or subjects, that may be claimed by this right—there are, I shall argue, distinct and compelling reasons why property lacks—*and should lack*—the presumptive power traditionally associated with rights, across a broad range of cases.

As a way to access these issues, I shall begin, in Part I, with an exploration of the nature of the idea of property in law. After an initial chapter which summarizes conventional attempts to capture the idea of property, I will proceed (in Chapter 2) to offer a different way to understand and analyse this difficult concept. Property, I shall argue, is a complex package of normative choices that is not fully or adequately illuminated by any of the conventional understandings of property that have been offered. Those understandings—which focus on the theories of rights that property may involve—identify and describe one dimension of common legal conceptions of property. Property is, however, considerably more complex. Selection of a theory of rights is necessary for any legally cognizable conception of property; in addition to this, we must (explicitly or implicitly) choose content for the dimensions of space, stringency, and time. It is only through specification of *all* of these dimensions that a legally cognizable conception of property can be constructed. And it is only through an examination of *all* of these dimensions and the questions they raise that we can illuminate all of the choices that property—as used in law—in fact involves.

In Part II, I will consider the broad question of what the power of individual property rights is—*and should be*—when they conflict with competing public interests. I shall begin (in Chapter 3) by analysing how the constituent dimensions of property that we identified in Part I are used to construct particular conceptions of property found in law. We will find, through this process, that two dominant conceptions of property emerge: the 'common' conception, in which property functions to protect the individual against collective interests; and the 'operative' conception, in which property performs a different—and far weaker—role. We will see, in Chapter 4, how the conception of property one chooses will have a practically determinative effect on whether individual property claims win or lose when confronted with conflicting public interests. We will also explore how the conception of property one chooses can influence our awareness of property's social context, and our idealized notions of the relationship between the individual and collective life.

The discovery of two entirely different conceptions of property in law is significant, in itself. This discovery does not, however, end our inquiry; in fact, it raises more questions than it answers. How can we have two conceptions of property in common usage, one of which gives the individual tremendous protection, and the other of which (in theory, at least) gives the individual no protection at all? Are there any articulable reasons why one conception is—*or should be*—used in some situations, and the other conception in others?

In the following chapters in Part II, I will attempt to explain, and justify, the use of protective and non-protective conceptions of property in law. I will argue, as the ensuing chapters unfold, that these different conceptions of property are not only explained—*they are commanded*—by the underlying nature of the property claims and the competing public interests that are involved in each case.

As a first step in this argument, I will begin, in Chapter 5, with a general discussion of the nature of legal rights and competing public interests. Under the traditional view of legal rights, rights are right-holders' demands that are fortified (by their classification as rights) against competing public interests. Rights, in this view, are discrete, conceptually 'bounded' entities which enjoy *prima facie* or presumptive power against public interests (and other non-rights interests) that oppose them.

Although this view of the rights/public interest relationship may describe many of the relationships between rights and competing public interests found in law, it does not describe all of them. In particular, for our purposes, it does not describe the lack of presumptive power that claimed property rights so often exhibit. In order to explain these seemingly aberrant cases, we must make a deeper inquiry into the nature of rights and opposing public interests, and the relationships between them. In particular, we must explore what I will call the 'core values' that claimed rights and competing public interests involve. These 'core values'—or the state of affairs that a particular demand is deemed to protect, and the reasons for that protection—identify the normative content of claimed rights and competing public interests. They also, I will argue, determine when—in the setting of particular claims—claimed rights will, and *should*, enjoy presumptive power.

In Chapters 6, 7, and 8, I will apply this discussion and the model that it generates to the particular question of the power of property claims in law. I will explore the 'core values' of various pairs of claimed property rights and competing public interests in an effort more completely to understand what they involve, and what (using our model) the presumptive power relations between them will—and should—be. We will see, by using our model, that the two conceptions of property that we previously identified are simply attempts to express (in concrete form) two different patterns of conflicting 'core values'— patterns which result, very predictably, in two different conceptions of rights/public interest relations. I will, in short, explain why—under existing law—claimed property rights sometimes have presumptive power and sometimes do not. I will also establish how property rights claims should be treated in cases in which the law is emerging or unsettled—such as those involving the body as property, personal information as property, cultural property, and state redistributive claims.

In the remaining chapters in Part II, I will further analyse these results, and will show how property is, indeed, *unique* among rights in the failure of its presumptive power across a broad range of cases. I shall argue that this result is grounded in the nature of the idea of property, and in the conflicts of that idea with competing public interests. Although the conditions necessary for the failure of a right's presumptive power occur only rarely (for instance) when speech is at issue, they are a routine occurrence in property cases. The fact that property claims so often fail to exhibit this power is, thus, not an aberrational or unprincipled result, as some critics have charged. Rather, it is an entirely predictable and justified one, particularly in cases involving external, physical, finite resources.

The idea that the presumptive power of property (or other claimed rights) will depend upon the values that these claims and their competitors assert may be frustrating to those who desire an across-the-board or simply mechanical outcome. It is certainly much easier to assert that property claims should be invariably powerful, or invariably not, than to assess the power of these claims on a case-by-case basis. However, the inability of across-the-board or similar theories to account for the clearly complex treatment of property claims in law—and our own conflicting intuitive views of this right—has long been identified as a profound, if not fatal, flaw in these theories.

There is, in addition, another great strength in the approach to property's power which this analysis advances. By rooting the presumptive power of property rights in the values that those claimed rights and opposing public interests assert, we can establish the relative power of competing claims *whatever* their nature and *whatever* their changing formulations. The truly difficult task that property theory has faced has been the construction of a workable theory for determining property's presumptive power while acknowledging that the values that property claims (and their competitors) assert are socially constructed, changeable, and often contentious in nature. There is a tendency in the pursuit of property theory either to ignore the socially constructed (and volatile) nature of property, in an attempt to provide predictive power for a proffered theory, or to acknowledge it and then—effectively—end the inquiry. One of the goals of this book is *both* to acknowledge the socially constructed nature of property *and* to proceed with a way to analyse difficult property questions.

In Part III, I shall explore the implications of all of these discoveries for the protection of property as a constitutionally entrenched guarantee. I shall argue that the nature of property, as we have discovered it, renders it fundamentally different—in very critical ways—from freedom of speech, freedom of conscience, due process of law, and other constitutional rights. This difference necessitates its different treatment, and lesser protection, as a constitutional right. Finally, I will argue that the nature of property itself—when constitutionally protected—compels state recognition of redistributive issues, and requires state assertion (in some circumstances) of redistributive claims.

*   *   *

Property has always involved an odd paradox. The idea that property rights are presumptively powerful, bounded, and protected is a deeply ingrained and enduring one. At the same time, this idea—when implemented by law—is deeply and seriously compromised in ways that other rights are not. It is the purpose of this book to explain, and justify, this seeming paradox in law. It is also to suggest—in the process—what questions we must ask, and what answers we should give, in determining what this socially, politically, and legally powerful idea will be.

PART I
PROPERTY AS IDEA:
THE HIDDEN STRUCTURE
OF PROPERTY IN LAW

1

What is Property?
The Question Posed

There is little doubt about the importance of property in our everyday lives, and as a fundamental concept in politics and law. Indeed, the universal human understanding of the importance of property has made it the rallying cry of diverse and often conflicting contemporary legal claims and political movements. The 'right to property' has been proclaimed by landowners who resist big government, activists who seek to preserve historic structures, feminists who demand reproductive control, privacy activists who fear an 'information society', and libertarians who demand protection for government-created largesse. Property—its privileges and powers—has been invoked by those who support environmental laws, and by those who oppose them; by those who demand land reform, and by those who oppose it; by those who claim reparations for historical injustice, and by those who oppose them. In virtually any critical social issue, and from virtually any perspective, the protection of property is hotly contested and of extreme importance.

Property reflects the ways in which we resolve conflicting claims, visions, values, and histories. Yet, despite this important role, there is remarkably little exploration of what property—as a socially and legally constructed idea—really is. Even in excellent scholarly work, it is usually assumed that the author and readers share a working understanding of property, and the discussion quickly moves to questions of property systems or desirable incidents of ownership. Large legal casebooks often devote hundreds of pages to the subject of property, with only the briefest discussion (if any) about what the *idea* of property— which unifies this discussion—really is.

The approaches of those who have addressed this question tend to fall into several broad categories. First, there is the layman's view that property is 'things'—tangible things, such as land, chattels, and body parts, and intangible things, such as patents, copyrights, stocks, and bonds. The idea that property is 'things' is, however, easily discredited by lawyers and philosophers for its awkwardness and incompleteness.[1] The idea of a man's coconuts being his property

---

[1] Most academics, at least, would agree with C. B. Macpherson that 'the current common usage of the word "property" [as 'things'] is at variance with the meaning which property has in all legal systems and in all serious treatments of the subject by philosophers, jurists, and political and social theorists'. C. B. Macpherson, 'The Meaning of Property', in C.B. Macpherson (ed.), *Property: Mainstream and Critical Positions* (Toronto: University of Toronto Press, 1978), 1, 2. Compare, however, J. W. Harris, *Property and Justice* (Oxford: Clarendon Press, 1996), 10–13 (arguing that the usage of the term 'property' 'to stand for things rather than rights over things' usually does no harm—and is often helpful—in understanding ownership relations).

makes no sense if he is stranded, irrevocably, on an uninhabited island; property has meaning only when human relations, or conflicting claims among people, are at stake. Furthermore, the idea of 'property as things' assumes a model of ownership—called, by J. W. Harris, 'full-blooded ownership'[2]—that involves a kind of complete freedom of individual choice regarding use, exclusion, and transfer that is (in fact) rarely conferred by law. Thus, although the idea of property as 'things' commands great cultural and rhetorical power, it fails to reflect the rich meanings of property in social discourse and law.

A more sophisticated approach is based upon Wesley Hohfeld's famous quadrumvirate. Under this approach, property (as enforced by law) involves claim-rights, privileges (liberties), powers, and immunities.[3] The virtue of this definition is its inclusiveness: since all legal rights are included, property rights—to the extent that they are legal rights—are undoubtedly included as well. With this virtue, of course, comes its vice. If all legal rights are property, then property—as a legally cognizable idea, at least—has no particular importance. Presumably, we could drop 'property' from our legal lexicon, and the universe of legal rights (otherwise defined) would be none the poorer. Although property might be understood this broadly, this approach does not capture, in any useful way, the distinctive features of this concept.

Acknowledging the problems of overbroad approaches, others have coupled the idea of 'property as rights' with more limiting ideas. In his famous essay, 'The Meaning of Property', C. B. Macpherson states that 'in law and in the writers, property is . . . *rights*, rights in or to things'.[4] The American Law Institute has adopted this approach, stating in its Restatement that property denotes 'legal relations between persons with respect to . . . thing[s]'.[5] This merger of the 'things' approach and the 'rights' approach seems to make sense; it adds to the theorist's sophisticated observation, that property involves relations among persons, our intuitive notion that property is somehow 'thing-based'. In one of the best statements of this approach, Stephen Munzer states that '[t]he idea of property—or, if you prefer, the sophisticated or legal conception of property—

[2] See Harris, n. 1 above, 29.
[3] See Wesley Newcomb Hohfeld, *Fundamental Legal Conceptions as Applied in Judicial Reasoning and Other Legal Essays* (New Haven, Conn.: Yale University Press, 1923), 23.
[4] Macpherson, n. 1 above, 2 (emphasis in original). For a similar formulation see Jeremy Waldron, 'Property Law', in Dennis Patterson (ed.), *A Companion to Philosophy of Law and Legal Theory* (Cambridge, Mass.: Blackwell Publishers, 1996), 3, 4 (emphasis in original) ('The law of property is about *things*, and our relations with one another in respect of the use and control of things.'). See also Kevin Gray and Susan Francis Gray, 'The Idea of Property in Land', in Susan Bright and John Dewar (eds.), *Land Law: Themes and Perspectives* (Oxford: Oxford University Press, 1998), 15, 15 ('The term "property" is simply an abbreviated reference to a quantum of socially permissible power exercised in respect of a socially valued resource.'); J. E. Penner, *The Idea of Property in Law* (Oxford: Clarendon Press, 1997), 2 (defending the view 'that property is what the average citizen, free of the entanglements of legal philosophy, thinks it is: the right to a thing').
[5] American Law Institute, *A Concise Restatement of Property* (St. Paul, Minn.: American Law Institute Publishers, 2001), 1. Those legal relations are 'designated by the words "right", "privilege", "power", and "immunity"'. *Ibid*. 2.

involves a constellation of Hohfeldian elements, correlatives, and opposites; a specification of standard incidents of ownership and other related but less powerful interests; and a catalog of "things" (tangible and intangible) that are the subjects of these incidents.'[6]

This 'rights plus' approach is lucid and useful; it is particularly useful when attempting to organize and understand legal relations that are easily cast in ownership terms. Natural resources, intellectual property, and even the human body[7] can be easily and productively discussed as 'rights' in 'things'. In addition, further discussion of the incidents of ownership—such as the rights to use, transfer, and exclude—can help to illuminate whether particular rights seem, as an intuitive matter, to be property rights or not.[8]

With the use of this approach, however, questions linger. Under this approach, one is uncertain whether the idea of property determines the list of 'things' that are property, or whether the list of 'things' is *itself* defining of what property means. For instance, do we consider certain rights in things to be transferable because (in common practice) they are property, or do we consider those rights in things to be property, because they are (in common practice) transferable? If, in fact, it is the latter idea that drives us—if things are property *because* they are transferable—then we need to know why this quality, apart from all other qualities, has been chosen as the core or cohesive idea that defines property interests. Although some writers intimate that there is a meaning for property which exists apart from simple descriptions of existing legal rules or social relations,[9] this meaning, and its source, are not obvious from the definitions themselves.

Some have attempted to provide criteria for the choice of particular rights, privileges, powers, and immunities as property by specifying what—as a policy matter—the goals of a property regime should be. For instance, theorists whose sympathies are rooted in economic liberalism argue that property

---

[6] Stephen R. Munzer, *A Theory of Property* (Cambridge: Cambridge University Press, 1990), 23 (emphasis deleted).

[7] For a particularly interesting discussion of body rights as property rights using ownership concepts, see *ibid*. 37–58. A compelling counter-argument can be found in Penner, n. 4 above, 111, 121–122 (arguing that only those 'things' in the world that are separable from human beings may be objects of property; and that this is not the case with our bodies).

[8] See, e.g., Munzer, n. 6 above, 47 (discussing the right to transfer as determinative of the identity and power of property rights); Lawrence C. Becker, *Property Rights—Philosophic Foundations* (London: Routledge and Kegan Paul, 1977), 18 (property rights of ownership include the rights to use, transfer, and exclude). Perhaps the most famous listing of the elements comprising 'full' or 'liberal' ideas of ownership is that offered by A. M. Honoré: ownership, in his vision, involves the right to possess, the right to use, the right to manage, the right to receive income, the right to capital, the right to security, the power of transmissibility, the absence of term, the prohibition of harmful use, liability to execution, and the incident of residuarity. A. M. Honoré, 'Ownership', in A. G. Guest (ed.), *Oxford Essays in Jurisprudence* (Oxford: Clarendon Press, 1961), 107, 113.

[9] See, e.g., Waldron, n. 4 above, 4 (emphasis in original) (distinguishing property, which 'require[s] [the law] to make certain decisions', from a chose-in-action, which 'exists only because the law has *already* settled certain disputes in a particular way. The philosophical issues raised by a chose-in-action are thus better regarded as issues in the law of contracts or corporate law, not issues in the law of property.').

should protect the fruits of individual labour,[10] while those who prize more intangible forms of human development argue that property should promote human flourishing[11] or the development of broad human capacities.[12] Such criteria usefully place flesh on the bones of property; they establish what—as an essential, normative matter—property should or should not accomplish. However, the specification of such goals does not tell us what, if any, essential qualitites—as an abstract matter—conceptions of property share. One can specify that property should protect the fruits of human labour, or promote human flourishing—yet neither goal consistently and invariably identifies what property is, and what it is not. It is clear that not all human labour or human flourishing involves property, and much is property that does not—under any ordinary understanding—fall within these rationales. In the end, we have a more sophisticated or detailed list of characteristics, perhaps, but a list still: property protects the rights to use, transfer, and exclude; or—property protects the fruits of human labour, or activities in which human beings flourish.

The seeming inability to advance the discussion of the idea of property beyond a simple list of incidents of ownership or desirable social goals has caused one commentator to charge that there is no structured or principled way to understand this idea. In his famous article, 'The Disintegration of Property', Thomas Grey begins by citing the tendency of modern scholars 'to dissolve the notion of ownership and to eliminate any necessary connection between property rights and things'.[13] With the dissolution of this bond, however, little is left:

> Property rights [are no longer] . . . characterized as 'rights of ownership' or as 'rights in things' by specialists in property. What, then, *is* their special characteristic? How do property rights differ from rights generally—from human rights or personal rights or rights to life or liberty, say? Our specialists and theoreticians have no answer; or rather, they have a multiplicity of widely differing answers, related only in that they bear some association or analogy, more or less remote, to the common notion of property as ownership of things.[14]

---

[10] See, e.g., Jeremy Bentham, 'Principles of the Civil Code', in C. K. Ogden (ed.), *The Theory of Legislation* (London: Kegan Paul, Trench, Trubner and Company, Ltd., 1931), 88, 111–119; Harold Demsetz, 'Toward a Theory of Property Rights' (1967) 57 *American Economic Review* (Papers and Proceedings) 347; Richard A. Posner, *Economic Analysis of Law* (4th edn., Boston, Mass.: Little, Brown and Company, 1992), 32–35. Other theorists, such as Carol Rose, accept the notion of property as a wealth-producing institution while rejecting many of the assumptions about human nature and appropriate social goals that often underpin liberal economic literature. See Carol M. Rose, *Property and Persuasion: Essays on the History, Theory, and Rhetoric of Ownership* (Boulder, Colo.: Westview Press, 1994), 3.

[11] See, e.g., Margaret Jane Radin, *Reinterpreting Property* (Chicago, Ill.: University of Chicago Press, 1993), 6 (emphasis omitted) (linking 'justifiable property relations' with the idea of human flourishing).

[12] C.B. Macpherson, 'Human Rights as Property Rights' (1977) 24 *Dissent* 72, 77 (property as a means to a 'full and free life', 'using and developing and exerting our capacities and energies').

[13] Thomas C. Grey, 'The Disintegration of Property', in J. Roland Pennock and John W. Chapman (eds.), *Nomos XXII: Property* (New York: New York University Press, 1980), 69, 69.

[14] *Ibid.* 71.

As Francis Philbrick famously stated, 'what is property may depend upon the action that is dependent upon the answer'.[15]

Distinguishing—on a consistent and abstract basis—the content of property rights from that of other rights may well be a hopeless task. Indeed, even commentators who believe that property remains a vital legal idea have modest expectations of what this kind of analysis, in the end, will yield. Munzer cautions, for instance, that 'the idea of property will remain open-ended until one lists the kinds of "things" open to ownership', with the compiling of the list an essentially descriptive or purely normative task.[16]

Is this, however, the *only* way usefully to approach, and critically analyse, this very important social and legal idea? As we shall see in the following chapter, although we may not always be able to establish—with any degree of certainty or predictive power—the *content* that distinguishes property rights from other rights, we *can* identify an underlying, organizational structure which property rights distinctively share. And, by recognizing this structure and its operation in law, we achieve new insight into the meaning and power of property.

---

[15] Francis S. Philbrick, 'Changing Conceptions of Property in Law' (1938) 86 *University of Pennsylvania Law Review* 691, 694. See also Jeremy Waldron, *The Right to Private Property* (Oxford: Clarendon Press, 1988), 26 (discussing the common view that the concept of property itself 'defies definition').

[16] Munzer, n. 6 above, 23.

2

Property's Four Dimensions: Theory, Space, Stringency, and Time

(i) THE FIRST DIMENSION OF PROPERTY: A THEORY OF RIGHTS

Let us begin with the familiar statement of the idea of property advanced in the previous chapter. Property, under this understanding, involves rights, privileges, powers, and immunities that govern the relative power of individuals over tangible and intangible things.[1] For instance, if land, trees, and water are at issue, property can be seen as the system of rules that governs control of these natural resources. If, further, we posit the existence of a system of *private* property, we can agree with Jeremy Waldron that property 'expresses the abstract idea of an object being correlated with the name of some individual, in relation to a rule which says that society will uphold that individual's decision as final when there is any dispute about how the object should be used'.[2]

There are obvious problems of indeterminacy in this understanding. The fact that property 'involves' such rights, privileges, powers, and immunities is hardly definitive; although this understanding apparently claims to define some property, it hardly purports—even by its own terms—to define all. Others have claimed that property properly includes much more than these 'object relations'; in the sixteenth and seventeenth centuries, for instance, 'property' or 'propriety' was widely used to include personal liberties as well as other interests.[3] This understanding of property went far beyond property as rules regarding physical objects and their analogues to include freedom of expression, freedom of conscience, free use of mental faculties, and free choice of occupations.[4] Although

---

[1] See, e.g., Stephen R. Munzer, *A Theory of Property* (Cambridge: Cambridge University Press, 1990), 17 (property as 'relations among persons with respect to things'); J. Roland Pennock, 'Thoughts on the Right to Private Property', in J. Roland Pennock and John W. Chapman (eds.), *Nomos XXII: Property* (New York: New York University Press, 1980), 171, 172 (property as the rights of ownership: liberties of use, powers of transfer, and claims to protection from interference by others).

[2] Jeremy Waldron, *The Right to Private Property* (Oxford: Clarendon Press, 1988), 47.

[3] See, e.g., Paschal Larkin, *Property in the Eighteenth Century* (Dublin: Cork University Press, 1930), 52–53; Casimir Czajkowski, *The Theory of Private Property in John Locke's Political Philosophy* (Notre Dame, Ind.: University of Notre Dame Press, 1941), 23 n. 62.

[4] For an extended discussion of the use of this conception of property in the American Founding Era, see Laura S. Underkuffler, 'On Property: An Essay', originally published in (1990) 100 *Yale Law Journal* 127, reprinted in Elizabeth Mensch and Alan Freeman (eds.), *Property Law: International Library of Essays in Law and Legal Theory* (New York: New York University Press, 1992), bk. i, 403, 409–418.

contemporary notions rarely go that far, many modern conceptions of property clearly extend beyond the simple notion of object—or even intangible object—relations. For instance, property has been powerfully argued to include reliance interests, a view adopted (to some degree, at least) by the United States Supreme Court.[5]

In addition, there are clearly *some* object relations that—while they involve rights, privileges, powers, or immunities—do not involve what we normally consider to be property relations. For instance, the rights or liberties of a bailee toward an object bailed, or the rights or liberties of a trustee toward the corpus of a trust, are not ordinarily considered to be property rights. One can attempt to rectify this problem by limiting property to 'ownership' rights; indeed, as many commentators have observed, identification of property with rights of ownership is the essence of the 'common' or 'ordinary' understanding of property.[6] However, this attempted refinement will also fail to provide the precision that we seek—ownership has such different meanings in different contexts as to have, in the end, little meaning at all. Ownership of land, chattels, ideas, jobs, and body parts involves such different configurations of rights, privileges, powers, and immunities that the addition of 'ownership' helps little, if at all. As Jeremy Waldron has written, there are 'as many ambiguities in the term "ownership" as there are distinct legal systems', rendering it, in the end, 'a mere . . . hook on which to hang various combinations of legal relations'.[7]

Despite these problems, our proposed definition clearly captures the essence of popular and academic notions about what property usually involves. Property 'as the rights, privileges, powers, and immunities granted over the tangible and intangible things of the world' may not be an unerring guide for sifting that which is property from that which is not, but it is a very useful starting point for our examination of the concept of property.

As a way to examine this concept further, let us take as an example a particular set of rights, privileges, powers, and immunities that enjoys virtually unanimous recognition (in our culture) as involving property: those that are involved in the ownership of land. Let us further posit, for the purposes of our discussion, a particular land-based power: the right of a title holder to use his land in the way that he, in his discretion, desires.

---

[5] See Joseph William Singer, 'The Reliance Interest in Property', originally published in (1988) 40 *Stanford Law Review* 611, reprinted in Mensch and Freeman (eds.), n. 4 above, 147; *Board of Regents of State Colleges* v. *Roth*, 408 US 564, 577 (1972); *Goldberg* v. *Kelly*, 397 US 254, 261–264 (1970). This view was recently restated with approval by the Court in *Nordlinger* v. *Hahn*, 505 US 1, 13 (1992).

[6] See, e.g., J. W. Harris, *Property and Justice* (Oxford: Clarendon Press, 1996), 5, 9 (ownership is the organizing idea in human property institutions; 'property talk, lay and legal, deploys ineliminable ownership conceptions').

[7] Waldron, n. 2 above, 29. Some authors are a bit more optimistic. J. W. Harris argues, for instance, that although 'any attempt to articulate a single conception of ownership . . . would be hopeless', invocations of ownership are united by the 'open-ended character' of the use-privileges and control-powers that they confer, their 'authorized self-seekingness, and the fact that they are relations between persons and assets'. Harris, n. 6 above, 75–76.

To provide a factual context for our discussion of this right, we will use the situation presented by *Lucas* v. *South Carolina Coastal Council*,[8] a case that was decided by the United States Supreme Court in 1992. The facts in *Lucas* present an individual claim that is—as a threshold matter, at least—clearly and unequivocally within the core of what are commonly believed to be property rights. It is therefore a particularly useful vehicle for beginning our exploration of the mysteries of property.

The operative facts in *Lucas* were straightforward. In the late 1970s, Lucas began residential-development activities on the Isle of Palms, a barrier island located near the city of Charleston, South Carolina. In 1986, he purchased two plots with the intention of erecting single-family residences on them. At the time of their purchase, these plots were within the area generally covered by the Coastal Zone Management Act.[9] This Act required owners of coastal land that was part of a 'critical area' to obtain a permit prior to the initiation of development activities. At the time of their purchase, Lucas's plots were not 'critical areas' under this Act.[10]

In 1988, the South Carolina Legislature passed the Beachfront Management Act.[11] The purpose of this Act was to protect the beach/sand dune coastal system from unwise development which could jeopardize the stability of the beach/dune system, accelerate erosion, and endanger adjacent property. As the result of the enforcement of this Act, in conjunction with the prior Act, development of Lucas's parcels was prohibited.[12]

Lucas challenged this result in the South Carolina courts, and later in the United States Supreme Court, claiming that it effected a taking of his 'property' without just compensation.[13] The South Carolina Supreme Court denied his claim,[14] and the United States Supreme Court reversed.[15] The results of this lawsuit are less important for our purposes than the questions that it raises about the nature and protection of what we call property.

Lucas's claim was that he—as the title holder—had a right to build upon his land, and that this right was, of itself, property. Recast in the general terms with which we began this chapter, we would say that Lucas claimed a property right, or *decisional power*, to determine how the object (land) should be used, regardless of the desires or interests of others.

It is apparent that the legal validity of this claim will depend upon what we consider property, as a substantive matter, to be. To express this more precisely, the validity of any property claim will depend upon the particular rights, privileges, powers, and immunities that we have decided (through our legal system)

---

[8] 505 US 1003 (1992).   [9] S.C. Code Ann. § 48–39–10 *et seq.* (1987) (U.S.).
[10] *Lucas*, n. 8 above, 1008.   [11] S.C. Code Ann. § 48–39–250 *et seq.* (Supp. 1988) (U.S.).
[12] *Lucas*, n. 8 above, 1008–1009.
[13] See US Const. amend. V ('No person shall be . . . deprived of . . . property, without due process of law; nor shall private property be taken for public use without just compensation.').
[14] See *Lucas* v. *South Carolina Coastal Council*, 404 SE 2d 895 (S.C. 1991) (U.S.).
[15] See *Lucas*, n. 8 above.

to confer. If the abstract idea of property is the 'concept' of property, then the particular rights, privileges, powers, and immunities that we choose to recognize are involved in determining the 'conceptions' of that abstract concept. We must know what these conceptions are—what particular decisional powers of individuals regarding things we will recognize—before we can know whether a particular claim, such as that made by Lucas, involves property that is recognized in law.

This brings us to what I shall call the first dimension of any legally cognizable conception of property. This dimension, which I shall call the 'theoretical' dimension, describes *the theory of the particular rights that is used for any particular conception of property*. It recognizes—with regard to private property— that *some theory of individual rights* must be adopted for a legally cognizable idea of property to have meaning.

One could object that the name for this dimension is misleading, since *all* of the dimensions of property that I will subsequently identify (as well as the resulting conceptions of property themselves) are, in fact, theoretical in nature. This is certainly true. However, for our purposes the dimension of 'theory' shall have particular meaning: it shall identify the 'theory of rights' that is used for a particular conception of property.

The theories of rights that have been used in American law for this necessary dimension are diverse and conflicting. For example, theories that have appeared at various times in the jurisprudence of the United States Supreme Court include the 'bundle' of 'traditionally' or 'commonly' recognized rights to possess, use, transport, sell, donate, exclude, or devise;[16] the 'fundamental attribute[s] of ownership';[17] the 'ordinary meaning' of 'property interest';[18] the right to protection of one's 'reasonable', 'investment-backed' or 'historical' expectations;[19] the right to 'anticipated [commercial] gains';[20] the rights enumerated in an executed

---

[16] See, e.g., *ibid*. 1031 (right to 'essential use' of land); *Hodel v. Irving*, 481 US 704, 716 (1987) (right to devise); *Keystone Bituminous Coal Association v. DeBenedictis*, 480 US 470, 496 (1987) (right to 'economically viable use'); *Loretto v. Teleprompter Manhattan CATV Corporation*, 458 US 419, 435 (1982) ('[p]roperty rights in a physical thing' include the rights to possess, use, exclude, and dispose of it); *Andrus v. Allard*, 444 US 51, 65–66 (1979) ('traditional' rights of possession, exclusion, and other powers of disposition; 'to possess and transport . . ., . . . to donate or devise').

[17] *Agins* v. *Tiburon*, 447 US 255, 262 (1980).

[18] *Nollan* v. *California Coastal Commission*, 483 US 825, 831 (1987).

[19] See, e.g., *Lucas*, n. 8 above, 1035 (Kennedy, J., concurring in the judgment) (protected expectations 'based on objective rules and customs that can be understood as reasonable by all parties involved', with such 'reasonable expectations . . . understood in light of the whole of our legal tradition'); *ibid*. 1055–1060 (Blackmun, J., dissenting) (discussing eighteenth- and nineteenth-century understandings of rights incident to land ownership as defining modern property interests); *Hodel*, n. 16 above, 715 ('investment-backed' expectations); *Keystone*, n. 16 above, 499 ('financial-backed expectations'); *Nollan*, n. 18 above, 847, 848 (Brennan, J., dissenting) ('reasonable expectations' possessed by landowners, and 'settled public expectations'); *Loretto*, n. 16 above, 441 (protection of 'historically rooted' expectations); *Kaiser Aetna v. United States*, 444 US 164, 179 (1979) (discussing 'a number of expectancies embodied in the concept of "property"').

[20] See, e.g., *Andrus*, n. 16 above, 66.

contract;[21] the recognition of the particular interest claimed as an 'estate in land' under state law;[22] the right to use, qualified by state nuisance law;[23] the 'common, shared understandings . . . derived from a State's legal tradition';[24] and the general body of individual rights existing under state law.[25] Legal scholars and other commentators have articulated similar and different theories. Property has, in different work, been defined as 'the rights of ownership', including rights to use, transfer, and exclude;[26] the 'twin notions of trespassory rules and the [principles established by] the ownership spectrum';[27] rights grounded in social convention, custom, practice, or law;[28] 'economically valuable legal rights' created by federal, state, or local law;[29] 'respect for reasonable expectations';[30] and interests that function like corporal property, in providing individual security.[31]

The complexities involved in the application of these theories can be illustrated by consideration of Lucas's claim. If the theory that we use is simply that of the 'traditionally' or 'commonly' recognized right to use, Lucas's claim may seem—at first blush, at least—clearly to involve a property right. However, we must also ask: *what is* the 'traditionally' or 'commonly' recognized right to use? Does it include the ability of a landowner to engage in activities that erode or otherwise endanger adjacent land? For instance, it is an established legal principle that landowners cannot engage in activities that constitute a nuisance to the land use of others.[32] Do Lucas's proposed activities meet this test?

If we were to use, instead, a theory based upon a landowner's 'reasonable', 'investment-backed', or 'historical' expectations, the answer is no clearer. Can

[21] See, e.g., *Louisville Joint Stock Land Bank* v. *Radford*, 295 US 555, 601–602 (1935) (rights under an executed mortgage contract); *Pennsylvania Coal Company* v. *Mahon*, 260 US 393, 414 (1922) (rights under a contract for sale of land subsurface rights).

[22] See, e.g., *Pennsylvania Coal Company*, n. 21 above, 414 ('support' estate recognized in Pennsylvania law).

[23] *Lucas*, n. 8 above, 1016, 1027–1030.

[24] *Palazzolo* v. *Rhode Island*, 533 US 606, 630 (2001).

[25] See, e.g., *Phillips* v. *Washington Legal Foundation*, 524 US 156, 164 (1998) (quoting *Board of Regents of State Colleges*, n. 5 above, 577 ('the existence of a property interest is determined by reference to "existing rules or understandings that stem from an independent source such as state law"'); *PruneYard Shopping Center* v. *Robins*, 447 US 74, 84 (1980) ('the several States [are] possessed of residual authority . . . to define "property" in the first instance').

[26] See, e.g., Lawrence C. Becker, *Property Rights—Philosophic Foundations* (London: Routledge and Kegan Paul, 1977), 18.

[27] Harris, n. 6 above, 5.

[28] See Robert C. Ellickson, *Order Without Law: How Neighbors Settle Disputes* (Cambridge, Mass.: Harvard University Press, 1991), 56–64, 240–264 (creation and enforcement of property rights on the basis of local custom and practice); C. B. Macpherson, 'The Meaning of Property', in C. B. Macpherson (ed.), *Property: Mainstream and Critical Positions* (Toronto: University of Toronto Press, 1978), 3 (property as 'a right in the sense of an enforceable claim to some use or benefit of something', 'enforced by society or the state, by custom or convention or law').

[29] Andrea L. Peterson, 'The Takings Clause: In Search of Underlying Principles (pt. 2)' (1990) 78 *California Law Review* 55, 62.

[30] Joseph L. Sax, 'Liberating the Public Trust Doctrine from Its Historical Shackles' (1980) 14 *University of California Davis Law Review* 185, 186–187.

[31] See Charles A. Reich, 'The New Property' (1964) 73 *Yale Law Journal* 733, 771–787.

[32] See, e.g., *Lucas*, n. 8 above, 1030–1031 ('principles of nuisance and [state] property law' are part of a landowner's title).

one 'reasonably' expect to engage in development activities which—although not prohibited (by statute) at the time of purchase—are subsequently so prohibited, on the ground that they endanger public resources and the lands of others? Furthermore, should a landowner's 'reasonable' or 'historical' expectations include knowledge of existing regulatory activity, which—although not, at the moment of purchase, restricting the particular property in question—might well, by its very nature, be extended to that property in the future?

Whether we may find a unifying core within these theories of property rights is a difficult question about which property theorists disagree. For our purposes, we need only appreciate that the theory of rights that we choose for our conception of property is clearly of critical importance. Until we have a detailed understanding of the particular rights that our conception entails, it is impossible to construct a legally cognizable conception of property.

(ii) The second dimension of property: space, or area of field

Our establishment of the need for a 'theory of rights' leads us to what I shall call the second dimension of property: that of 'space', or area of field. The adoption of a theoretical dimension—for example, positivist concepts of existing law, or justified expectations, or 'historical' understandings—means nothing until we know *to what* this theory is to be applied. If we choose, for example, the property holder's 'reasonable expectations' as the theoretical dimension for our conception of property, the question arises: 'reasonable expectations *with respect to what?*'. If we choose legal rules as the theoretical dimension for our conception of property, the question arises: 'legal rules *as applied to what?*'. The chosen theory of rights has meaning as property only with reference to a particularly described field of application. Our first, theoretical dimension must be accompanied by a second dimension: an understanding of *the space, or area of field*, to which the theoretical dimension applies.

The idea of a 'spatial' dimension for a conception of property is obviously (as a literal matter) more readily applicable to land or other corporeal property than it is to property of a different sort. For instance, where property of an incorporeal nature is concerned, descriptions such as 'scope', 'extent', or 'limits' may more appropriately apply. However, for the sake of simplicity, we shall label as the 'spatial' dimension that field, corporeal or incorporeal, to which our theory of rights applies.

This dimension of property is a curious one. In most common contexts, it is obvious and uncontroversial: rights in land pertain to land; rights in kidneys pertain to kidneys; rights to trade secrets pertain to trade secrets. If, indeed, a distinct (and uncontroverted) 'thing' is the subject of the property right, and if the 'thing' is (as an essential matter) simply equated with that right, this dimension will have little visible impact upon our resulting conception of property.

Often, however, property conceptions are much more complex. Let us take, for example, the ideas of property that are involved in 'takings' cases—cases where it is claimed that the government has taken an individual's property without paying for it, as required by law.[33] In the nineteenth and early twentieth centuries, it was assumed that the Takings Clause in the United States Constitution governed cases of governmental exercise of eminent domain or their functional equivalents;[34] in such cases, there was generally little question—from a spatial, geographic, or otherwise conceptually described point of view—as to what the property in question was. If title to a parcel of land is transferred from an individual to government, there is little doubt what the 'property' in issue (from a spatial perspective) should be deemed to be.

As the twentieth century progressed, however, a new kind of 'taking' by government was recognized: the taking of property by government regulation.[35] In these cases, it was held that if government action went 'too far'—if its economic impact on the property concerned was too great—its action would be a 'taking' of property, even if title remained in the private owner.[36] With the recognition of so-called 'regulatory' takings, the question of the spatial dimension of the property involved became of critical importance. Whether the regulation went 'too far'—whether the 'property' was too greatly impaired—would depend on what the 'property', as a spatial or conceptual matter, was deemed to be. Consider, for example, the *Lucas* claim. The degree of impairment of the 'property' interest in a case of this type will depend on whether the property at issue is understood to be a smaller area, on which development is (perhaps) entirely prohibited, or is understood to be a larger area, of which only part is subject to the development restriction.

Indeed, the importance of the spatial dimension of property in takings cases has been the subject of increasing commentary by the members of the Supreme Court. In *Keystone Bituminous Coal Association v. DeBenedictis,*[37] for instance, members of the Court disagreed sharply about whether the 'property' for takings purposes was the particular coal that the challenged legislation affected, or was, instead, the whole of the plaintiff's mining operation.[38] As Justice Scalia has candidly observed, '[r]egrettably, the rhetorical force of [the Court's takings test] . . . is greater than its precision, since the rule does not make clear the "property interest" against which the loss of value is to be measured. When, for example, a

---

[33] See n. 13, above.

[34] See *Lucas*, n. 8 above, 1014 (quoting *Legal Tender Cases*, 12 Wall. 457, 551 (1871) (U.S.)) (discussing historical assumption that 'the Takings Clause [of the United States Constitution] reached only a "direct appropriation" of property . . . or the functional equivalent of a "practical ouster of [the owner's] possession"'); *Transportation Company v. Chicago*, 99 US 635, 642 (1878).

[35] See, e.g., *Pennsylvania Coal Company*, n. 21 above, 415.

[36] See *ibid.*; *Lucas*, n. 8 above, 1014–1015.   [37] 480 US 470 (1987).

[38] Compare *ibid.* 496–501 (property interest in question was the entire mining operation, which was little impaired by the government action) with *ibid.* 517 (Rehnquist, J., dissenting) (affected coal was an 'identifiable and separable property interest', the use of which was completely impaired by the government regulation).

regulation requires a developer to leave 90% of a rural tract in its natural state, it is unclear whether we would analyse the situation as one in which the owner has been deprived of all economically beneficial use of the burdened portion of the tract, or as one in which the owner has suffered a mere diminution in value of the tract as a whole.'[39]

The spatial dimension of property can also involve whether particular rights should be severed from other rights, and treated as a separately identifiable property interest.[40] In *Penn Central Transportation Company* v. *New York City*,[41] for instance, the Court considered whether the 'property' in question was the 'air rights' above the building, which were completely 'taken' by the City's development prohibition, or was the owner's rights in the parcel as a whole.[42] In the *Lucas* case, we are required by this dimension to determine not only what the physical boundaries of the parcel of property are, but also whether the right to use should be severed—and separately considered—from the remaining bundle of ownership rights.

The spatial dimension of property is of obvious importance in 'takings' cases, since the recognition of particular rights—or other smaller, conceptually defined pieces—as the 'property' interest at stake will increase the impact (on that property) of the proposed government action, and make more pressing the owner's compensatory claim.[43] Although often less visible in other contexts,

[39] *Lucas*, n. 8 above, 1016, n. 7. In a recent case, the Court held that '[a]n interest in real property is defined by the metes and bounds that describe its geographic dimensions and the term of years that describes the temporal aspect of the owner's interest.' *Tahoe-Sierra Preservation Council, Inc.* v. *Tahoe Regional Planning Agency,* 122 S Ct, 1465, 1484 (U.S.).

Recent legislative attempts to determine the occurrence of a taking by specifying a threshold percentage of 'diminution of value' required suffer from this same difficulty. As Carol Rose has written, '[w]hatever else might be said of percentage limits, they ultimately fail to clarify one of the central issues of takings jurisprudence. To posit a 10% or 20% or 30% diminution in value as a taking still does not answer the question that has always dogged the diminution in value test for regulatory takings—"a percentage of what?".' Carol M. Rose, 'A Dozen Propositions on Private Property, Public Rights, and the New Takings Legislation' (1996) 53 *Washington and Lee Law Review* 265, 289 (footnote omitted).

[40] This question has been described by Margaret Radin as that of 'conceptual severance'. See Margaret Jane Radin, 'The Liberal Conception of Property: Cross Currents in the Jurisprudence of Takings' (1988) 88 *Columbia Law Review* 1667, 1676.

[41] 438 US 104 (1978).

[42] *Ibid.* 130–131. The latter conception prevailed. See *ibid.* 130–131, 136–137.

[43] See *Lucas*, n. 8 above, 1065 (Stevens, J., dissenting) ('The smaller the estate, the more likely that a regulatory change will effect a total taking.').

In an interesting and controversial approach, Hanoch Dagan proposes that the choice of what I call the spatial dimension of property be used 'as a proxy for egalitarian considerations'. Under his proposal, the 'preexisting value of the affected property' should encompass 'the value of [the] . . . parcel as a whole and, in the event that [the claimant] . . . owns other parcels within the relevant local community, the total value of these holdings'. As a result, public projects would be imposed as uncompensated costs on those most able to bear them. Hanoch Dagan, 'Takings and Distributive Justice' (1999) 85 *Virginia Law Review* 741, 767, 783 (footnote omitted). Cf. Kevin Gray and Susan Francis Gray, 'The Idea of Property in Land', in Susan Bright and John Dewar (eds.), *Land Law: Themes and Perspectives* (Oxford: Oxford University Press, 1998), 15, 38 and n. 131 (quoting *Wik Peoples* v. *Queensland* (1996) 187 CLR 1, per Kirby, J. at 244, 246 (Austr.)) ('There have been suggestions, particularly in Australia, that the scale of a landholding may impact upon the degree to which that land can properly be subjected to an estate owner's comprehensive regulatory

this dimension is, in fact, of critical importance in every legally cognizable conception of property: until we know the space or conceptual area of field to which our theory of rights applies, we cannot know—as an actual or functional matter—what our conception of property is.

* * *

The dimensions of theory and space, so far identified, are those that are used—consciously and unconsciously—in most ordinary and theoretical discussions of the nature of property. Property (it is argued) describes our rights, defined by the relevant theory, and applied to a space, object, or other conceptual field. Property is, for example, an individual's right to possession, disposition, and use of land, chattels, or other corporeal or incorporeal things. It is an individual's rights under an executed contract; it is an individual's rights under existing patent law.

This two-dimensional model is certainly useful; it is, indeed, as far as most theorists go. But does it in fact describe *all* of the dimensions that are involved in legally cognizable conceptions of property?

Upon closer examination, we find that identification of theoretical and spatial dimensions, without more, is woefully inadequate. We may know that a particular theory (such as the 'right to possess, use, devise, and exclude') has been chosen, and that this theory is to apply to a particular piece of land, geographically defined. However, this does not tell us *how*—to what degree—these rights are protected, or *when*—in time—their content is determined. These additional dimensions are rarely recognized by commentators or courts; however, they are, as we shall see, critical parts of any legally cognizable conception of property.

(iii) THE THIRD DIMENSION OF PROPERTY: STRINGENCY (OF PROTECTION)

So far, we have established that any legally cognizable conception of property involves the specification of a theory of rights, and an understanding of the space or conceptual area of field to which the chosen rights apply. From these dimensions, we can begin to assemble the structure of a particular conception of property. For instance, the 'absolute right to exclude', as applied to land, has a certain, definite meaning; it is different from the 'right to use' that land, 'subject to reasonable regulation'. However, identifying the theory of rights that our conception of property involves, and the field of application of those rights, tells only part of the story. The question remains: *if* a particular right falls within our understanding of property, *how* is it protected? With what *stringency—to what degree*—is it protected?

control'. For instance, it is difficult to justify 'absolute exclusory power under pastoral leases covering "huge areas as extensive as many a county in England and bigger than some nations"'.).

We shall call this dimension of property '*stringency*', or *the degree to which property rights* (otherwise defined by theoretical and spatial dimensions) *are protected*. Although this dimension is rarely recognized, it plays a crucial role in the construction of any legally cognizable conception of property.

To illustrate this dimension, let us consider some common property rights as portrayed in American constitutional jurisprudence. The rights to use, possess, exclude, devise, and so on are often cited as the usual incidents of corporeal property ownership. Because these rights are almost always described in the same breath, one might expect that they are equally held and equally protected. In fact, we find that this is not true. Suggesting a hierarchical ordering of these rights, the right to exclude has (for instance) been called ' "one of the *most essential* sticks in the bundle of rights that are commonly characterized as property" '.[44] It is '*one of the most treasured strands* in an owner's bundle of property rights';[45] violation of this right is '*qualitatively* more severe' than the violation of other property rights[46] and leads to an almost automatic right to compensation.[47] The right to pass property to one's heirs has been afforded a similarly important, rigidly protected status. Complete abrogation of the right to devise has been deemed 'extraordinary'—and compels compensation.[48]

This almost absolute protection for rights to exclude and devise must be contrasted with the 'sliding scale' of protection afforded to other property rights. Other rights, although recognized as property interests, are simply not held with the same sense of inviolable protection; their protection is far more a matter of collective whim. For example, the right to use—in particular, the right to protect or to enhance value through continuation of pre-existing, permitted use—has been consistently characterized as 'less protected' or 'less compelling' than other property interests.[49] Use restrictions, such as those imposed by zoning, do not 'extinguish a *fundamental* attribute of ownership'.[50] As a result, there is ' "no appropriation of private property" ' when there is ' "merely a lessening of value" ' due to government action.[51] The right to sell is similarly unprotected, particularly where the rights 'to possess and transport . . ., to donate or devise' the property remain.[52] Indeed, the Court's differing treatment of different property

[44] *Loretto*, n. 16 above, 433 (quoting *Kaiser Aetna*, n. 19 above, 176) (emphasis added).

[45] *Ibid*. 435 (footnote omitted) (emphases added).   [46] *Ibid*. 436 (emphasis added).

[47] See, e.g., *ibid*. 434–435; *Nollan*, n. 18 above, 831–832. '[T]his Court's most recent cases . . . have emphasized that physical invasion cases are special'. *Loretto*, n. 16 above, 432 (emphasis deleted). This view of the right to exclude has not remained unchallenged. See, e.g., Gray and Gray, n. 43 above, 38–39.

[48] See *Hodel*, n. 16 above, 716–718. For a very interesting critique of such simple formulations of justified testamentary powers see J. W. Harris, 'Inheritance and the Justice Tribunal', in Stephen R. Munzer (ed.), *New Essays in the Legal and Political Theory of Property* (Cambridge: Cambridge University Press, 2001), 106.

[49] See, e.g., *Andrus*, n. 16 above, 66 ('[T]he interest in anticipated gains has traditionally been viewed as less compelling than other property-related interests.').

[50] *Agins*, n. 17 above, 262 (emphasis added).

[51] *Andrus*, n. 16 above, 67 (quoting *Jacob Ruppert, Inc.* v. *Caffey*, 251 US 264, 303 (1920)).

[52] *Ibid*. 66. See also *James Everard's Breweries* v. *Day*, 265 US 545 (1924) and *Jacob Ruppert, Inc.*, n. 51 above, 302–303 (upholding sales bans on previously acquired goods).

interests has prompted some commentators to draw an analogy between prop-
erty-protection hierarchies and the hierarchical ordering of liberty interests in
American constitutional law.[53]

One could argue that this difference in treatment is due not so much to differing stringencies with which these interests are protected, as to differing sever-
ities of deprivation. In cases of physical invasion, for instance, the right to
exclude might have been totally abrogated, while in cases involving regulation
of use, residual uses might have remained. Although such theories may explain
some of the Court's holdings, they do not explain others. In *Loretto* v.
Teleprompter Manhattan CATV Corporation,[54] for instance, the physical invasion at issue—the presence of a cable wire and junction box on the exterior of
the owner's apartment building—was admittedly trivial in nature:[55] it was small
in size and was granted to only one entity. Although the landowner's general
right to exclude was far from totally abrogated, the Court upheld her takings
claim. Compare—with this—*Andrus* v. *Allard*,[56] in which a federal law that
prohibited all commercial transactions in the property in question was challenged. Despite the far more serious impact on the owner's claimed right to dispose in *Allard*, the Court denied this takings claim.

Indeed, in a recent case the Court discussed two wartime takings cases as
'instructive' on the question of different interests' levels of protection.[57] In the
first case, the government seized and directed the operation of a coal mine; this
was held to be a taking.[58] In the second case, the government ordered a gold
mine closed; this was held *not* to be a taking.[59] Although conceding that the
effects of the actions on the owners' rights were—as a practical matter—
the same in both cases, the different outcomes of these cases are explained (the
Court reasoned) by the intrinsic natures of the interests involved. The first case
involved 'physical possession' by the government; the second did not. As a
result, compensation was required in the first case; in the second, it was not.[60]
The different ways in which the claimed rights were treated cannot be explained
by differing degrees of severity in the deprivation of these rights; it can be
explained only by the differing degrees of stringency with which these rights are,
as an initial matter, protected.

So far, we have explored the dimension of stringency as it is apparent in the
differing protection afforded to different *kinds* or *theories of rights:* the right to
exclude or devise is more stringently protected than the right to use or sell, and
so on. The dimension of stringency may also be apparent in a second way: the

---

[53] See, e.g., John J. Costonis, 'Presumptive and Per Se Takings: A Decisional Model for the
Taking Issue' (1983) 58 *New York University Law Review* 465, 513 (arguing that the Court has
elevated 'property's dominion' (right to exclude) 'to a status coequal with . . . conventional civil liberties interests'—a status not accorded to other property rights).

[54] 458 US 419 (1982).   [55] See *ibid*. 438 & n. 16.   [56] 444 US 51 (1979).

[57] See *Loretto*, n. 54 above, 431.

[58] *United States* v. *Pewee Coal Company*, 341 US 114 (1951).

[59] *United States* v. *Central Eureka Mining Company*, 357 US 155 (1958).

[60] *Loretto*, n. 54 above, 431–432.

degree to which property rights are protected may depend upon the *kinds of 'things'* that are the objects of those rights. For instance, the Supreme Court has indicated that money is less protected than real or personal property, since money is fungible in nature.[61] Even things that are of roughly the same kind—such as those within the broad class of tangible objects—may be protected more or less stringently. For instance, although the rights to possess and exclude may be similarly defined with respect to one's kidneys and one's car, the degrees of protection that are afforded to these rights as applied to these things may be of vastly different characters. Finally, property rights—although involving the same 'things' and the same theories of rights—may be afforded more or less stringent protection because of the *different contexts* in which those rights appear. The differing degrees of protection that are afforded to property claims in different human contexts are explored by Margaret Radin in her seminal article, 'Property and Personhood'.[62] In this article, Radin observes that human beings feel far more attachment to objects that are 'closely bound up with personhood', such as 'a wedding ring, a portrait, an heirloom, or a house', than they do to objects that are held instrumentally, or are 'perfectly replaceable with other goods [or currency] of equal . . . value'.[63] This greater attachment which we feel for 'personal' property is, she argues, 'implicit in our law'.[64] It explains, for instance, the greater legal protection that is afforded to personal objects than to general wealth, and the greater willingness of courts to permit legislatures to destroy (without legal consequence) the expectation of gain from fungible development rights than to destroy (without legal consequence) 'personality ties . . . invested in a home or land'.[65]

The idea of 'contextual' protection for claimed property rights is also illustrated by the redistributive notions that are accepted parts of our culture and our laws. The stringency with which completely fungible and otherwise 'impersonal' property (such as money, stocks, bonds, and other kinds of general wealth) is protected often depends upon the size of the individual holdings involved. It is an intuitive and widely accepted principle that an individual's protective claims weaken as one moves from a limited core of personal wealth into the penumbra of larger and more widespread property claims. Because of this view, we accept as fair those laws that impose heavy taxes on luxury goods or that use graduated rates for income and estate taxation.

All of the different ways in which issues of stringency of protection may arise can be illustrated through use of the *Lucas* case. Lucas claimed the right to build on his land in contravention of state legislation which precluded additional shoreline development. Even if we were to decide, in this case, that our conception of

[61] See *United States* v. *Sperry Corporation*, 493 US 52, 62 n.9 (1989).
[62] Margaret Jane Radin, 'Property and Personhood' (1982) 34 *Stanford Law Review* 957.
[63] *Ibid*. 959.　　　　　　　　[64] *Ibid*. 991.
[65] *Ibid*. 1007. The greater stringency with which personal ties are protected may also explain the myriad of 'homestead exemptions' found in our laws. See, e.g., 11 U.S.C § 522 (b)(2)(A) (2001) (qualified exemption for the value of a debtor's domicile under federal bankruptcy law).

property includes (as a matter of theory) the right to use, and that this right applies (as a spatial matter) to the particular parts of the lots in question, an additional question would remain. To what extent—with what stringency—should this right be protected? Should it be afforded more protection, or less, than other land-based rights? Does it matter that this right, in this case, involves land rather than other corporeal or incorporeal 'things'? Should our decision be affected by the fact that this claim is essentially 'land-based', or 'wealth-based', or involves commercial investment (rather than 'personal' property protection) objectives?

In short, the dimension of stringency is of great importance, and appears in many forms. It may be a function of the particular theory of rights in issue, or of the particular 'thing' or 'object' that the chosen conception of property involves. It may also be a function of the extent to which particular objects of property are believed to be important for human 'flourishing' or human personality. In each instance, this dimension answers a crucial question: *how—with what degree of stringency*—the property rights (otherwise defined) will be protected.

(iv) THE FOURTH DIMENSION OF PROPERTY: TIME

We have now described the following dimensions necessary for any legally cognizable conception of property: theory, space, and stringency. We must have a theory of the particular rights that our conception of property entails; those rights must be understood to apply to a particular space, or conceptual area of field; and we must know how—with what stringency—those rights will be protected. Are these dimensions all that are necessary to construct a legally cognizable conception of property?

Let us consider, for instance, the conception of property that we could use in the *Lucas* case. For our theory of rights, we could use the bundle of rights that is usually associated with land ownership, and as are reflected in existing common-law land ownership and nuisance principles.[66] We could further agree that the space or conceptual field to which we will apply these rights will be the particular land parcel purchased by Lucas, as legally defined.[67] Further, we will agree that this 'property', involving land-based use rights, will be afforded an intermediate level of protection—less than the right to exclude strangers from one's homestead, perhaps, but more than simple income subject to taxation. Despite the understandings established so far, we find that critical questions remain unanswered. For instance, *when* were Lucas's rights—defined, as they are by 'existing law'—established? Were they established—and defined by 'existing law'—at the time of purchase, at the time that the use of the land commenced, or at some other time? Obviously, this question is of crucial importance: at the time of his purchase, Lucas had (in theory, at least) the legal right to build on his land, but by the time that building was to begin, he did not.

---

[66] See, e.g., *Lucas*, n. 8 above, 1027–1030.   [67] See *ibid.*

In addition, we discover another, lurking question. Even if a moment for 'fix-ing' his rights is chosen, were his 'rights'— as then defined—his 'property rights' forever after? Or did those rights change, as conditions changed? As Justice Stevens argued in the *Lucas* case, '[t]he human condition is one of constant learning and evolution—both moral and practical.' As a result, legislatures 'often revise the definition of property and the rights of property owners'. 'New appreciation of the significance of endangered species . . .; the importance of wetlands . . .; and the vulnerability of coastal lands . . . shapes our evolving understandings of property rights.'[68] Before we can evaluate Lucas's claims, we must have an answer to this question.

These reflections bring us to the final dimension of property: what I shall call the dimension of *'time'*. This dimension is as essential as the others in con-structing a legally cognizable conception of property. We may know the theory that our conception of property will employ; we may know the spatial dimen-sion to which it is to be applied; and we may know the stringency of protection that 'rights', recognized by our conception, will be afforded. The question remains: *at what moment, or point in time, is the content of these dimensions determined?* And is that content, once determined, *fixed and unchanging, or does it vary, potentially, thereafter?*

The importance of this dimension can be easily illustrated. Whether property (under our conception) is understood to be the 'ordinary meaning' of owner-ship, the 'reasonable expectations' of purchasers, the 'historically rooted expec-tations' of landowners, or the 'applicable background principles' of common and/or statutory law—applied to a particular spatial dimension, and protected with a particular stringency—the content of each of these dimensions must be determined with reference to a particular point in time for that content to have meaning. This content may be determined, for example, at the moment of purchase or acquisition,[69] at the moment of useful employ,[70] at a particular his-torical moment,[71] or at another time. However, *some* point in time must be chosen, as the referent for each.

In addition, once this point in time is chosen, we must make another decision: whether the content that we have chosen will remain fixed thereafter, or

---

[68] *Ibid.* 1069–1070 (Stevens, J., dissenting).

[69] See, e.g., *ibid.* 1027 (discussing the 'bundle[s] of rights' acquired by citizens 'when they obtain title to property'); *Nollan*, n. 18 above, 854–856 (Brennan, J., dissenting) (discussing landowner's 'reasonable' expectations at the moment of purchase, in view of existing encumbrances and laws). Cf. *Palazzolo*, n. 24 above, 626–630 (fact that laws were in place when land was purchased does not make them 'a part' of title).

[70] See, e.g., *Penn Central Transportation Company*, n. 41 above, 136 (discussing impact of the challenged regulation on the building's 'present uses' and, hence, on the owner's 'primary expecta-tion'); *Russian Hill Improvement Association* v. *Board of Permit Appeals*, 118 Cal Rptr 490, 494 (1974) (U.S.) (rights to develop site fixed at the moment that substantial on-site construction was begun).

[71] See, e.g., *Hodel*, n. 16 above, 715–716 (discussing 'investment-backed expectations' in land at the time of purchase, and rights which have inhered in property ownership as a 'part of the Anglo-American legal system since feudal times').

whether it will—in fact—vary in time. We could, for example, choose to protect—with utmost stringency—an individual's right to use land, with the content of that right determined (on the basis of 'reasonable expectations', 'existing
state law', or other understandings) at the moment of the individual's purchase.
The question remains: what if expectations, 'reasonable' at the moment of
purchase, become unreasonable thereafter? What if state law, existing at the
time of purchase, is thereafter changed? Does our conception of property fix
these rights—as of a moment of time—forever, or does it allow change in their
content, with the passage of time?

Few would deny that regimes of private property, as generally conceived,
include consideration of the public's interests. To the extent that individual
property rights are collectively conceived and collectively enforced, they will
(almost certainly) consider not only the interests of property owners but also the
interests of others in the community. With the consideration of collective needs,
however, comes the question of collective change. The dimension of time captures that question.

(v) THE DIMENSIONS OF PROPERTY, APPLIED

As was noted above,[72] academic efforts to capture the essence of the idea of
property have clustered around several dominant approaches. First, there is
recognition of the layman's idea that property is 'things'—an idea of property
that is easily discredited in view of property's clearly relational qualities.[73] At
the other extreme is an approach that simply describes property (as enforced by
law) as the claim-rights, privileges (liberties), powers, and immunities of whatever type that the law confers.[74] This approach has also been criticized, as fail-
ing to distinguish property from other legal rights and powers. The most
developed approaches to the question have coupled the idea of 'property as
rights' with more limiting ideas, such as rights (variously defined) in or to
things.[75] Although efforts of the last type are not without problems or controversy—for instance, what 'things' are the proper subject of property?— they
seem to capture, most accurately, what we believe property (as a socially and
legally constructed idea) to be.

The idea of (private) property as rights, privileges, powers, and immunities
that govern the relative powers of individuals over tangible and intangible
things is also useful in its obvious illumination of normative choices involved in

---

[72] See Ch. 1, above.

[73] See, e.g., Bruce A. Ackerman, *Private Property and the Constitution* (New Haven, Conn.: Yale University Press, 1977) (describing the layman's understanding of property).

[74] See Wesley Newcomb Hohfeld, *Fundamental Legal Conceptions as Applied in Judicial Reasoning and Other Legal Essays* (New Haven, Conn.: Yale University Press, 1923).

[75] See, e.g., Macpherson, n. 28 above, 2; Munzer, n. 1 above, 23; J. E. Penner, *The Idea of Property in Law* (Oxford: Clarendon Press, 1997), 49–50.

the enforcement of property rights in law. By focusing on the idea of property as *rights*, these theorists expose, very directly, the question of what—as a policy matter—the goals of a property regime should be. In response to this question, theorists have advanced answers that range from the traditionally individual-protectionist[76] to the broadly communitarian. Indeed, the development of theories of property that are explicitly different from traditional, individual-protectionist ones has been the objective of many recent commentaries.[77]

To place this work into the context of the analytical structure developed in this chapter, it is—we may say—a critical and detailed examination of what the theoretical dimension of property should be. This work is of obvious import-ance: whether the theoretical dimension of particular property is individual-protectionist, communitarian, or otherwise defined will obviously affect the nature, structure, and function of the resulting conception of property. The discussion that follows is in no way meant to detract from the importance of this work. However, the choice of a theoretical dimension for property—as import-ant as it is—only partially illuminates the issues that legally cognizable concep-tions of property involve.

To illustrate this truth, we will consider one of the very best recent efforts to examine systematically the idea of property as legally understood. In his book, *The Idea of Property in Law*,[78] J. E. Penner examines the rules, rights, and duties that make up what is commonly regarded as 'the law of property', in an effort to distil what property (in the legal context) means.[79] He believes that there is a coherent idea of property in law—one which can be distinguished from other legal relations (such as contractual relations)—and his book is an effort to articulate this idea.[80]

Penner begins with the proposition that the law, through imposing duties on others, protects our interests in things. In particular, '[t]he interest in property is the interest in *exclusively* determining the use of things.'[81] As Penner elabor-ates, this 'exclusion thesis' 'is a statement of the driving analysis of property in

[76] See, e.g., Richard A. Epstein, *Takings: Private Property and the Power of Eminent Domain* (Cambridge, Mass.: Harvard University Press, 1985).

[77] See, e.g., Gregory S. Alexander, *Commodity & Propriety: Competing Visions of Property in American Legal Thought 1776–1970* (Chicago, Ill.: University of Chicago Press, 1997), 4–7 (prop-erty as a way to choose and support a proper and just social order); John Christman, *The Myth of Property: Toward an Egalitarian Theory of Ownership* (New York: Oxford University Press, 1994), 125–146 (separating 'control' rights and 'income' rights in constructing a justified theory of prop-erty ownership); Kevin Gray, 'Equitable Property' (1994) 47 (pt. 2) *Current Legal Problems* 157, 208–209 (property as including the values of human dignity and the 'sense of the reciprocal respon-sibility which each citizen owes to his or her community'); Carol M. Rose, 'Environmental Lessons' (1994) 27 *Loyola Los Angeles Law Review* 1023, 1042–1043 (ideas of stewardship and trusteeship as a part of property-rights ideas); Joseph William Singer, *Entitlement: The Paradoxes of Property* (New Haven, Conn.: Yale University Press, 2000), 207–209 (arguing that obligations to others are an inherent part of traditional understandings of property); Underkuffler, n. 4 above, 409–423 (advocating the idea of property as encompassing a broad range of human liberties, within a collec-tive context of support and restraint).

[78] (Oxford: Clarendon Press, 1997). [79] *Ibid.* 3. [80] *Ibid.* 37.
[81] *Ibid.* 49 (emphasis in original).

legal systems. It characterizes property primarily as a protected sphere of indefinite and undefined activity, in which an owner may do anything with the thing he owns.'[82] Exclusion is, furthermore, intimately tied to the idea of alienabilty: 'it includes the rights to abandon [a thing] . . ., to share it, to license it to others (either exclusively or not), and to give it to others in its entirety'.[83]

In addition, '[i]f property is a right to things, we must provide some characterization of the things that can be property.'[84] Penner distinguishes ' "things" which lack personality, whether objects, space, ideas, and even particular concretely specified relations between people, such as debts', from 'things' which significantly involve 'personality-rich relationships with other people'.[85] It is only the former that the law treats as property in conventional terms, and Penner argues that this distinction should—as an analytical matter—be largely maintained. He restates this distinction in terms of what he calls the 'separability thesis': that property involves only those things in the world 'which are contingently associated with any particular owner', that is, they are separable from that owner, and 'in theory nothing of normative consequence beyond the fact that the ownership has changed occurs when [the] . . . object of property is alienated to another'.[86]

We have, in Penner's work, a carefully detailed and intuitively resonant account of the understanding of property that one finds in law; indeed, there is no doubt but that Penner's work is one of the best accounts one can find of the kinds of rights that property—as legally understood—involves. However, when one considers this account of property in light of the dimensions of property that we identified in the last chapter, it is apparent that vital pieces of the puzzle are missing. For instance, although property may indeed involve rights to exclude others from separable things—thus providing, in effect, understandings of the theoretical and spatial dimensions of property—critical questions remain unanswered. With what *stringency* are these rights protected? And, once protected, must these rights remain protected forever? Or does their content, or enforceability, vary in *time*?

One can, perhaps, guess at Penner's answers to these questions. For instance, his emphasis on the interest in property as involving the individual's interest in 'exclusively determining the use of things',[87] and as a 'protected sphere of indefinite and undefined activity',[88] seems to imply a stringency of protection that is very high. And to the extent that individual protection is the paramount feature and purpose of property rights, the idea that collective change of those rights is permissible—as a part of our understanding of property—seems highly unlikely. Elsewhere, however, Penner stresses the normative dimension

[82] (Oxford: Clarendon Press, 1997), 72.   [83] *Ibid.* 103.   [84] *Ibid.* 105.   [85] *Ibid.*
[86] *Ibid.* 111.
[87] *Ibid.* 49. See also *ibid.* 75 ('The important feature of property is the individual's *determination of the disposition* of a thing'.) (emphasis in original).
[88] *Ibid.* 72.

of property rights, and their existence in social context,[89] so the answers to these questions are far from clear.

In even the best theoretical work on the nature of property, one tends to find rich accounts of the theoretical dimension of property, occasional mention of the spatial dimension, and little or no attention to the dimensions of stringency or time. It is perhaps understandable that these accounts are missing discussions of these dimensions of property, since the body of property law—with which these accounts are primarily concerned—almost always omits discussion of them as well. We must remember, however, that the theoretical and spatial dimensions of property—as important as they are—only partially tell the deeper story of property. If we are to be aware of *all* of the normative choices that property involves—if we are not simply to assume, to our detriment, certain characteristics of property rights, without critical evaluation—we must remember all of the dimensions of property: theory, space, stringency and time. Only then will we be fully aware of what the idea of property involves, and—as is the subject of the following chapters—how it operates, and *should* operate, as a protective force in law.

---

[89] See, e.g., *ibid.* 50.

PART II
PROPERTY AS PROTECTION: THE CLASH BETWEEN PROPERTY RIGHTS AND COMPETING PUBLIC INTERESTS

3

The Power of Property Claims in Law: The Emergence of Two Visions

In Part I, we identified the four constituent dimensions of any legally cognizable conception of property: theory, space, stringency, and time. We also saw how we must be aware of all of these dimensions, and the questions that they raise, if we are to understand in any depth how the idea of property operates in law.

In Part II, we will consider the broad question of what the power of individual property rights is—and should be—when they conflict with competing public interests. We will begin (in this chapter) by using the insights developed in Part I to analyse the common conceptions of property found in American jurisprudence. We will find, curiously, that two different conceptions of property emerge, with very different structures and very different functions; and that these conceptions provide radically different answers to questions of individual protection against collective interests.

The primary focus for our examination will be the conceptions of property found in the Supreme Court's interpretations of the Takings Clause of the Fifth Amendment to the United States Constitution, and related commentary. These cases deal predominantly with individual/collective conflict over the rights, privileges, powers, and immunities exercised over land and other resources. The American preoccupation with constitutional cases—in particular, takings cases—as the battleground for determining the meaning of rights of private property has been a subject of some mystification to observers abroad.[1] Clearly, issues about the nature, scope, and legitimacy of private property claims occur in contexts far more varied than simply that of constitutional constraints on government action. Indeed, most governmental issues, and all disputes between private citizens, do not involve constitutional questions at all. It is, however, the struggle between individual and collective, refracted through various constitutional guarantees, that has fired the American debate about the meaning of rights in private property.[2] In particular, the Takings Clause has provided the

---

[1] See, e.g., A. J. van der Walt, 'Subject and Society in Property Theory—A Review of Property Theories and Debates in Recent Literature: Part II', 1995–2 *Journal of South African Law* 322, 332 (discussing the 'typically American' framing of property issues in terms of the 'constitutional struggle about takings and due process').

[2] For discussion of the history of property in American life, as mirrored through constitutional issues, see Gregory S. Alexander, *Commodity & Propriety: Competing Visions of Property in*

contemporary stage for real and symbolic struggles among different visions of individual prerogative and state power.[3] As a result, takings cases and commentary provide a rich trove of ideas about these issues. In addition, since—as a matter of apparent constitutional and common assumption—the meaning of 'property' in the constitutional context is the same as that used in private law,[4] the conceptions of property found in takings cases should—roughly speaking—mirror the conceptions of property found in private law.

(i) PROPERTY AS PROTECTION: THE 'COMMON'
CONCEPTION OF PROPERTY IN LAW

(a) **Starting points**

Let us begin, then, our examination of the conceptions of property that are used in Supreme Court takings jurisprudence. In sketching its conceptions of property, the Court invariably begins with the adoption of a theory of the particular rights that comprise its idea of property—the choice, in our parlance, of a 'theoretical' dimension of property. For instance, the Court has stated that cognizable property interests are determined by reference to the 'common, shared understandings . . . derived from a State's legal tradition'.[5] Or the Court has described '[p]roperty rights in a physical thing' 'as the rights "to possess, use and dispose of it"'.[6] Or the Court has declared that property is comprised of the holder's 'distinct investment-backed expectations'.[7]

In addition, the Court has established—explicitly or implicitly—the space, or conceptual area of field, to which its theory of property applies. This 'spatial'

American Legal Thought 1776–1970 (Chicago, Ill.: University of Chicago Press, 1997); James W. Ely, Jr., *The Guardian of Every Other Right: A Constitutional History of Property Rights* (New York: Oxford University Press, 1992).

[3] For instance, in very recent years property-rights activists have proposed a host of national legislative initiatives which attempt to change the balance between government action and citizen protection that has been struck by the Supreme Court. See, e.g., Private Property Protection Act of 1997, H.R. 95, 105th Cong. (1997) (U.S.); Private Property Rights Implementation Act of 1997, H.R. 1534, 105th Cong. (1997) (U.S.); Private Property Rights Act of 1997, S. 709, 105th Cong. (1997) (U.S.). For a description of initiatives on the state level see Nancie G. Marzulla, 'State Private Property Rights Initiatives as a Response to "Environmental Takings"' (1995) 46 *South Carolina Law Review* 613, 633–635.

[4] See, e.g., *Lucas* v. *South Carolina Coastal Council*, 505 US 1003, 1030 (1992) (quoting *Board of Regents of State Colleges* v. *Roth*, 408 US 564, 577 (1972)) (describing 'traditional resort to "existing rules or understandings that stem from an independent source such as state law" to define the range of interests that qualify for protection as "property" under the Fifth and Fourteenth Amendments'); *Nollan* v. *California Coastal Commission*, 483 US 825, 857 (1987) (Brennan, J., dissenting) ('It is axiomatic . . . that state law is the source of those strands that constitute a property owner's bundle of property rights [under the Takings Clause]'). Whether public and private understandings should be interchangeable in this sense is, of course, another question. See Ch. 14, below.

[5] *Palazzolo* v. *Rhode Island*, 533 US 606, 630 (2001).

[6] *Loretto* v. *Teleprompter Manhattan CATV Corporation*, 458 US 419, 435 (1982) (quoting *United States* v. *General Motors Corporation*, 323 US 373, 378 (1945)).

[7] *Penn Central Transportation Company* v. *New York City*, 438 US 104, 127 (1978).

dimension has been established in some cases in physical terms, such as the parcel of land described in the landowner's title.[8] In other cases, this dimension involves purely conceptual matters as well—such as one right being severed, as 'property', from others. For instance, the 'property' (in various cases) has been held to involve 'the city tax block designated as the [historic] "landmark site"', rather than the more limited notion of the 'air rights' above a particular building;[9] the whole of the owner's mining operation, rather than the particular segment of the owner's coal that is affected by the challenged regulation;[10] the right to exclude, rather than all of the rights that comprise a landowner's 'bundle' of rights;[11] and so on.

Using these dimensions, the Court has constructed—in many cases—an idea of property that is in rough accordance with how we ordinarily think about property. Under this 'common' conception, property describes our rights (defined by the relevant theory), as applied to a space, object, or otherwise conceptually defined field. It is, for example, the individual's right to unfettered possession, disposition, and use of land, chattels, or other corporeal or incorporeal things.[12] It is that which identifies and protects individual interests against collective power. It is that 'private sphere of individual self-determination securely bounded off from politics by law'.[13] This familiar conception of property, when combined with Takings Clause protection, has very concrete meaning. It means the protection of possessions; it means the protection of one's business; it means the protection of 'expectations' of development of one's land. The 'right to property', under this conception, is of a very definite character; it is envisioned as a box, with all objects or interests within that box protected strongly and equally.

The Supreme Court's opinions are replete with this image. For instance, Justice Marshall has written that property, protected by this Clause, has a 'normative dimension'; it 'establish[es] a sphere of private autonomy which government is bound to respect'.[14] Indeed, so powerful is the appeal of this conception of property that members of the Court who have opposed its results in practice have been loathe to depart from it in rhetoric. In *Nollan* v. *California Coastal Commission*,[15] for example, Justice Brennan—although dissenting from the Court's holding of a compensatable taking—insisted that 'state law is the source of those strands that constitute a property owner's bundle of . . .

---

[8] See *Lucas*, n. 4 above, 1029.

[9] *Penn Central Transportation Company*, n. 7 above, 130–131.

[10] *Keystone Bituminous Coal Association* v. *DeBenedictis*, 480 US 470, 498 (1987).

[11] See, e.g., *Nollan*, n. 4 above, 686; *Loretto*, n. 6 above, 435.

[12] See, e.g., Richard A. Epstein, *Takings: Private Property and the Power of Eminent Domain* (Cambridge, Mass.: Harvard University Press, 1985), 22–24.

[13] Frank Michelman, 'Takings, 1987' (1988) 88 *Columbia Law Review* 1600, 1626. See also Joan Williams, 'The Rhetoric of Property' (1998) 83 *Iowa Law Review* 277 (describing the ubiquitous presence—as a rhetorical matter, at least—of this 'intuitive image' of property in American law).

[14] *PruneYard Shopping Center* v. *Robins*, 447 US 74, 93 (1980) (Marshall, J., concurring).

[15] 483 US 825 (1987).

rights', and that '[t]he State [in this case] has not sought to interfere with any [of those] pre-existing property interest[s]'.[16]

This common conception of property does not, of course, deny the exercise of collective power; to the extent that this conception is a legally cognizable one, its dimensions—its characteristics—are obviously the product of collective choice. The important characteristic of this conception, however, is this: once its dimensions are chosen, the area of individual autonomy and control is established. Any subsequent, attempted diminution in the interests protected is an infringement of property rights.

This, then, is the conception of property that takings jurisprudence seems to assume. Under this conception, property identifies and protects individual interests against collective forces. Property is asserted, *as an entity*, against collective power. Collective forces, under this conception, are clearly external to the protection that property, as an entity, affords.

So far, we have analysed this conception of property in terms of the dimensions that it is usually acknowledged to involve: the dimension of theory, and the dimension of space. What about the remaining, less obvious dimensions of stringency and time?

If we examine the common conception of property, we discover that it *assumes* particular content for these dimensions. Under this conception's essential meaning, once a claimed right (defined by theoretical and spatial dimensions) is found to be 'property', it falls within the protected sphere of individual autonomy and control. It is then—of necessity—held with the same intensity, and afforded the same protection, as all other property rights. There is no analytical basis, under this conception, for some property to be protected with great stringency, and others with less. The core idea of property, under this conception, is property as a 'bounded sphere' which represents and protects an area of individual autonomy. Once triggered, the idea of autonomy is—by its very nature—absolute. Indeed, the very notion of rights being granted varying degrees of protection is intuitively inconsistent with the idea that those rights exist within a bounded sphere of individual autonomy and individual control. The common conception of property assumes, very definitely, particular content for the dimension of stringency; although unarticulated, it assumes the equal stringency—the equal protection—of all property rights.

The treatment of the dimension of time by this conception of property is more complex. First, this conception assumes that *some* moment in time must be chosen for the establishment of property's protected rights. Whether property (under this conception) is understood to be rooted in the 'ordinary meaning' of ownership, the 'reasonable expectations' of purchasers, the 'historically rooted' expectations of landowners, the 'applicable background principles' of common law, or some other idea, the content of this theoretical dimension must be ident-

---

[16] 483 US 857, 855 (1987). As Joseph Singer has observed, this conception of property is usually assumed in academic discourse as well. Joseph William Singer, *Entitlement: The Paradoxes of Property* (New Haven, Conn.: Yale University Press, 2000), 4.

ified at a particular moment in time for this conception of property to have meaning. This content may be determined at the moment that the property was purchased, at the moment its productive use began, at a particular historical moment, or at another time; the key point is that *some* moment in time must be chosen as the referent for each.

Once this moment in time is chosen, and the content of these rights 'fixed', this conception of property assumes, further, that the collective cannot thereafter change these rights. The dimension of time, under this conception, involves not only the identification of an initial point of reference for the content of included rights, but also the 'freezing' of that content from that moment forward. Once property rights (under this conception) are defined and recognized, they establish an area of individual autonomy and control; they cannot—consistently with this understanding—be subject to collective change thereafter.

It is possible, of course, that the theory of rights chosen may *itself* permit some degree of future flexibility. For instance, property rights could be defined as a landowner's 'reasonable expectations', understood in light of future laws, social assumptions, or other factors reasonably anticipated at the time of purchase, or as the 'traditional rights of ownership', subject to the rights of encroachers acquired (later) through adverse possession.[17] However, to be consistent with the common conception of property, such theories of rights are subject to two restraints. First, it is assumed that, *once established*, the theory of rights cannot (itself) be changed. 'Reasonable expectations' cannot be changed, after purchase, to reflect another theory, more favourable to collective interests. In addition, and perhaps more importantly, this conception *assumes the creation of a sphere of individual autonomy and control*. Indeed, it is in precisely this quality that this conception's premise of concreteness and protectiveness inheres. Any theory of rights that destroys this quality, by granting broad powers of collective change, would not create 'property' in the terms of this vision.

The operation of these restraints can be seen in the Supreme Court's articulation of this conception of property. For instance, in a recent takings case, the Court held that an expressly reserved ability to change an alleged 'contractual right' created by social security laws destroyed any claim that this right was 'property'. The Court remarked that since the 'contractual right' at issue 'was simply part of a regulatory program over which Congress retained [general amendatory] authority', it bore 'little, if any, resemblance to rights held to constitute "property"'.[18]

---

[17] The idea that property interests can be gained or lost through usage and time is an old one. See Morton J. Horwitz, *The Transformation of American Law 1780–1860* (Cambridge, Mass.: Harvard University Press, 1977), 43–44.

[18] *Bowen* v. *Public Agencies Opposed to Social Security Entrapment*, 477 US 41, 55 (1986). Under this conception of property, an *implied* power by government to change what appear to be statutory entitlements will likewise defeat claims of deprivation of property (without just compensation). See, e.g., *Bowen* v. *Gilliard*, 483 US 587, 608 (1987) (quoting *Reichelderfer* v. *Quinn*, 287 US 315, 319 (1932)) (there is no property interest in a statutory entitlement 'subject to modification by the "public acts of government"').

The conjunction of property claims and familiar ideas of harmful, nuisance, or noxious uses also illustrates the identity and restraints of this conception of property. It is often stated that principles of common-law nuisance are an inherent part of a landowner's title.[19] In such formulations, the 'theory of rights' chosen does not include harmful, noxious, or nuisance uses within the individual's protected sphere. Such formulations are compatible with the common conception of property if they establish a protected individual sphere with sufficient substance and clarity, and if that sphere—once established—is protected from collective change thereafter. If, for instance, what is a 'harmful', 'noxious', or 'nuisance' use is based upon the meaning of those terms at the time of a landowner's purchase; if those terms have an understood meaning, which provides concreteness; and if they cannot (by the collective) be changed thereafter—the 'property' described is of this common conception. If it fails to have those qualities, it is not.

(b) Implementation issues

We have, then, the common conception of property with (in fact) four dimensions: the explicit, articulated dimensions of a theory of rights and spatial reference, and the implicit, unarticulated dimensions of stringency (equal protection for all property rights) and time (rights established in time, and unchanged thereafter). What are the problems with this conception? What are the problems with the legal implementation of 'property as protection'—established by rights that are defined by theory, applied in space, protected equally, and frozen in time?

There are, for the theoretical dimension, obvious problems of articulation and choice. Particular theories may fail to establish the protected area with sufficient clarity or concreteness to yield legally identifiable or workable boundaries. What are a landowner's 'reasonable expectations' about land use? What are the 'ordinary understandings' that accompany chattel ownership? What is the 'right to control' one's body? The inherent vagaries of these theories are in fundamental conflict with the concrete articulation of legal rights that this conception demands.

Articulating the spatial dimension can be difficult as well. Although geographical boundaries in land may be easily identified, the spatial dimensions of other, more 'conceptually' defined property—such as 'autonomy over one's body'[20] or the 'coal mining operations'[21]—are not. In addition, the identification of a particular spatial dimension may fail to reflect the actual breadth of the

[19] See, e.g., *Lucas*, n. 4 above, 1022–1023, 1029–1031

[20] See, e.g., Lori B. Andrews, 'My Body, My Property', originally published in (1986) 16 *Hastings Center Report* 28, reprinted in Elizabeth Mensch and Alan Freeman (eds.), *Property Law: International Library of Essays in Law and Legal Theory* (New York: New York University Press, 1992), bk. ii, 27.

[21] See *Keystone Bituminous Coal Association*, n. 10 above, 499.

rights involved. The right to use land, for instance, is rarely restricted (in its effects) to a particular, definable parcel; it often affects neighbouring land as well. The common conception of property, with it simple application of theories of rights to particular spatial dimensions, may fail to capture the external or 'spillover' effects of such rights, and the practical limitations that they imply.[22]

Determining the temporal dimension, and the content of the rights arrested at that moment, can also be highly problematic. What moment, in time, should we choose? If the property in question is conventional in nature, we could choose the moment of its acquisition. Even this, however, may prove to be more difficult than it appears. Some methods of acquisition, such as inheritance, may have quite complicated origins. If, for instance, we are protecting 'expectations', should we protect the 'expectations' of forebears, as well? Even if acquisition is conceptually simpler, such as by purchase or gift, other problems remain. If our theory uses state laws or regulations as part of protected 'expectations', what content does this yield? Do we include regulations authorized by existing law, but actually promulgated later? Do we include laws or regulations in existence at the time of purchase or other acquisition, but which become factually applicable to the particular property (due to changed conditions) only *after* the 'magic moment' chosen? The more that we examine this conception of property, the more difficult the achievement of its concreteness, boundaries, and protections becomes.

Moreover, even if we manage—somehow—to meet these challenges, a deeper problem remains. In the words of C. B.Macpherson, '[p]roperty is not thought to be a right because it is an enforceable claim: it is an enforceable claim because it is thought to be a human right.'[23] Human society is not static. Values will change; scientific and social discoveries will be made; crises of war, pestilence, and economic deprivation will require collective action. As human conditions and needs change, so will the bases on which prior property regimes were constructed. What may have been an appropriate configuration of property rights in one era may be an undesirable or intolerable burden in another. If property describes an area of individual autonomy and control, defined by dimensions of theory, space, and stringency, established in time and protected from collective change thereafter, the protection of property—when human needs are bound to change—presents a very difficult problem.

Some property-rights advocates have argued that this is not a 'problem' at all; rather, it is a highly desirable social and legal outcome. Property, in their view, means (and *should* mean) protection; and it is to enforce this protection that

---

[22] As Joseph Sax has written, '[w]e can talk about a landowner having a property interest in "full enjoyment" of his land, but in reality [the full enjoyment] . . . of one tract [is often] . . . incompatible with full enjoyment of the adjacent tract.' Property is more accurately described as 'the value which each owner has left after the inconsistencies . . . have been resolved'. Joseph L. Sax, 'Takings and the Police Power' (1964) 74 *Yale Law Journal* 36, 61 (footnote omitted).

[23] C. B. Macpherson, 'The Meaning of Property', in C. B. Macpherson (ed.), *Property: Mainstream and Critical Positions* (Toronto: University of Toronto Press, 1978), 11.

legal guarantees against the collective impairment of property rights, such as the Takings Clause, exist. Conditions may change; the area ceded to individual autonomy and control may be altered; but this can be fairly done, under the Takings Clause and other such guarantees, only if compensation is paid. It is, they argue, in such guarantees that the essential meaning of property lies. Attempts to change the configuration of individual property interests are 'takings', requiring compensation.[24]

The idea of absolute protection for unchanging property interests is, of course, completely untenable as a practical matter. As Justice Holmes wrote in a famous observation, '[g]overnment hardly could go on if to some extent values incident to property could not be diminished without paying for every such change in the general law.'[25] The idea that compensation must be paid whenever the individual's pre-existing property rights are changed by government is one at which '[c]ommon sense revolts'.[26] To 'compel government to regulate by *purchase*',[27] would, in practical effect, return us 'to the era of *Lochner* v. *New York* . . ., when common-law rights were . . . found immune from revision by State or Federal Government'.[28]

This situation is ameliorated, to some extent, when we remember that the notion of 'property rights' in law is comprised of two parts: a conception of property, and a conception of rights. Although property may (under the common conception) describe an area of individual autonomy and control, defined by dimensions of theory, space, and stringency, established in time and protected from change thereafter, the extent to which this interest is protected *as a legal right* is a separate question. To put it simply, property may indeed be 'x' (a particular—even absolute—conception of protection); but 'x' is embedded, in turn, in a conception of rights. The extent to which 'x' is protected by law, as a legally enforceable right, is a different—and analytically separate—question.

Although the common conception of property may assume an individual's interest will (always) be protected, the idea of a legal *right* does not. No legal right is of absolute power; indeed, even the right to life may offer no protection to the holder of that right under particular facts and circumstances. In cases of individual/collective conflict, legal rights confer *prima facie* power: interests protected by rights are deemed, as a *prima facie* or presumptive matter, to be more powerful, more normatively compelling, than competing (non-rights) public interests. In this regard, property rights are no different from the right to free speech, the right to free religious exercise, or any other right. These rights estab-

---

[24] See, e.g., Epstein, n. 12 above; Richard A. Epstein, 'Property, Speech, and the Politics of Distrust' (1992) 59 *University of Chicago Law Review* 41.

[25] *Pennsylvania Coal Company* v. *Mahon*, 260 US 393, 413 (1922).

[26] *United States* v. *Causby*, 328 US 256, 260–261 (1946).

[27] *Andrus* v. *Allard*, 444 US 51, 65 (1979) (emphasis in original).

[28] *PruneYard Shopping Center*, n. 14 above, 93 (Marshall, J., concurring).

lish (only) the *presumptive superiority* of the interests that they protect; they can be overridden, but only by public interests of a sufficiently compelling nature.

Therefore, the protection that common-conception property provides, when implemented as a right by law, can be restated as follows. Property rights, under this understanding, protect an area of individual autonomy and control. They protect individual interests that are, as an essential matter, defined by dimensions of theory and space; protected equally; and protected from collective change thereafter. The individual interests protected by property are presumptively superior to competing public interests. They can be overridden (without legal consequence) by public interests of a particularly dire or compelling nature, but *only* by interests of that nature. They cannot be overridden by the simple or routine goals of government.

Although some advocates of common-conception property may call for an absolute conception of property rights, it is this more nuanced version that is advanced by most property-rights advocates. For instance, Richard Epstein argues that property rights protect individual interests in the possession, disposition, and use of corporeal or incorporeal objects; that the content of these interests is established at the moment of acquisition, or other historical moment; that these interests are presumptively protected; and that only in very narrow circumstances—such as those involving threats to human health or safety—is this presumption overcome.[29]

Some Supreme Court cases also reflect this approach. In *Hadacheck* v. *Sebastian*,[30] for instance, the Court upheld a city ordinance that made the operation of a brickyard unlawful, even though the brick-making operation predated (by many years) the annexation of this land by the city. The Court apparently agreed with the plaintiff that the 'property' in question included the previously recognized land-use rights; however, the Court held, this interest must yield to public-health claims.[31] Using a similar rationale, the Court upheld laws that prohibited the continued operation of a livery stable,[32] prohibited the operation of a previously lawful brewery,[33] permitted the destruction of private property to prevent the spread of fire,[34] and prohibited the continued operation of a quarry in a residential area.[35] These cases, and others like them, are sometimes said to illustrate a 'police power exception' to the Takings Clause: previously recognized property interests, which are later

---

[29] See Epstein, n. 12 above, 35–104, 107–125, 161–194. John Christman describes this idea of 'liberal ownership' as one in which 'the more or less full rights that I have over my possessions are part of the sanctum of activity that the state has no business invading, except perhaps for some tremendously weighty social goal'. '[I]n this way of thinking, . . . citizens [are afforded] the greatest possible range of independence, privacy, and personal sovereignty allowable in a social order.' John Christman, *The Myth of Property: Toward an Egalitarian Theory of Ownership* (New York: Oxford University Press, 1994), 6.

[30] 239 US 394 (1915).   [31] *Ibid.* 410–412.

[32] *Reinman* v. *Little Rock*, 237 US 171 (1915).   [33] *Mugler* v. *Kansas*, 123 US 623 (1887).

[34] *Bowditch* v. *Boston*, 101 US 16, 18–19 (1879).

[35] *Goldblatt* v. *Hempstead*, 369 US 590 (1962).

determined to be inimical to public health or safety, may simply be prohibited, with no compensation paid.[36]

Thus, in some cases, the Court's treatment of the problem of property protection and change is consistent with the common conception of property. Property rights, in these cases, are viewed as rights which protect fixed and determinate individual interests. There is no question, in these cases, but that the competing public interests *impair* the property rights at issue; the only question is whether that impairment is *justified*. And in making that determination, property rights have great presumptive power. Property rights, previously granted, can be changed—public interests can *override* property rights[37]—only in the most dire and unequivocal of circumstances.

In other cases, however, the Court's reconciliation of property rights and change is starkly incompatible with common-conception property. In these cases, the Court has upheld routine government interests against clearly staked property rights, with little mention of the individual interests—so far described—that this action obviously transgresses. In these cases, common-conception property has, in fact, been replaced by a very different vision: what we shall call the 'operative' conception of property in law.

(ii) Change as a part of property: the 'operative'
conception of property in law

Although the disregard of property interests can be justified—under the common conception of property—in situations of dire public circumstance, it clearly is *not* justified when property interests clash with the ordinary or routine goals of government. Yet, that is precisely the result in many takings cases. In many cases, the Court has seemed to disregard what appear to be clearly established, pre-existing rights in property, in favour of what are simply 'desirable' instances of public regulation.

In zoning cases, for instance, the Court has upheld all but the most extreme impairments of land use against asserted takings claims. It has held that the

---

[36] See, e.g., *Calhoun v. Massie*, 253 US 170, 175 (1920) ('An appropriate exercise by a state of its police power is consistent with the Fourteenth Amendment although it results in serious depreciation of property values; and the United States may . . . [impose] restrictions upon property which produce like results.'); *Corn Products Refining Company v. Eddy*, 249 US 427, 431–432 (1919) ('The right of a manufacturer to maintain secrecy as to his compounds and processes must be held subject to the right of the state, in the exercise of its police power . . ., to require that the nature of the product be fairly set forth'.).

This narrow understanding of the 'police power' must be contrasted with a much more expansive understanding that is also—sometimes—found in these cases. See sect. (ii) of this ch., below.

[37] The same result—i.e., the supremacy of the competing public interest—could be achieved, of course, in another way: the theoretical dimension of the property in issue could simply be defined in a way that excludes (from the first) uses which are now deemed undesirable. Under this approach, for instance, an individual's 'property' would simply be understood not to encompass the right to engage in harmful or noxious uses. This, of course, does not involve property *and change*; it simply involves the choice of limited content for the theoretical dimension of (common-conception) property.

general diminution in value of land through zoning, short of the prohibition of *all* economically viable use, is not a compensatable taking.[38] A similar approach, with similar results, has been employed by the federal courts in cases involving environmental laws,[39] historic-preservation laws,[40] and laws that preserve one person's commercial interests at the expense of another's.[41] When—for instance—'a state tribunal [has] reasonably concluded that "the health, safety, morals, *or general welfare*" would be promoted by prohibiting particular contemplated uses of land', the Supreme Court has upheld land-use regulations that 'destroyed or adversely affected recognized real property interests'.[42]

The Supreme Court has sometimes attempted to explain these results on the ground that non-monetary compensation—or, as it is sometimes called, 'reciprocity of advantage'— has been provided to the claimant by the government action.[43] Although compensation (in the traditional sense) has not been paid, the Court has argued that the burdens that the government action in question has placed upon others (and which, arguably, inure to the claimant's benefit) work to offset the claimant's loss. Although such arguments may be persuasive in situations where benefits and burdens are roughly equal and widespread,[44] they have no appeal in the far more common situations that lack their characteristics. When a landowner must preserve his wetlands for ecological reasons, or when the owner of an isolated historic building must forego developing his property in order to preserve its historic character,[45] or when the owner of cedar trees must allow their destruction in order to preserve the apple orchards of others,[46] 'compensation'—in the form of the community's general ecological, preservationist, or commercial goals—may be of little consolation.[47]

---

[38] See, e.g., *Agins* v. *Tiburon*, 447 US 255, 260–261(1980); *Gorieb* v. *Fox*, 274 US 603, 607 (1927); *Village of Euclid* v. *Ambler Realty Company*, 272 US 365 (1926).

[39] See Richard J. Lazarus, 'Changing Conceptions of Property and Sovereignty in Natural Resources: Questioning the Public Trust Doctrine' (1986) 71 *Iowa Law Review* 631, 693 ('The thrust of recent developments in environmental and natural resource law has been to replace already eroding traditional notions of private property rights in natural resources with a scheme . . . explicitly premised on continuing sovereign regulatory authority.').

[40] *Penn Central Transportation Company*, n. 7 above, 124–138.

[41] See, e.g., *Walls* v. *Midland Carbon Company*, 254 US 300 (1920) (law prohibiting the continued manufacture of carbon black); *Miller* v. *Schoene*, 276 US 272 (1928) (law ordering the destruction of cedar trees to preserve others' apple orchards).

[42] *Penn Central Transportation Company*, n. 7 above, 125 (quoting *Nectow* v. *Cambridge*, 277 US 183, 188 (1928)) (emphasis added).

[43] See, e.g., *Keystone Bituminous Coal Association*, n. 10 above, 491; *Agins*, n. 38 above, 262.

[44] Examples of such situations include the requirement that pillars of coal be left in underground mines to protect miners working in adjacent mines: see *Plymouth Coal Company* v. *Pennsylvania*, 232 US 531 (1914), and uniform zoning regulations that protect pre-existing uses. See *Agins*, n. 38 above, 262 ('The [general] zoning ordinances benefit the [claimants] . . . as well as the public by serving the city's interest in assuring careful and orderly development of residential property'.).

[45] See *Penn Central Transportation Company*, n. 7 above.   [46] See *Miller*, n. 41 above.

[47] Indeed, it is often stated that the essential purpose of the Takings Clause is to 'prevent . . . the public from loading upon one individual more than his just share of the burdens of government'. *Monongahela Navigation Company* v. *United States*, 148 US 312, 325 (1893). See also *Armstrong* v. *United States*, 364 US 40, 49 (1960).

The ease with which the Court disregards what appear to be clearly established, pre-existing rights in these cases is, of course, not uniform. In many recent cases, for instance, the Court has emphasized its protection of 'traditionally' or 'commonly' recognized rights to possess, use, exclude from, and dispose of land against regulation that restricts these rights.[48] However, even in these cases—in which common-conception property seems to be strongly emphasized—uncertainty enters. In the *Lucas* case, for instance, the Court found that Lucas's land-use claim was of a 'categorically compensatable' nature, but nonetheless remanded the case to South Carolina's courts to determine whether common-law principles of property law allowed the imposition of land-use controls of the kind that the State desired. This analysis, the Court explained, would 'entail . . . [consideration of] the degree of harm to public lands and resources, or adjacent private property, posed by the claimant's proposed activities, . . . the social value of the claimant's activities and their suitability to the locality in question, . . . and the relative ease with which the alleged harm can be avoided through measures taken by the claimant and the government (or adjacent private landowners)'.[49]

Consistent rhetoric about the 'concreteness' of property, or about property as that which delineates a sphere of 'individual security, autonomy, and control', cannot obscure the fact that the conception of property that the Court uses in these cases is quite different from that which it professes. The idea that property protects individual interests against collective change often gives way, in these cases, to one which envisions change *as a part of* the idea of property. For instance, the Court observed in one case that a property owner '*necessarily expects* the uses of his property to be restricted, from time to time', by subsequent legislative enactments.[50] In another, it stated that the 'interests that . . . constitute "property"' do not include the continuation of previously approved and beneficial uses, if those uses are later deemed, '"in the judgment of the legislature, . . . [to be subordinate to others] of greater value to the public"'.[51]

Indeed, the alacrity with which the Court will apparently uphold collective efforts to curtail previously permitted uses of land has been the subject of sharp judicial dissent[52] and extensive scholarly commentary. For instance, Joseph Sax

[48] See, e.g., *Lucas,* n. 4 above, 1029–1031; *Nollan,* n. 4 above, 831.

[49] *Lucas,* n. 4 above, 1030–1031.

[50] *Ibid.* 1027 (emphasis added). See also *Block* v. *Hirsh,* 256 US 135, 155 (1921) (property rights in tangible property, although often envisioned in concrete terms, 'are [not] exempt from . . . legislative modification'). This understanding extends, of course, beyond constitutional law to common-law property cases. See, e.g., Williams, n. 13 above, 358 ('Highly fictionalized . . . arguments allow American courts to preserve the intuitive image of property as eternal, absolute, and unchangeable, even while they regularly redistribute property rights [for example] in the context of adverse possession cases, doctrine of agreed boundary cases, and implied easement and covenant cases.').

[51] *Penn Central Transportation Company,* n. 7 above, 125–126 (quoting *Miller,* n. 41 above, 279). See also *Keystone Bituminous Coal Association,* n. 10 above, 491 (quoting *Mugler,* n. 33 above, 665) (property is held '"under the *implied obligation* that the owner's use of it shall not be injurious to the community"') (emphasis added).

[52] See, e.g., *Keystone Bituminous Coal Association,* n. 10 above, 513 (Rehnquist, J., dissenting) (objecting to the broad and uncompensated abridgment of previously recognized property rights in favour of 'multifaceted health, welfare, and safety regulations').

has argued that wetlands- and coastal-protection laws, open-space zoning, growth controls, and the resurgent public-trust doctrine are evidence of 'a major transformation in which property rights are being fundamentally redefined to the disadvantage of property owners'—with little constitutional consequence.[53]

Before we proceed, a potential objection to our analysis must be addressed. Wait, the reader could say; this is not a new idea of property, but merely a different form of the old one. Couldn't one simply choose a theoretical dimension for common-conception property that includes this feature? For instance, couldn't property be understood, under the common conception, to protect a landowner's 'reasonable expectations'—with those defined, and redefined, as circumstances warrant?

Although some collective ability to change conferred rights could—as we have previously indicated[54]—be compatible with the common conception of property, the power to change conferred rights ' "as the . . . exigencies of the moment may require" '[55] goes far beyond these limits. It is the concreteness of the common conception of property, and its protection *against* the collective, that gives it its essential character. The elimination of this concreteness, through the choice of a theoretical dimension that repudiates it, would destroy this conception's most important quality. For extreme or dire social circumstances (involving public health or safety) to *override* the protection that property rights provide, under this conception, is one thing; for property rights to *simply change,* as general social needs change, is quite another. If—for example—an owner's 'expectations' were simply understood to change, as collective needs change, this conception of property and its purported protection would be rendered meaningless.[56]

What, then, is this alternative conception of property? This conception of property, which we shall call the 'operative' conception, shares some characteristics with the other. Like the common conception of property, it involves the choice of a theory of rights, often in very similar terms. For instance, theories of rights that operative-conception property involves include the 'reasonable expectations' (of the property holder), the 'rights traditionally associated' with land or chattel ownership, rights afforded by 'existing law', and so on. It also involves the application of these rights to a particular space, object, or other conceptual field—again, in terms similar to the common conception. Neither the existence of these dimensions, nor the terms in which they are generally described, distinguishes these conceptions of property.

---

[53] Joseph L. Sax, 'Some Thoughts on the Decline of Private Property' (1983) 58 *Washington Law Review* 481, 481–482. Indeed, 'we are already so far long in diminishing developmental rights that owners are viewed, in important respects, as already on notice'. *Ibid.* 494.

[54] See sect. (i) (a) of this ch., above.

[55] *Mugler,* n. 33 above, 669 (quoting *Stone* v. *Mississippi,* 101 US 814, 819 (1879)).

[56] In the words of Justice Kennedy, if 'the owner's reasonable expectations' are simply 'what courts allow as a proper exercise of governmental authority, [then] property tends to become[, simply], what courts say it is'. *Lucas,* n. 4 above, 1034 (Kennedy, J., concurring in the judgment).

This situation changes when we consider the remaining dimensions of stringency and time. Although these dimensions are essential to both conceptions of property, the content of these dimensions is, in each, very different. Under the common conception of property, as described above, the content of these dimensions is assumed in a way that protects individual interests. Under the operative conception, the content of these dimensions is understood in a way that empowers opposing (collective) forces.

Let us consider, first, the dimension of stringency. Under the common conception of property, as we have already discovered, all property rights are protected with (presumably) equal stringency because all are within the sphere of individual control which property, itself, defines. Once a right is protected as 'property', it is held with the same intensity—and protected to the same degree—as all other property rights. There is no analytical basis, under this conception, for different degrees of protection for different property rights.

The operative conception of property, on the other hand, makes no such assumption. Under this conception, all property interests are *not* held with the same intensity and are *not* protected equally. For instance, the right to exclude is protected more strongly than the right to use;[57] the right to devise is protected more strongly than the right to sell;[58] and so on. The assumption of equally stringent, rigid protection—which is a defining characteristic of common-conception property—is not made here.

These conceptions of property also differ, quite radically, in the crucial dimension of time. Under the common conception of property, it is assumed that property rights are determined at a particular moment in time, and 'frozen' against change thereafter. Under the operative conception, we find something quite different. In case after case, the Court has upheld unilateral changes in what were clearly previously existing property rights, with *no* compensation required. Rights to use, protect, or transfer are routinely curtailed, without legal consequence, if deemed to be necessary for general public welfare. The common conception of property—consisting of individual rights, determined in time, and protected from change thereafter—is replaced, in these cases, by another: property as an individual right, *fluid* in time, *established and re-established* as 'new . . . circumstances . . . justify'.[59]

By employing content for the dimensions of stringency and time that acknowledge collective definition, redefinition, control, *and* change, the operative conception of property presents an approach to property that is fundamentally different from that advanced by the common conception of property. Both conceptions involve the resolution of conflicts between individual interests and collective goals. However, the critical difference that these conceptions of property present is this. Is this individual/collective tension seen as something that is

---

[57] See, e.g., *Loretto*, n. 6 above, 433–436.
[58] See, e.g., *Hodel* v. *Irving*, 481 US 704, 716–718 (1987); *Andrus*, n. 27 above, at 66.
[59] *Loretto*, n. 6 above, 454 (Blackmun, J., dissenting).

external to the concept of property, or as something that is *internal* to it? Put another way, is property, protected by law, something that protects individual interests *against* collective goals? Or is it a kind of Trojan horse, which carries the prospect of ready collective change within it?

* * *

We have discovered two different conceptions of property in law: the common conception of property, in which property represents individual interests, defined and protected against collective change, absent dire threats to public health or safety; and the operative conception of property, in which property represents individual interests, fluid in time, established and re-established as circumstances warrant. The conception of property that we choose will—as we shall see in the next chapter—deeply and irrevocably affect what 'property rights' mean in law, and what social choices—through those rights—we make.

4

Two Conceptions of Property: Their (Hidden) Influence in Law

In the prior chapter, we found that there are, in fact, two conceptions of property that appear in the Supreme Court's takings cases: the common conception of property, in which property describes the individual's protected sphere, asserted against the collective; and the operative conception of property, in which particular individual/collective tensions have been settled, at the moment, but which incorporates those tensions—and their changes—within the concept of property. Although the common conception of property is that which is usually presented by the Court as the 'idea' of property, it is the operative conception that is often used by the Court in the resolution of takings claims.

In this chapter, we will explore how these different conceptions of property influence our thinking about property and its role in law. We will consider this question from three perspectives: first, from the perspective of the protection afforded by the Takings Clause; next, from the perspective of the meaning of property, as a general legal matter; and lastly, from the perspective of the implications that the idea of property holds for our idealized notions of personal autonomy, social context, and the relationship—that we assume—between them.

(i) THE TAKINGS CLAUSE, REVISITED

To frame our consideration of the common and operative conceptions of property and the Takings Clause, we will begin with facts that mirror those of the *Lucas* case.[1] In that case, Lucas asserted the following 'property' interest: the right to develop his shoreline land in the manner and to the extent that he pleased. The State of South Carolina (in the exercise of its regulatory authority) decreed that Lucas could not develop his land, on the ground that his proposed actions would jeopardize the stability of the beach/dune system, accelerate erosion, and endanger adjacent property.[2]

Let us assume, further (as Lucas argued), that this state decree *is*, in fact, a change in the law: that the principles upon which it rests were not a part of the common law or other applicable law at the time of Lucas's purchase. Let us

---

[1] *Lucas v. South Carolina Coastal Council*, 505 US 1003 (1992).   [2] *Ibid*. 1008–1009.

further assume (as the Court apparently did) that the theoretical dimension for Lucas's property interest is comprised of 'existing legal rights' and that this theory of rights is applied (as a spatial matter) to the land as legally described.

So far, so good. Now we must choose a conception of property. If, at this point, we choose the common conception, our analysis proceeds as follows. Under this conception, the stringency of protection afforded to property rights is simple: all are within the individual's autonomous sphere, and all are—as a consequence—fully and equally protected. Lucas's right to use, as a 'property' right, is therefore (under this conception) a fully protected right. Furthermore, this conception of property assumes that property rights are established at a particular point in time, and protected from change thereafter. Assuming (as Lucas argued) that the moment of purchase established Lucas's rights, his claimed right to develop—permitted at that time—is a protected property right, and is protected from change thereafter.

From these premises, the result in our 'takings' case is clear. Under the common conception of property, 'property' describes Lucas's rights, bounded and protected; his right to use—as we have defined it—is one of those rights; and the 'taking' of this right is a 'taking' of property. This property right might be overridden (without legal consequence) by a public interest of a particularly dire or compelling nature, but *only* by an interest of that nature. Since ecological considerations of the kind involved in the case do not involve public health, public safety, or like concerns, the result is clear: under this conception of property, Lucas has suffered a 'taking' of property, for which the State (presumably) must pay.

In the next chapter, we will discuss why the use of the common conception of property or any similar, 'strong' view of rights is (in fact) inappropriate in this case and others like it.[3] For the present, it is sufficient for us to appreciate the power of this conception of property when applied in takings cases. When this conception is used, the nature of the property *itself* imposes limits on collective action. If, under this conception, a collective goal impairs an individual's property right, compensation is—almost always—paid.

What if we were to use, instead, the operative conception of property? Under this conception, all rights are not necessarily protected equally; some rights (for public policy reasons) may be protected less stringently than others. There is, therefore, no particular degree of protection that is assumed for Lucas's right to use, or anyone's right to use; indeed, as we have previously seen, the right to use is often less protected in law than other property rights.[4] Furthermore, under this conception of property, tensions between individual interests and collective

---

[3] Indeed, the *Lucas* Court—although rhetorically wedded to a common conception of property—used, in fact, what amounts to an operative one. See *ibid.* 1014, 1029–1031 (government may 'redefine the range of interests included in the ownership of property'; and land use is subject to 'background [common law] principles of nuisance and property law', which include the balancing of individual interests and public claims).

[4] See Ch. 3, sect. (ii), above.

goals are simply a part of the meaning of property; although particular individual interests may be cognizable 'property' at one moment, there is no guarantee that they will be at another. Although Lucas's claimed right to develop may be a property right *at the time of purchase*, this right is understood to incorporate—as an inherent part of it—a societal power to alter it later.

From these premises, the result in our 'takings' case is also clear. Under the operative conception of property, the idea of property, itself, confers no rights; it simply describes, or mediates, the tensions between individual interests and collective goals, which are resolved and re-resolved as circumstances warrant. The change in permissible use, of which Lucas was informed, is not an *impairment* of 'property', for which compensation is owed; it is simply an adjustment of the tensions between individual interests and collective goals, something that is an inherent part of this conception of property.

Whatever claimed property rights one considers, the conclusions that we draw—under our two conceptions of property—are the same. The different conceptions of property that we have identified provide radically different protection for individual interests under legal guarantees such as the Takings Clause. If the common conception of property is used, individual interests are afforded strict protection. If the operative conception is used, individual interests are—as a practical matter—afforded none.

Before we leave the subject of these different conceptions of property and the Takings Clause, one cautionary note must be added. It may be tempting, when considering these issues, to contrast these conceptions of property in the following way: that property under the common conception is an 'extra-political' institution, free from social forces, while property under the operative conception is not. This dichotomous conclusion is, of course, a false one. Property is, under *any* conception, quintessentially and absolutely a social institution. Every conception of property reflects, through its constituent dimensions, those choices that we—as a society—have made. What are an individual's 'justified expectations'? What is 'existing law'? What values do the dimensions, chosen for 'property', serve? Why should we, as a society, promote or preserve those values? The common conception of property does not avoid these questions. It simply proclaims that such questions—once answered—cannot be considered again.

(ii) THE MEANING OF PROPERTY, AS A GENERAL LEGAL MATTER

In the last section, we explored the roles that the common and operative conceptions of property play in the resolution of claims under the Takings Clause. In this section, we will broaden our inquiry. Is the recognition of these conceptions of property of importance only when considering the Takings Clause, and similar legal guarantees? Or are there deeper, more pervasive reasons to recognize and understand the use of these differing conceptions of property in law?

As a way to approach these questions, we will consider (at some length) an analysis of property law recently offered by J. W. Harris. In his seminal book, *Property and Justice*,[5] Harris sets out to refute what he sees as unjustified attacks on the coherence of what he calls property as 'conventionally' or 'ordinarily' understood.[6] Although—as some scholars have argued—'all rights [can] be termed "property rights"',[7] Harris argues that this is not the way that property is understood as a social, political, and legal institution. Rather, there is something that 'constitutes an essence of propertiness' in these institutional contexts, something that allows us to 'share an intuitive sense of what property is'.[8] He argues that we can, through an examination of these institutional contexts, identify those characteristics of property that philosophers, lawyers, and lay people intuitively use to distinguish property relations from other relations.[9]

A property institution, Harris writes, is a 'social and legal institution which constitutes the background for conventional property-talk among both laymen and lawyers'.[10] The 'essentials of a property institution' are, in turn, 'the twin notions of trespassory rules and the ownership spectrum'.[11] Harris explains these 'twin notions' as follows:

By 'trespassory rules' is meant any social rules, whether or not embodied in law, which purport to impose obligations on all members of a society, other than an individual or group who is taken to have some form of open-ended relationship to a thing, not to make use of that thing without the consent of the individual or group. The most hallowed such trespassory rule embodies the commandment 'thou shalt not steal.' . . .

By 'the ownership spectrum' is meant the open-ended relationships presupposed and protected by trespassory rules. All attempts in the history of theorizing about property to provide a univocal explication of the concept of ownership, applicable within all societies and to all resources, have failed. Yet property talk, lay and legal, deploys ineliminable ownership conceptions.[12]

'Property' institutions, then, are built upon trespassory rules, or obligations imposed upon 'an open-ended range of persons' (with 'owners' excepted), and upon ownership relations themselves. Ownership relations, in Harris's understanding, include a broad range of use-powers and control-powers; they extend from 'mere property', or the simple notion 'that something that pertains to a person is, maybe within drastic limits, his to use as he pleases', to 'full-blooded ownership', or 'the assumption that, *prima facie*, the person is entirely free to do what he will with his own, whether by way of use, abuse, or transfer'.[13]

After property is defined by particular trespassory rules and by particular ownership relations, there may be—superimposed upon these—'"property-limitation rules" and "expropriation rules", whereby ownership privileges and powers [are] . . . curtailed or taken away'.[14] Property-limitation rules and expropriation rules are typically part of the minimal structure of property institutions.

[5] (Oxford: Clarendon Press, 1996).   [6] *Ibid.* 161, 149.   [7] *Ibid.* 148.   [8] *Ibid.* 7.
[9] *Ibid.* 7–8.   [10] *Ibid.* 141.   [11] *Ibid.* 5.   [12] *Ibid.* 5 (footnote omitted).
[13] *Ibid.* 25, 28–29.   [14] *Ibid.* 29.

These rules are not strictly necessary elements of property institutions, since '[o]ne could [imagine] . . . a property institution in which owners were literally free to do anything they liked to or with their things . . ., and where there was no power in others or in the State to strip them of their ownership interests.' 'However', as Harris no doubt correctly asserts, 'no such system exists today and probably none ever did.'[15] As a practical matter, and '[a]lthough their content and scope varies in time and place, we may say that any property institution must . . . comprise property-limitation rules and expropriation rules'.[16]

It is the idea of property-limitation rules, and their function, that are particularly interesting for our purposes, and that we will therefore explore in some detail. Harris explains property-limitation rules in the following terms:

An important feature of all complex property institutions resides in property-specific limitation rules whereby *prima facie* normative claims founded on the prevailing ownership conception are overridden. Property-limitation rules . . . are premised on the assumption that, but for the restrictions they contain, the owner would be free to act in a certain way. Some positive or negative mode of using a thing which would otherwise be privileged to X by virtue of his ownership interest in it is negated by the imposition of a corresponding negative or positive duty, enforceable by civil or criminal sanctions or by both. Or the exercise of some power, otherwise inherent in ownership, is qualified or curtailed.[17]

Examples of such property-limitation rules include nuisance restrictions, limitations on a testator's power to dispose of property to the detriment of her dependents, limitations on ownership-transmission freedoms to curtail the development of monopolies, and so on. Perhaps the most familiar examples to most people are 'environmental conservation rules [which] impose drastic limits on ownership privileges and powers'. In these cases, '[o]wnership use-privileges are overridden where there is a public interest in conservation. Public regulation has superimposed restraints on deleterious uses going well beyond those flowing from the common law of nuisance.'[18]

Let us stop at this point and take stock of where we are. Harris has described property, as it is institutionally understood, as comprised of trespassory rules and ownership interests, which confer certain privileges and powers of personal use and control of others. Those conferred privileges and powers are, in turn, overridden by other rules, imposed on public-interest grounds.

Harris is careful, in his analysis, to stress that the final package of individual use-privileges and control-powers that are implemented by property institutions are rarely absolute; 'totality ownership', as he describes it, is more a figment of academic imaginations than of existing property institutions. Under such a conception, 'to "own" something would entail that one could use it in any fashion, however anti-social or even lethal. There is . . . a consensus that no-one ever "owns" anything in this sense'; and that consensus is not limited to lawyers.

---

[15] *Property and Justice* (Oxford: Clarendon Press, 1996) 33 (footnote omitted).
[16] *Ibid*. 33–34.   [17] *Ibid*. 34.   [18] *Ibid*. 35 (footnotes omitted).

'Even a child who supposed he could ride a bicycle over the neighbour's flowers provided he "owned" the bicycle would be "perverse".'[19]

Recognition that absolute use-powers and control-powers are rarely conferred by property systems edges us closer to a description of property as actually, institutionally understood. However, an important question remains. If we begin with the idea of a set of complete use-privileges and control-powers that could, in theory, be conferred (what Harris calls 'full-blooded' or 'totality' ownership), it is apparent that something less than this could be conferred in several ways. In particular:

—*the individual could be granted full-blooded privileges and powers, and then—in a next step—those privileges and powers could be restricted through property-limitation rules.* For instance, a landowner could be given full-blooded powers to use his land, and environmental controls could—as property-limitation rules—restrict those powers.

—*the individual could be granted a less-than-full-blooded set of ownership privileges and powers, in the first place.* This lesser set of privileges and powers is, however—once granted—determinate in nature. For instance, a landowner could be given limited powers to use his land, with environmentally damaging uses excluded from that bundle of powers. If additional environmental controls are determined to be necessary at a later date, these are imposed through property-limitation rules.

—*the individual could be granted ownership privileges and powers—of a full-blooded **or** lesser kind—that are understood to be changeable if circumstances warrant.* For instance, a landowner could be given full-blooded powers (or lesser powers) to use his land, with the understanding that environmental controls (if needed) are an inherent part of the idea of property.

Does the manner in which we do this matter? Indeed, as we examine this issue, we see that this choice is in fact a crucial one—often an *outcome determinative one*—in our resulting treatment of property claims.

What would the differences be? The ramifications of these choices are apparent from the terms that Harris employs. If the first choice is made—if property is defined in 'full-blooded' ownership or other broad terms, with collective power to restrict use imposed as a property-limitation rule—the presumptive powers of individual landowner and community, in the case described above, are clear. The collective power to enforce environmental and conservation rules must 'override' the '*prima facie* normative claim founded on the prevailing ownership conception' of broad individual use-privileges and control-powers. One begins with the perception that individual use and individual control are *normatively* justified; as a necessary corollary of this presumption, collective use and collective control are *not;* accordingly, environmental and conservation

---

[19] *Ibid.* 136 (footnote omitted).

rules are seen as (presumptively) unjustified incursions of normatively superior and historically entrenched property rights.

If the second choice is made—if property is more narrowly defined, but still determinate in nature—the result is similar. Although those uses that are excluded from the defined ownership powers have no recognized normative power, those that are included as a part of property's powers do. And since—under our example—environmental and conservation rules that are *later* deemed to be necessary must be imposed as property-limitation rules, they will be seen as (presumptively) unjustified incursions of property's justified powers.

If the third choice is made—if collective powers to control are seen as an inherent part of the initial configuration of ownership privileges and powers—then the result is very different. Under this choice, there is *no particular normative response* to this limitation of theoretically available ownership interests. The reservation of this collective power is simply seen as a choice, like any other choice involved in our conception of 'property' interests, with no particular normative objection to it. Under this choice, environmental and conservation rules—whenever authorized—face no particular presumptive hurdle.

It is immediately apparent, from this discussion, that we have again uncovered the two conceptions of property that we identified in Chapter 3. The first and second choices—in which property represents entrenched, protected interests, defined broadly or narrowly, which collective powers must later attempt to override—are examples of the common conception of property. Property is seen as individual protection, with the exercise of collective powers a potential impairment of previously conferred property rights. The third choice—in which collective powers are simply seen as a part of the initial configuration of ownership privileges and powers—is an example of the operative conception of property. Tensions between individual and collective are seen a part of property, with adjustments of relative privileges and powers made as circumstances require.

The subtle (and often unrecognized) power and influence of these conceptions of property can be seen in Harris's discussion of attitudes toward environmental controls. In this discussion, he clearly recognizes that limitations on theoretically available ownership privileges and powers could be accomplished in two ways: through the imposition of property-limitation rules (on otherwise determinate ownership conceptions), or through a change in the conception of ownership itself. He writes:

Reformers may insist that settled ownership conceptions ought to be altered, not merely restricted by particular property-limitation rules. . . . The predominant approach seems to be that environmental harms override ownership use-privileges and control-powers which . . . need to be restricted. *A more radical stance would be to claim that, whatever may have been assumed in the past, we should now persuade people to accept that ownership itself confers no prima facie privileges to engage in, or prima facie powers to permit, uses of resources which are environmentally deleterious.*[20]

[20] *Property and Justice* (Oxford: Clarendon Press, 1996) 78 (footnote omitted) (emphasis added).

This 'more radical stance' is, of course, our third choice or operative conception of property: a conception in which collective power to alter privileges and powers is assumed to be a part of the idea of property, itself. Harris is aware of the potential 'pay-off' of this approach, as he puts it:

Perhaps the pay-off from such a shift in the way which ownership functions as an organizing idea would be that constraints could not then be viewed as taking anything away from owners. Supposing, for example, it were to be discovered that the use of a certain kind of pesticide in agriculture had intolerable side-effects on the human food chain and it was therefore agreed on all hands that its use should be completely banned. Now— so the radical critic might argue—conceived of as a property-limitation rule the new measure will raise questions of compensation for farmers, whereas that would not be the case if we educated people to accept that decisions about what (if any) pesticides should be employed is exclusively a public matter and not something reached by use-privileges and control-privileges inherent in ownership.[21]

After posing this possibility, however, Harris seems to reject it:

First, the proposal has unwelcome implications. Are inhabitants of the developed world to instruct their brethren in poorer countries that, not only should they cease to destroy rainforests, but that no question of compensation for complying with such strictures can arise because the fact that the forests were theirs carried no rights to engage in or permit deforestation in the first place? Secondly, as we shall see, there are in any case many kinds of property-limitation rules which escape the compensation principle notwithstanding that they are recognized to be property-limitation rules.[22]

Is the use of this alternative conception of property as improbable or objectionable as Harris apparently believes? To address the first point, the idea (for example) that owners of rainforests cannot engage in their destruction could be implemented in two ways: it could be accomplished by *excluding* the right to destroy from the owner's determinate set of privileges and powers, or it could be accomplished by retaining the idea of evolving social norms *as a part* of the idea of property privileges and powers. Harris himself—by acknowledging elsewhere that 'full-blooded' ownership is rarely conferred—seems to acknowledge the viability of the first approach. The idea that use rights preclude destruction is not unknown to the world's legal systems. If, however, we *assume* that the right to destroy is a part of the privileges and powers of ownership—an assumption that Harris, in this passage, seems to make— there is still no reason why the second approach (in which change is a part of property) is not a valid one. Many thoughtful people, when considering these issues, would agree that the deforestation of the planet is not something which—in light of current knowledge— we consider to be an unquestioned part of the powers and privileges of 'property', for the 'owner's' sole determination, and in which the other

---

[21] *Ibid.*

[22] *Ibid.* 79 (footnote omitted). The position which Harris takes in this passage must be contrasted with the positions that Harris occasionally takes elsewhere in his book—for instance, at another point, he describes the privileges of ownership as 'imprecise and *fluctuating* product[s] of cultural assumptions'. *Ibid.* 64. See also *ibid.* 68.

inhabitants of the planet have no cognizable interest. Rather, issues of this kind
can be seen to involve highly complex and evolving social, economic, and scientific matters, which *all* should consider, and which no configuration of property
rights—determined years ago—can answer.

To address the second point, the fact that many kinds of property-limitation
rules *escape* the compensation principle, in practice, in fact *supports* the use of
this alternative conception of property in law. Harris notes that '[i]n most cases
of health and amenity regulation in England over the past century and a half it
has been assumed that the privileges and powers taken from owners were not
accorded to them as of right so that the uncompensated recapture of this aspect
of their private wealth into undifferentiated social wealth was not unjust.'[23]
Assuming that the regulations that Harris describes changed previously recognized ownership privileges and powers—which those regulations, as 'property-
limitation' rules, would clearly imply—the denial of compensation in these
cases would be justified *only* if the ownership powers and privileges involved
were *not* in fact established once and for all time, but were deemed to be subject
(as in American takings cases) to continuing social control. These cases do not
present reasons why the operative conception of property should not be used;
they are—instead—illustrations of the use of it.

The core of Harris' objection to thinking of property in 'operative' terms
seems to be that he does not see such a conception of property as 'property', at
all. By establishing ownership as the premise for the institutional idea of property,[24] and by defining ownership as an 'open-ended set of *prima facie* use-
privileges [and] control powers',[25] Harris presents a *particular* conception of
property (the 'common' conception of property) as, in fact, the *only* one. Harris
criticizes the work of Bruce Ackerman, Joseph Singer, and other scholars who
have articulated understandings of 'ownership' and 'property' which do not
depend upon simple individual-protectionist understandings.[26] He argues that
these accounts are implausible, because they render ownership 'an empty
premise'.[27] However, such critiques hold only if one begins with the assumption
that property must involve the normative judgement that individual interests,
once recognized and protected, shall be deemed presumptively superior to all
conflicting claims thereafter—a conception of property which, although often
involved in common parlance and political rhetoric, is—for very good reasons,
as we shall see—often *not* the one that is implemented by law.

The assumption that underlies these passages—that we begin, as a normative
matter, with the common conception of property, and its presumed priority of

[23] *Property and Justice* (Oxford: Clarendon Press, 1996) 98–99.
[24] *Ibid*. 138.   [25] *Ibid*. 136.
[26] See, e.g., Bruce A. Ackerman, *Private Property and the Constitution* (New Haven, Conn.: Yale
University Press, 1977); Joseph William Singer, 'The Reliance Interest in Property', originally published in (1988) 40 *Stanford Law Review* 611, reprinted in Elizabeth Mensch and Alan Freeman
(eds.), *Property Law: International Library of Essays in Law and Legal Theory* (New York: New
York University Press, 1992), bk. i, 147.
[27] Harris, n. 5 above 137.

individual interests—may not, in the end, be that which Harris himself favours. In the portion of his book from which these passages were taken, Harris sets out to describe property institutions as we find them, not as they (necessarily) should be. Indeed, his compelling consideration of distributive issues and other justice issues in the latter part of his book can be interpreted to entail a considerably more fluid understanding.[28] To the extent, however, that property is believed to be grounded in 'ineliminable ownership conceptions'[29]—and to the extent that ownership is believed to 'preserve . . . to . . . individuals an open-ended set of use-privileges and powers of control'[30]—the problem which we have identified has been joined. A particular conception of property has been chosen; a particular normative baseline has been cast; and all attempts toward social control and change thereafter will be seen as 'impos[ing] drastic [and presumptively illegitimate] limits on ownership privileges and powers'.[31] As Joseph Singer has observed, if ownership means presumptive control by owners, then our discussion of limitations on the rights of owners becomes a discussion about whether the limitations are 'justified by sufficiently strong reasons to overcome the presumption of legitimacy'.[32]

Our choice of a conception of property is not, in short, a simply 'descriptive' or 'neutral' one. We determine—through our choice of a conception of property—what is assumed and what is not, what is 'radical' and what is not, what is presumptively legitimate and what is not, what is 'owed' (as a normative matter) to the individual and what is not.

It is apparent that the importance of our choice of a conception of property goes far beyond 'takings' questions or other legal compensation schemes. If we assume—*as a part of property's very nature*—a particular institutional understanding, or a particular (immutable) configuration of individual rights and collective powers, we have, in effect, gone very far toward predetermining the question of how much protection property does or should provide.

(iii) 'COMMON PROPERTY', 'OPERATIVE PROPERTY', AND THE QUESTION OF SOCIAL CONTEXT

We have seen, thus far, how the choice of a conception of property is critical to the outcome of conflicting individual and collective claims. If the common conception of property is used, the individual's interest (as the 'property' interest) is strictly protected; it has *prima facie* superiority over public claims that seek to

---

[28] See, e.g., *ibid.* 14 (describing his ultimate conclusions that the protection of individual interests under the mantle of property must 'be assessed in the light of the community's obligation to discharge citizens' basic needs and the pervasive danger of illegitimate domination'.) Although these concerns could be addressed through a very limited, determinate understanding of property privileges and powers, they are more easily addressed through an operative conception of property.
[29] *Ibid.* 5.   [30] *Ibid.* 44.   [31] *Ibid.* 35.
[32] Joseph William Singer, *Entitlement: The Paradoxes of Property* (New Haven, Conn.: Yale University Press, 2000), 4.

erode or change previously recognized individual privileges and powers. As a result, individual claims that were recognized as 'property' in the past will be honoured, absent a dire threat to public health or safety. Such honouring could be in the form of a constitutional-compensation guarantee, or in another form of legal protection; the important point is that the individual claim is seen as a 'right' which has presumptive power against conflicting public claims.

If the operative conception of property is used, there is no such presumptive outcome. 'Property', in this case, does not represent the individual's interest, alone; rather, it represents the outcome of individual/collective tensions, determined and redetermined as circumstances warrant. As a consequence, individual claims—even if protected in the past—are afforded no special or assumed right to continued legal protection.

Our choice of a conception of property, then, has a very real impact on the way that conflicting individual and collective claims are—as a practical matter—legally resolved. It also has more subtle impacts on the ways in which we regard and resolve these claims. For instance, our choice of a conception of property tends to influence, very strongly, the degree to which we openly and expressly acknowledge the individual/collective conflicts that all property claims involve. Every legally cognizable conception of property is comprised of choices for its dimensions of theory, space, stringency, and time; these choices are those that we, as a society, have chosen to make and to enforce through law. If the operative conception of property is used—with its express acknowledgement of conflict, fluidity, and change—these choices are readily seen and explicitly assessed. We understand, when using this conception, that property claims involve interests that compete with other interests, expectations that conflict with the expectations of others.

The common conception of property, on the other hand, tends to deny or obscure these choices. When we see property as protection, we tend not to ask *why* or *how* such protection exists. A simple claim, for instance, that land-use rights must be honoured because they are 'historic' in nature tends to ignore the social and political contexts in which such claims were initially established, and in which they (as enforceable legal principles) unavoidably exist thereafter. If currently permitted use pollutes the air we breathe, or if the 'right' to build on shoreline land accelerates erosion and endangers adjacent property, there is simply no way to honour the 'pre-existing' or 'historic' rights of everyone involved. Property must be seen, in such cases, in more complex terms. To the extent that the common conception of property denies or obscures such issues, we lose the opportunity to evaluate consciously the social and political choices that all property involves.

There is, finally, a deeper, symbolic function which our choice of a conception of property consciously or unconsciously serves. The common conception of property proceeds from a vision of property as that which protects and separates the individual from the collective sphere. Indeed, the image of property as that which gives the individual a bulwark of isolated independence from his fellows has been cited as a central symbol of a vision of antagonism between the individual and collective life.[33] In recent years, there has been widespread dissatisfaction in the United States and elsewhere with political and legal traditions that reflect the view—rhetorically, at least—that the self is the final, ultimate political entity, absolute and inviolate. Recognition of an alternative conception of property will help us to remember that the idealized notion of the individual as a detached and autonomous entity is a choice, like other choices. It will also help us to remember that individual autonomy and social context are—in fact, and unalterably—deeply intertwined.

* * *

We have, to this point, identified two different conceptions of property in law: one (the common conception) which strongly protects individual interests, and one (the operative conception) which does not. We have also seen how the choice of one conception or the other will have dramatic implications for how we presumptively resolve conflicting individual and collective claims. Our identification of these conceptions, however, leaves important questions unanswered. Although use of the operative conception of property may make the accommodation of change easier, or accomplish other goals, the use of this conception in any particular case seems, thus far, to be simply a matter of arbitrary policy choice. As many of the champions of the common conception of property point out, we could as easily argue that the protection of the individual and the prevention of change are the appropriate goals of our legal and political systems. Are there any other reasons why one conception of property or the other should be used in particular cases? Put another way, are there any reasons— *intrinsic to the nature of property, and opposing public interests*—why property should protect so powerfully in some cases, and so very little in others? It is these questions that we will explore in the chapters that follow.

---

[33] See Jennifer Nedelsky, 'Reconceiving Autonomy: Sources, Thoughts, and Possibilities' (1989) 1 *Yale Journal of Law and Feminism* 7, 11, 17.

5

The Variable Power of Rights: A Normative Hypothesis

Conceptions of property are important in law because of their roles in determining the meaning of legal rights and obligations. If the common conception of property is used, 'property rights' are powerful, indeed: they identify individual interests, determined in time, which—once established—are protected from collective change thereafter. If the operative conception of property is used, the result is (as we have seen) very different. Although one begins with the identification of (presumably) protected individual interests here as well, change as the result of societal needs *is an accepted part* of this conception of property. Accordingly, 'property rights'—if this conception is used—offer little resistance to collective forces. Although established in time, with apparently protective functions, such rights are simply 'established and re-established', again and again, as collective interests warrant.

The use of the operative conception of property in law raises an obvious question. The essence of a legal right, under the traditional view, is that it protects the interests of its holder. How can we have a 'right to property' that yields so readily to collective interests—that protects, in fact, so little?

To answer this question, we will consider the phenomena that we have observed in slightly different terms. Up to this point, we have described the different degrees of protection afforded to individual interests in these cases as a function of the choice of different conceptions of property: one in which individual interests (once established) are protected against collective change, and one in which individual interests (once established) are not. If, however, we ponder these conceptions further, we realize that the core difference between them is the *relative power* that is afforded to individual interests and to the collective interests that oppose them. Put another way, it appears that individual interests (protected as property) have tremendous presumptive power against collective interests in some cases, and little (if any) presumptive power in others.

Is there a way to explain this result? Is there a way to explain—and justify—this variable power of property rights? In order to answer these questions, we must first examine more deeply the general nature of rights and opposing public interests, and the possible relations between them.

(i) THE TRADITIONAL STARTING POINT: RIGHTS AS 'TRUMPS' AGAINST
COMPETING PUBLIC INTERESTS

A declaration of right clothes an interest with awesome rhetorical, political, and legal power. 'I have a right' is a challenge to the world; my interest, which I assert, is—presumptively, at least—superior to all non-rights interests with which it may conflict. The assertion of an individual right carries with it a powerful message of individual autonomy and the protection of the asserted individual interest from the claims or predations of others.

The division of demands into those that are rights-based and those that are not is deeply entrenched in political rhetoric, moral philosophy, and law. The common view of rights as normative demands with particular strength which 'trump'[1] (at least as a *prima facie* matter) non-rights interests that conflict with them can be found in the discussion of any contemporary social issue. Property owners claim a 'right' to develop their land, in violation of state or local environmental laws.[2] Politicians and donors claim a 'right' to be free of spending limits and limits on campaign contributions.[3] Purveyors of pornography and adult entertainment claim a 'right' to be free of government regulation.[4] Citizens claim a 'right' to doctor-assisted suicide.[5]

Scholarly explorations of the precise nature of rights has generated an immense literature. Competing notions of rights include rights as the absence of prohibitions, rights as positive authorizations, rights as reflections of obligations, rights as powers, and rights as immunities.[6] Although these conceptions often overlap—for instance, rights as reflections of obligations or rights as powers may be expressed, in a legal system, as positive authorizations—all are common understandings of legal rights. Indeed, as Carl Wellman has noted, a legal right (in particular) may be seen as all of these: typically, it is a 'complex cluster

---

[1] See Ronald Dworkin, *Taking Rights Seriously* (Cambridge, Mass.: Harvard University Press, 1977), p. xi. Some have argued that—at least in the constitutional context—the relationship of rights to competing interests is one of balancing, not trumping. See, e.g., T. Alexander Aleinikoff, 'Constitutional Law in the Age of Balancing' (1987) 96 *Yale Law Journal* 943. However, even those who hold this view concede that rights are, by their very nature, accorded greater presumptive power than are non-rights interests. For a critique of the balancing or 'cost-benefit' approach to constitutional rights, see Jed Rubenfeld, 'Affirmative Action' (1997) 107 *Yale Law Journal* 427, 437–443.

[2] See, e.g., James V. DeLong, *Property Matters: How Property Rights Are Under Assault—And Why You Should Care* (New York: The Free Press, 1997); Nancie G. Marzulla and Roger J. Marzulla, *Property Rights: Understanding Government Takings and Environmental Regulation* (Rockville, Md.: Government Institutes, 1997).

[3] See, e.g., *Buckley* v. *Valeo*, 424 US 1 (1976).

[4] See, e.g., *Barnes* v. *Glen Theatre, Inc.*, 501 US 560 (1991) (challenge to statute prohibiting nude dancing); *Paris Adult Theatre I* v. *Slaton*, 413 US 49 (1973) (challenge to statute prohibiting exhibition of sexually explicit films).

[5] See, e.g., *Washington* v. *Glucksberg*, 521 US 702 (1997) and *Vacco* v. *Quill*, 521 US 793 (1997).

[6] See, e.g., Carlos Nino, 'Introduction', in Carlos Nino (ed.), *Rights: International Library of Essays in Law and Legal Theory* (New York: New York University Press, 1992), pp. xi, xiii–xix (discussing competing theories of rights).

of legal liberties, claims, powers, and immunities involving the first party who possesses the right, second parties against whom the right holds, third parties who might intervene either to aid the possessor of the right or the violator, and various officials whose diverse activities make up the legal system under which . . . [these] parties have their respective legal liberties, claims, powers, and immunities'.[7]

Commonly believed to unify all of these conflicting conceptions of rights is the idea that a legal right protects the right-holder's interest (however defined) by providing grounds for the imposition of constraints on the actions of other people.[8] Rights are inherently relational; they deal with the imposition of restraints, or duties (of non-interference, at least) upon others. As J. E. Penner has written, a solitary individual on an isolated planet 'can have interests regardless of the presence of others'; but 'it would be odd to say that he has rights'.[9]

In the individual/collective context, legal rights of individuals are usually contrasted with public-interest demands. 'Public interests' are usually understood, in law, to be utilitarian or otherwise derived aggregative social concerns that provide reasons for coercive legal action. Legally cognizable public interests are, thus, *also* relational in nature: they describe not only the interests that members of the public hold, but also the duties that may be imposed to vindicate those interests.[10]

The idea that legal rights function to protect individuals from public-interest demands is deeply ingrained in Anglo-American jurisprudence.[11] The assump-

[7] Carl Wellman, 'Upholding Legal Rights,' originally published in (1975) 86 *Ethics* 49, reprinted in Nino (ed.), n. 6 above, 61, 62–63.

[8] See, e.g., Joseph Raz, *The Morality of Freedom* (Oxford: Clarendon Press,1986), 166 (footnote omitted) ('"X has a right" if and only if X can have rights, and, other things being equal, an aspect of X's well-being (his interest) is a sufficient reason for holding some other person(s) to be under a duty.'); Jeremy Waldron, *The Right to Private Property* (Oxford: Clarendon Press, 1988), 3 (a right is afforded when an interest is sufficiently important from a moral point of view that others have a duty to respect it). Rights, under this understanding, ground certain duties, 'whether [the right holder] . . . wishes it or not'. Raz, above, 170.
This 'interest theory' of rights is, of course, not without its competitors. It has been argued, for instance, that it is the protection of the right-holder's will—not the right-holder's interest—which rights more accurately entail. See, e.g., H. L. A. Hart, 'Bentham on Legal Rights', in A. W. B. Simpson (ed.), *Oxford Essays in Jurisprudence 2nd Series* (Oxford: Clarendon Press, 1973), 171. The idea that rights protect interests is, however, that most commonly associated with legal rights, and it is within that tradition that we will operate here.

[9] J. E. Penner, *The Idea of Property in Law* (Oxford: Clarendon Press, 1997), 14.

[10] The name 'public interest' is, in a way, a misleading one for such concerns. An 'interest'—public or otherwise—is not, of itself, relational or coercive in nature; yet 'public interests', in law, are understood to be inherently so. 'Public interests', as understood in law, are in fact public interest *demands*—they describe interests with asserted coercive power. However, because the short-hand term 'public interest' is used so ubiquitously to describe these demands, that nomenclature will be retained here.

[11] See, e.g., Dworkin, n. 1 above, 193–194, 269 (discussing the 'anti-utilitarian' functions of individual rights); Alan Gewirth, 'Human Rights and Conceptions of the Self' (1988) 18 *Philosophia* 129, 138 (rights recognize 'morally justified position[s]' which individuals can claim 'even if majority preferences decree otherwise').

tion that individual rights and collective interests *conflict*—which is so often found in law—has been challenged by commentators. It has been pointed out that rights often (in fact) further collective goals, and that many collective goals (in fact) further individual rights.[12] For example, individual freedom of speech furthers the collective goals of maintaining a society characterized by open and free debate, and the collective goal of public health furthers the individual right to life. The fact that individual rights and collective interests may be mutually reinforcing or congruent in some instances does not, however, obscure the fact that they are clearly conflicting or incompatible in others. If an individual demands the right to speak in the face of state censorship, or if an individual demands the right to fill wetlands that must be preserved under public environmental laws, such rights and public interests clearly involve conflicting goals, in an adjudicative sense—or, if they involve the same abstract goals (such as 'the maintenance of a democratic society' or 'proper land use'), they assert quite different (and conflicting) means of getting there. When we think of the function of legal rights, in law, we generally think of these cases—and it is these instances of conflict between individual and collective interests, means, or goals that are our focus here.

When we declare an individual demand to be a right, in such situations, it is because we take the individual and his interests seriously.[13] To honour this grounding, individual rights must, as a *prima facie* matter at least, be deemed more powerful, more normatively compelling, than conflicting public interests.[14]

Prima facie power does not, of course, mean absolute power; in our legal system, many individual demands that are recognized as rights must ultimately yield to the conflicting interests of other individuals or collectivities. However,

---

[12] See, e.g., Robert Alexy, 'Individual Rights and Collective Goods', in Nino (ed.), n. 6 above, 163, 169–174 (discussing possible means-end relations between rights and collective goods); Joseph Raz, 'Rights and Individual Well-Being', in his *Ethics in the Public Domain: Essays in the Morality of Law and Politics* (Oxford: Clarendon Press, 1994), 29, 43–44 (arguing that the protection of civil and political rights furthers common or public goods, and that '[l]iberal political thought has often been guilty of overemphasizing the degree to which politics is a process of reconciling conflicting interests.'). Some have argued that courts in fact consistently accord rights a wider range of functions than is generally thought. See, e.g., Richard H. Pildes, 'Why Rights Are Not Trumps: Social Meanings, Expressive Harms, and Constitutionalism' (1988) 27 *Journal of Legal Studies* 725, 732 (arguing that rights often function—in constitutional adjudication—'not [to enhance] . . . the autonomy or atomistic self-interest of the right holder but [to realize] . . . various common goods', such as democratic self-governance, public education, a bounded religious sphere, and so on).

[13] The individual's fundamental interest in such rights schemes has been described as being afforded equal concern and respect: see Dworkin, n. 1 above, 272–278; as being treated as an end rather than as a means: see Robert Nozick, *Anarchy, State, and Utopia* (New York: Basic Books, Inc., 1974), 30–31; or as maintaining control over the important factors in one's life: see T. M. Scanlon, 'Rights, Goals, and Fairness', in Stuart Hampshire (ed.), *Public and Private Morality* (Cambridge: Cambridge University Press, 1978), 93, 106.

[14] See Alexy, n. 12 above, 178–179 (the postulate of taking the individual seriously requires 'a general *prima facie* priority in favour of individual rights'; 'there [must] be stronger grounds in favour of . . . [a] resolution required by collective goods than exist for that required by individual rights').

to be a 'right' under the traditional understanding, an individual demand must have presumptive power when it conflicts with other, non-rights demands.[15] Ronald Dworkin has described this power of rights, in the individual/collective context, in familiar terms. Rights 'may . . . be less than absolute; one principle might have to yield to another, or even to an urgent policy with which it competes on particular facts'. However, '[i]t follows from the definition of a right that it cannot be outweighed by all social goals.' It must have 'a certain threshold weight against collective goals in general'. '[I]t cannot be defeated by appeal to any of the ordinary routine goals of political administration'; it can be defeated 'only by a goal of special urgency'.[16]

Legal rights, then, are traditionally understood as right-holders' demands that are fortified,[17] by their classification as rights, against competing public interests. The heavy hand that this model lends in the resolution of conflicting individual and collective interests can be seen throughout American jurisprudence. Individual rights (in this view) have tremendous presumptive power despite the substantial public interests that may oppose them. For instance, in constitutional law, free-speech rights are stringently protected by law, with conflicting public interests—even those based upon national security concerns—bearing a heavy presumption of invalidity.[18] Similar power has been afforded to the right to free religious exercise,[19] the right to reproductive freedom,[20] the right to private association with whom one chooses,[21] the right to bodily

---

[15] A 'right' can be understood in two different ways: as an asserted claim, with *prima facie* power, or as a claim that is honoured (as an ultimate matter) in particular instances of conflict with other claims. The 'right to free speech', for instance, could be understood to mean a claim (made under the First Amendment) which has *prima facie* power and validity, or it could be understood to mean only those claims that are *ultimately* deemed valid *vis-à-vis* other, conflicting interests. It is in the first sense that we generally speak of rights in law, and it is that sense that is intended here: a right is a demand with presumptive validity *vis-à-vis* other (non-rights) demands.

[16] Dworkin, n. 1 above, 92. See also Alexy, n. 12 above, 179 (the '*[p]rima facie* priority [of rights] does not exclude the setting aside of individual rights' in favour of other interests; it simply demands that there be 'stronger grounds' in favour of the resolution required by other interests than is required for rights); Frederick Schauer, 'A Comment on the Structure of Rights' (1993) 27 *Georgia Law Review* 415, 429 ('[W]hat I get when I move from nonright to right is not (necessarily) the ability to have θ or to engage in the θ-ing to which a right to θ pertains, but rather simply the right to put the state to a higher burden of justification. A right to θ then just is the right to have the state not restrict the ability to θ without showing a compelling interest or the like.') (emphasis deleted).

[17] I am indebted to Alon Harel for this locution.

[18] See, e.g., *New York Times Company* v. *United States*, 403 US 713, 714 (1971) (*per curiam*).

[19] Under traditional constitutional tests, individual claims to religious free exercise could be denied only if compelling government interests opposed them. See *Hernandez* v. *Commissioner*, 490 US 680, 699 (1989); *Wisconsin* v. *Yoder*, 406 US 205, 221 (1972). The United States Supreme Court later changed its approach, and held that the individual right to free religious exercise is presumptively subordinate to otherwise neutral state laws. See *Lyng* v. *Northwest Indian Cemetery Protective Association*, 485 US 439 (1988); *Employment Division* v. *Smith*, 494 US 872 (1990). This provoked Congress to restore the traditional test: see Religious Freedom Restoration Act of 1993, 42 U.S.C. § 2000bb (1995), which effort was in turn invalidated by the Supreme Court: *City of Boerne* v. *Flores*, 521 US 507 (1997).

[20] See, e.g., *Roe* v. *Wade*, 410 US 113 (1973); *Eisenstadt v. Baird*, 405 US 438 (1972).

[21] See *NAACP* v. *Alabama*, 357 US 449 (1958); *Schware v. Board of Bar Examiners*, 353 US 232 (1957).

integrity,[22] the right to determine one's medical treatment,[23] and others. Although such rights may occasionally lose, there is no doubt but that in all of these cases the conflicting public interests—to overcome the rights' presumptive power—must have unusual force. For instance, in the case of symbolic speech, the Supreme Court has stated that the quality of the government interest which must appear in order to justify regulation must be 'compelling; substantial; subordinating; paramount; cogent; strong'.[24]

Other rights have less presumptive power; in constitutional law, they may (for instance) be defeated by state initiatives that are rationally related to legitimate state purposes.[25] Examples of such rights include the right to equal protection of the law when race, national origin, or other suspect category is not at issue;[26] the right to due process of law in the termination of government benefits;[27] the right to freedom from unreasonable searches and seizures by law enforcement officers;[28] and so on. However, even in these cases, the identity of the individual demands as 'rights' dictates that they are presumed (as a threshold matter, at least) to win, and that the opposing public interests are presumed (as a threshold matter, at least) to lose. Indeed, if individual demands do not have this presumptive power, one wonders how (under the traditional understanding) they can be 'rights' at all.

The image of rights and public interests that this traditional model of rights presents is simple and straightforward. Rights are demands that are discrete, conceptually 'bounded', and fortified against conflicting claims. They are asserted as entities against the public interests that oppose them.

This model of the rights/public interest relationship seems to describe many of the relationships between rights and conflicting public interests that we find in law. However, does it *always* capture the nature of this legal relationship?

Let us consider, for instance, our prior examination of American takings jurisprudence. The traditional rights of property ownership—the rights to possess, use, exclude, and dispose of property—are among the most foundational individual rights in the American legal system.[29] They have been, in the words of the United States Supreme Court, 'part of the Anglo-American legal system since feudal times'.[30] Although one may question the wisdom of this system, few would disagree with the expressed Congressional sentiment that the

---

[22] See *Winston* v. *Lee*, 470 US 753 (1985); *Rochin* v. *California*, 342 US 165 (1952).

[23] See *Cruzan* v. *Director, Missouri Department of Health*, 497 US 261 (1990).

[24] *United States* v. *O'Brien*, 391 US 367, 376–377 (1968) (footnotes omitted).

[25] See, e.g., *Pennell* v. *City of San Jose*, 485 US 1, 14 (1988).

[26] See, e.g., *Vance* v. *Bradley*, 440 US 93 (1979) (classification based upon age); *San Antonio Independent School District* v. *Rodriguez*, 411 US 1 (1973) (classification based upon wealth).

[27] See, e.g., *Mathews* v. *Eldridge*, 424 US 319 (1976).

[28] See, e.g., *Michigan Department of State Police* v. *Sitz*, 496 US 444 (1990) and *United States* v. *Martinez-Fuerte*, 428 US 543, 555 (1976).

[29] For a judicial expression of this view, see *Loretto* v. *Teleprompter Manhattan CATV Corporation*, 458 US 419, 435 (1982).

[30] *Hodel* v. *Irving*, 481 US 704, 716 (1987).

American political system 'was founded on principles of ownership, use, and control of private property'.[31] Because of the ubiquity and importance of property rights, one would expect to see the rigorous protection of such claims in law, with their protection in all but the most compelling circumstances. Indeed, the 'common' conception of property, described in the preceding chapter, seems to express what this traditional view of rights demands: property as protection, property as that which is effectively asserted by the individual against collective power. Yet we have seen that the individual protection which this conception of property rights envisions is often not what we find in takings cases. Rather, we find that claimed property rights in land, chattels, and other resources—otherwise well recognized in law—have been repeatedly sacrificed to general social interests on a routine basis. This result—which we have attributed to the use of an alternative, 'operative' conception of property—appears to be the antithesis of what our traditional understanding of rights generally, and our traditional understanding of property rights in particular, would demand.

The apparent failure of the presumptive power of property rights claims in these cases is puzzling. The treatment of the claimed property rights in these cases seems to be anomalous and inexplicable under traditional ideas of rights alone. Is there a way to explain—and justify—the treatment of property rights claims in these cases?

Our task, in the chapters that follow, is to explain why the traditional power afforded to rights is not afforded—and *should not* be afforded—to certain kinds of property claims. Before we can proceed to answer this question, we must first deepen our understanding of the nature of rights and their relationships with opposing public interests.

(ii) The presumptive power of rights: toward a deeper understanding

(a) **Identifying the concerns of rights and competing public interests**

As stated above, legal demands involved in individual/collective conflicts are generally of two types: rights-based demands and public-interest demands. The former are demands couched in the language of individual rights, such as one's right that the government not censor one's speech, or one's right that one's property not be confiscated without compensation. Collective demands, such as the government's demand that national security be preserved or that environmental regulations be enforced, are typically classified as public-interest demands.

---

[31] Private Property Owners Bill of Rights, S. 239, H.R. 790, 104th Cong. (1995) (U.S.).

If we probe further, we find that legal rights are—as Alon Harel has illuminated—both *content-specific* and *reason-dependent*.[32] The first quality, or the
content-specificity of rights, is well recognized in legal discourse. There is a certain content—a certain protected state of affairs—that we associate with every
legal right. If, for instance, we consider the right to free speech, there is a certain
content—the ability of individuals to speak freely—that we associate with that
right. The same is true of other rights. The right to property protection involves
the right to build, or to destroy, or otherwise to act in specified ways in connection with that property; the right to free exercise of religion involves the right to
worship, or to speak, or otherwise to believe or act in accordance with one's
beliefs; and so on.

The reason-dependent nature of legal rights is less obvious but no less critical.
Rights do not only involve particular content, i.e., they do not only protect certain states of affairs—they protect those states of affairs (only) for particular
reasons.[33] For instance, the right to free speech is often justified on the ground
that it promotes individual autonomy[34] or contributes to the marketplace of
ideas.[35] The reasons for protection of free speech are regarded as essential to
that right. To fall within the right to free speech, a demand must not only
involve the content of this right, but the reasons that the right in question protects this right, as well.[36]

The way in which content-specificity and reason-dependency work together
to identify demands that involve rights can be illustrated by consideration of

[32] See Alon Harel, 'Revisionist Theories of Rights: An Unwelcome Defense' (1998) XI *Canadian
Journal of Law and Jurisprudence* 227; Alon Harel, 'What Demands are Rights? An Investigation
into the Relation between Rights and Reasons' (1997) 17 *Oxford Journal of Legal Studies* 101. For
another account of reason-dependency in the particular context of property rights see Penner, n. 9
above, 13, 70.

[33] See Harel, 'What Demands are Rights? An Investigation into the Relation between Rights and
Reasons', n. 32 above. The reason-dependency of rights is grounded in the interests that rights are
intended to serve. See Raz, n. 8 above, 180–183.

[34] See, e.g., *Cohen* v. *California*, 403 US 15, 24 (1971) (interpretation of constitutional free speech
rights must 'comport with the premise of individual dignity and choice'); *Consolidated Edison
Company* v. *Public Service Commission*, 447 US 530, 534 n.2 (1980) ('Freedom of speech . . . protects the individual's interest in self-expression.'). See also Kent Greenawalt, *Fighting Words:
Individuals, Communities, and Liberties of Speech* (Princeton, N.J.: Princeton University Press,
1995), 5 (freedom of thought and expression promote individual autonomy, which is regarded as
intrinsically valuable in liberal democratic societies).

[35] See *Abrams* v. *United States*, 250 US 616, 630 (1919) (Holmes, J., dissenting) (constitutionally
protected free speech assumes that 'the best test of truth is the power of the thought to get itself
accepted in the competition of the market'). In Thomas Emerson's famous formulation, freedom of
speech is protected to promote individual self-fulfilment, allow the pursuit of truth in the marketplace of ideas, encourage participation in public life, and enhance the maintenance of a stable community through interaction and exchange. Thomas I. Emerson, *The System of Freedom of
Expression* (New York: Random House, 1970), 6–7.

[36] See Harel, 'What Demands are Rights? An Investigation into the Relation between Rights and
Reasons', n. 32 above, 105. See also Penner, n. 9 above, 13 ('If a duty not to interfere with others'
property were imposed on people generally in order to serve the interests of owners, then owners
[would] have rights in respect of their property [under the common understanding]. If it were
imposed instead in the public interest to avoid conflict or bloodshed, then the owners of property
would [not]').

whether a particular demand is an instance of a general, legally recognized right.[37] Consider, for example, a demand that the publication of pornography be protected as an instance of the right to free speech. When we consider this demand, we must consider not only whether this demand involves the content that we associate with a free speech claim—i.e., whether this demand involves 'speech' of the requisite character—but also whether this demand is justified by reasons that underlie the right to free speech. If the person making this demand can establish that it involves both the appropriate content and the right reasons—i.e., reasons (such as individual autonomy or the marketplace of ideas) that are essential (or intrinsic) to the core right of free speech—then his demand may be properly classified as an instance of the right to free speech. If, however, his demand is justified for other reasons—such as the financial cost of suppressing pornography, the administrative impossibility of suppressing pornography, and so on—his demand may be important, or well founded, but may not be classified as an instance of the right to free speech.[38]

Determining the content of a particular right and the reasons for its protection may, of course, be quite contentious. For instance, the extent to which particular expressive activity falls within the 'content' of free speech, or the extent to which certain values—such as the marketplace of ideas—are essential to that right, have been the subject of intense debate. Moreover, determinations of whether a demand involves the 'content' of a right, and whether it involves the 'reasons' for a right, are often mutually and inextricably dependent. For instance, in rejecting obscenity as involving 'speech' content, judges often rely upon the fact that obscenity fails to promote what are seen as free-speech values.[39] But, despite these qualifications, it is apparent that a demand's content and its reasons are both critical to its classification as an instance of a particular legal right. Demands involve legal rights if they involve certain content and certain reasons—that is, if they are concerned with the protection of a particular state of affairs, for particular reasons, as defined by law.[40]

When we turn to public-interest demands, we find a similar structure. Although public-interest demands are often stated in very general terms—e.g., the 'public interest in national security' or the 'public interest in environmental protection'—these demands also involve both content-specificity and reason-dependency. For instance, the public interest in national security or the public interest in environmental protection is content-specific: it is concerned with the achievement or protection of a certain state of affairs. In addition, to be a valid

[37] Cf. Raz, n. 8 above, 169–170 (discussing general rights and particular instantiations of those rights).
[38] See Harel, 'What Demands are Rights? An Investigation into the Relation between Rights and Reasons', n. 32 above, 107. Cf. Raz, n. 8 above, 168–170 (for one right to be an instance—or derivative—of another, the premises of the latter must provide a justification for the existence of the former).
[39] See, e.g., *Roth* v. *United States*, 354 US 476, 484 (1957).
[40] Understandings about a right's content and reasons are, obviously, subject to societal redefinition and legal change. For further discussion of this issue, see Ch. 6 , below.

public-interest demand, this demand must be made for the right reasons[41]—e.g., for the reason that citizens be protected, or that the natural environment be preserved. Although public-interest demands are typically framed by courts in very general terms, we find that they involve, in operation, the same content-specificity and reason-dependency that rights involve. That is, a particular demand is a legally cognizable public-interest demand if it is concerned with the protection of a particular state of affairs, for particular reasons, as collectively understood and defined by law.

The qualities of content-specificity and reason-dependency are perhaps more easily seen *vis-à-vis* rights than they are *vis-à-vis* public interests; we are more accustomed in legal analysis separately to identify the states of affairs to be achieved by rights, and the reasons that rights involve for the protection of those states of affairs, than we are to ask—and answer—those same questions about public interests. However, both elements in fact play an equally important role in both contexts.

We find, then, that particular demands involve legal rights, or particular demands are legally cognizable public interests, because of what we shall call their *'core values'*, i.e., *their protection of particular states of affairs for particular reasons*. We can now proceed to understand when—and why—claimed rights (such as the claimed right to property protection) may have *prima facie* or 'trumping power' in some situations, but not in others.

(b) Differing presumptive powers of claimed rights: a normative hypothesis

Under the traditional understanding of the nature of rights in law, rights are seen as demands with particular strength which 'trump' (at least as a *prima facie* matter) non-rights interests that conflict with them. In individual/collective conflicts, the purpose of rights is to protect individual interests against public-interest demands. Individual rights can be overridden by collective goals, but only by collective goals of special or compelling urgency. They cannot be defeated by the ordinary or routine goals of government.

Is this, however, all that our implementation of the notion of rights in law involves? Do we simply—and mechanically—(1) determine whether the individual interest asserts a right (as legally defined), (2) determine whether the public interest is—in fact—a collective one, and (3) afford the right 'trumping' power, if the public interest is not—by its very nature—'compelling'?

---

[41] For an interesting discussion of reasons as a part of common goods and the public interests that assert them see Pildes, n. 12 above, 739–740. As Pildes states, '[f]or constitutional and other purposes, it is a mistake to treat an action as independent from the reasons behind it, for those reasons give actions their distinct social meanings. Two state actions are not the same—ethically, expressively, and sometimes legally—if they are taken for different reasons. How an action comes about shapes its social meaning—and therefore what it is.' *Ibid.* 753.

In fact, there is far more to this power than our description so far allows. When we assign to an individual demand the presumptive power afforded to rights, we assume that we have done so on some kind of principled basis. Although we could explain this assignment on purely institutional grounds—we could say that legal rights are simply those demands that citizens, through the political process, have designated as 'rights', and that the presumptively less powerful public interests are simply the remaining (non-rights public) interests—this explanation is viscerally unsatisfactory. We assume that the process of designating particular demands as rights involves something more than completely arbitrary political action. We assume that there are reasons why some demands have been granted 'rights power', and others have not.

We assume, in short, that there is something about the nature of the demands that rights protect—*something about the nature of the interests that these demands assert*—that justifies their presumptive power. The most commonly held (and, in the end, the most persuasive) rationale for the presumptive power of rights is that the interests that underlie those rights involve values that are—as a *prima facie* matter, at least—more important or more worthy (as a societally determined matter) than competing non-rights interests. Thus, for example, freedom of speech has been granted 'rights' status and power because the core values that it involves are more important than those involved in the competing (public) interests.

This 'normative hypothesis' for the power of rights is certainly in keeping with common notions of what rights are and why they are recognized in law. Freedom of speech, freedom of religion, the protection of property, equal protection, and so on involve core values that we particularly prize in our society and are, accordingly, interests to which we grant special legal protection. This explanation for the power of rights has, however, an important and often overlooked corollary. Under this hypothesis, the presumptive power of rights adheres only if the values that the right involves are *not shared, in fact, by the competing public interest*. If the core values that the claimed right involves *are the same, in kind,* as the core values that are involved in the competing public interest, there is no basis for a conclusion that the right involves normatively superior values and no basis for affording the right presumptive power.

By combining this fundamental insight with our understanding of the constituent elements of rights and public interests, previously set forth, we can now develop a simple yet powerful model which will predict when (in law) claimed rights will—*and should*—have *prima facie* or trumping power over competing public interests, and when they will—*and should*—not. This model, and its operation, are described in the following chapter.

6

Predicting the Power of Claimed Rights: A Two-Tiered Model of Rights' Presumptive Power

We are now in a position to set forth a model that predicts when—in law—claimed rights will (and should) have *prima facie* or trumping power, and when they will (and should) not. This model is as follows:

- Claimed rights *will (and should) have presumptive power* over competing public interests when the core values that underlie the claimed right and the core values that underlie the competing public interest are *different in kind*.

  In this situation, the claimed right and the competing public interest are entirely different and unrelated entities. They are in the traditional, opposing relation associated with rights. The claimed right—in this case—enjoys presumptive or *prima facie* power.

- Claimed rights *will (and should) not have presumptive power* over competing public interests when the core values that underlie the claimed right and the core values that underlie the competing public interest are *the same in kind*.

  In this situation, the claimed right and the competing public interest are, in fact, integrally related. They are viewed—most accurately—as presenting competing interpretations about the nature of a 'foundational' right that both, in fact, involve. The conflict between them is a struggle that is *internal* to that right, over that right's definition, scope, and meaning. The claimed right and the competing public interest are of presumptively equal power, with neither favoured—as a threshold matter—over the other.

These different relations between claimed rights and competing public interests can be seen as different levels or tiers of analysis. The first relation presents the traditional, '**Tier One**' case: the claimed right and the competing public interest are opposing and unrelated entities, with the claimed right enjoying presumptive power. This relation can be schematically represented as shown in Figure 1, below:

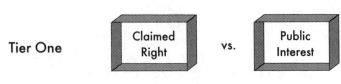

Figure 1

- claimed right and competing public interest involve *different core values*
- claimed right—as an entity—is asserted against competing public interest that is conceptually external to it
- claimed right has presumptive power

The second relation can be seen as presenting a '**Tier Two**' case—or, in other words, an internal struggle over what the right (in Tier One) means. We can schematically illustrate this as shown in Figure 2, below:

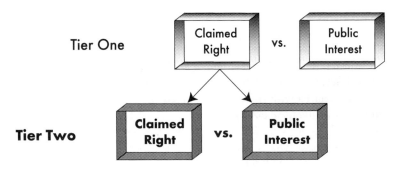

Figure 2

- claimed right and competing public interest involve the *same core values*
- conflict between claimed right and competing public interest presents an internal question as to what the foundational right (in Tier One) is
- claimed right and competing public interest are of presumptively equal power

By determining whether—under our model—the conflict involved presents a Tier One or Tier Two case, we can predict the relative power of the claimed right and the competing public interest in law.[1]

---

[1] Richard Pildes has suggested that there is yet another class of cases in which claimed rights lack 'trumping power' in constitutional adjudication: those in which the claimed right—although framed in individual-interest terms—in fact presents little more than a competing conception of a common good which the public interest also involves. For instance, a public employee's challenge to an 'English only' workplace law is not (truly) 'about "the rights" of public employees to free speech, at least not in the atomistic conception of rights', since '[p]ublic employees do not have rights of free speech' in this sense. 'It is the interests of those whom government serves, not employs,

We can illustrate these two relations with familiar examples involving the right to free speech. Let us take, for example, a newspaper's claimed right to publish a story, and the competing government interest in stopping publication to preserve national security. To predict the presumptive power of the claimed right, we must determine what the core values that underlie this right and its competitor are. We will assume that the newspaper's right is claimed on free-speech grounds—that is, that the right to publish involves a claimed right to 'speak' and that the reasons cited by the newspaper are those traditionally cited as grounding the right to free speech, such as the promotion of individual autonomy or the marketplace of ideas. Under these circumstances, it is clear that the core values that underlie the newspaper's claim are those that are traditionally associated with the right to free speech. The state of affairs that the claimed right seeks to protect is the ability to speak freely, and the reasons that are advanced for this claimed right are those that we generally associate with the right to free speech.

Consider, now, the competing government interest. The core values that are generally assumed to underlie the government's claim to national security are very different. The state of affairs that this claim attempts to achieve involves the physical security of the nation's citizens. This content is unrelated to the preservation of speech. Furthermore, whatever the reasons for the preservation of national security may be, they are generally not those that are associated with the protection of speech (such as the promotion of individual autonomy, or the enhancement of the marketplace of ideas).

When analysed in this way, it is apparent that this conflict presents a Tier One case. Since this claimed right and competing public interest do not involve the same core values, they are simply opposing and unrelated entities which present a right/public interest conflict of the traditionally envisioned kind. Our model predicts that this Tier One case will—and should—involve a claimed right with presumptive or trumping power. This is, in fact, the relation that one finds, for instance, between this claimed right and this competing public interest in American constitutional discourse.[2]

that are . . . at stake in this context.' Accordingly, '[t]he constitutional clash . . . is not between the "rights" of public employees versus the strength of governmental interests in regulating those rights. The clash is over competing conceptions of a particular common good: the official public culture of the State, as expressed through its language commitments.' Richard H. Pildes, 'Why Rights Are Not Trumps: Social Meanings, Expressive Harms, and Constitutionalism' (1988) 27 *Journal of Legal Studies* 725, 742–743.

The significance of Pildes' observation will depend upon one's assessment of the number of cases which do not present genuinely conflicting rights/public interest claims. As Pildes notes, '[r]ights play many roles, and no doubt many problems must continue to be understood to involve direct conflicts between rights and state interests.' *Ibid*. 761 n. 114. To the extent that a case is one which Pildes describes, however, one could see it as a kind of Tier Two case—only one in which the meaning of a public interest (rather than a foundational right) is at stake.

[2] See, e.g., *New York Times Company* v. *United States*, 403 US 713 (1971). *Presumptive* power does not, of course, mean *ultimate* power. It is quite possible that the competing public interest in national security might ultimately prevail over the claimed right to publish, because of the particularly compelling nature of the competing public interest. If, for instance, the national security interest were

Let us consider, now, another claimed speech right/public interest conflict that has been the subject of much current controversy. In recent years, a debate has raged over whether there should be a right to publish pornography as an instance of the right to free speech. The publishers of pornography frame their demand in free-speech terms: they claim that it involves the right to speak, for reasons (such as promotion of personal autonomy and the marketplace of ideas) that are essential or intrinsic to free speech rights.[3]

Feminist theorists (among others) challenge the pornographers' claims on the ground that the public interest demands that women are entitled to live in a pornography-free environment. In particular, the claimed public interest in a pornography-free environment is based upon a 'silencing' claim: it is argued that the publication of pornography 'silences' women, who are degraded by it.[4]

In this situation, it is apparent that the same core values underlie both the claimed right and the competing public interest. Both seek to protect states of affairs of the same kind: both are concerned with the ability of (particular) individuals to speak freely. Furthermore, the reasons that are advanced by both sides are those that are classically associated with free-speech rights, such as the promotion of personal autonomy and the need for a vibrant and varied public discourse.

Indeed, if we reflect further, we realize that the claimed right and the competing public interest in this case are, in fact, integrally related. They present, essentially, different interpretations of what the foundational or core right to free speech should be—a right which both attempt, in different ways, to implement. The publishers of pornography claim that the ability to publish pornography is an intrinsic part of the right to free speech. The public interest in a pornography-free environment, as advanced by feminist theorists and others, claims that the right to free speech (of women) requires the opposite: that the publication of pornography be suppressed. The conflict between the claimed

---

deemed to involve values associated with an immediate right to life—such as the protection of troops in a time of war—those values may well be normatively more compelling than those that the right to publish asserts. See *ibid.* 726–727 (Brennan, J., concurring) (danger must be of a type 'kindred to imperiling the safety of a transport already at sea'.). In such a case, however, the reason for the claimed right's ultimate failure is not that it lacks presumptive or *prima facie* power; rather, that power is simply overcome—in that case—by the strength of the competing public interest.

The question that our model explains is why rights sometime lack presumptive power—i.e., why they sometimes yield so easily to routine (rather than compelling) government interests. The model does not preclude the possibility that rights which *have* presumptive power might still, in the end, be overcome by particularly compelling public interests.

[3] See, e.g., *American Booksellers Association, Inc.* v. *Hudnut*, 771 F 2d 323 (7th Cir. 1985), aff'd, 475 US 1001 (1986) (in which publisher of pornography argued, and the Court agreed, that pornography is protected speech).

[4] See, e.g., Catharine A. MacKinnon, 'Pornography as Defamation and Discrimination' (1991) 71 *Boston University Law Review* 793; Rae Langton, 'Speech Acts and Unspeakable Acts' (1993) 22 *Philosophy and Public Affairs* 293. See generally Alon Harel, 'The Boundaries of Justifiable Tolerance: A Liberal Perspective', in David Heyd (ed.), *Toleration: An Elusive Virtue* (Princeton, N.J.: Princeton University Press, 1996), 114 (discussing situations in which intolerance of the speech of others can be considered to be a necessary and justified part of free-speech rights).

right and the competing public interest in this case is a struggle that is internal to the definition, scope, and meaning of the right to free speech. However one may resolve this conflict, our model predicts that in this Tier Two case, the claimed right will—and should—have no presumptive power over the competing public interest. The difficulty that courts and commentators have had in the resolution of cases involving this conflict attests to the inapplicability of the usual, 'trumping' relation between claimed rights and competing public interests when evaluating these claims.[5]

A similar analysis can be made of the conflict between the demand to publish 'hate' speech, as an incident of the right to free speech, and the competing public interest in a hate-speech-free environment, if the public interest is grounded in the tendency of hate speech to 'silence' members of targeted groups.[6] In this case, the core values that underlie the claimed right and the competing public interest are the same in kind. Both are concerned with the ability of individuals to speak, for reasons that are associated with free-speech rights. The claimed right and the competing public interest are integrally related, both presenting (in effect) internal, defining interpretations of the nature of the foundational right to free speech. As a result, this is a Tier Two case, in which the claimed right and the competing public interest are—and should be—of equal presumptive power.

The principles of our two-tiered model are often reflected, on an unarticulated basis, in the work of theorists who oppose the publication of pornography or hate speech. They often argue that pornography or hate speech is not a form of speech that the right to free speech should encompass.[7] These theorists assert, essentially, that the dispute is centred upon what the right to free speech *is*—an assertion that is well supported when the core values that underlie the claimed right are of the same kind as those that ground the claimed public interest. In this circumstance, the conflicts involved are not between two unrelated

---

[5] Compare *American Booksellers Association*, n. 3 above (holding Indianapolis anti-pornography ordinance unconstitutional) with *Regina* v. *Butler* [1992] SCR 452 (Can.) (holding that pornography may be censored because of the harm that it causes to women, among others). See also Steven G. Gey, 'The Case Against Postmodern Censorship Theory' (1996) 145 *University of Pennsylvania Law Review* 193, 193–195 (discussing the erosion of assumed priority of free speech rights in the face of 'silencing' and like claims).

[6] See, e.g., Mari J. Matsuda, 'Public Response to Racist Speech: Consider the Victim's Story,' in Mari J. Matsuda, Charles R. Lawrence III, Richard Delgado, and Kimberlè Williams Crenshaw (eds.), *Words That Wound: Critical Race Theory, Assaultive Speech, and the First Amendment* (Boulder, Colo.: Westview Press, 1993), 17; Patricia Williams, 'Spirit-Murdering the Messenger: The Discourse of Fingerpointing as the Law's Response to Racism' (1987) 42 *University of Miami Law Review* 127, 129–130 (discussing the psychological effects that victims of hate speech experience). Such claims may be made on the basis of individual or group identity. See Calvin R. Massey, 'Hate Speech, Cultural Diversity, and the Foundational Paradigm of Free Expression' (1992) 40 *University of California at Los Angeles Law Review* 103, 158–166.

[7] See, e.g., Catharine A. MacKinnon, 'Pornography, Civil Rights, and Speech' (1985) 20 *Harvard Civil Rights-Civil Liberties Law Review* 1; John M. Finnis, '"Reason and Passion": The Constitutional Dialectic of Free Speech and Obscenity' (1967) 116 *University of Pennsylvania Law Review* 222.

demands; they are disputes over the meaning of the foundational right itself. Accordingly, the usual, *prima facie* power that we associate with claimed rights does not apply to these conflicts.[8]

Before we proceed, several observations are required at this point. First, our analysis of the presumptive power of the claims that we have examined is dependent, of course, on our understandings of the core values that underlie these claims. If the content or reasons for either of the competing claims is different from those that we have specified, their legal relation may be different as well. For instance, if hate speech is opposed (in the public interest) not on 'silencing' grounds, but on the ground of its tendency to incite violence and disorder,[9] then the relation that we have previously described between these claims would change. The prior situation—in which the core values that underlie these claims are of the same kind—would be replaced by one in which the core values that underlie these claims are very different. Under this new assumption, neither the state of affairs that the claimed right and the competing public interest attempt to achieve (ability to speak vs. community peace) nor the reasons for these objectives (promotion of personal autonomy, varied public discourse, and so on vs. promotion of individual security, interpersonal harmony, and so on) are the same. As a result, this would be a Tier One case, and the claimed right would enjoy presumptive power.

In addition, the application of our model to determine the relative strength of claimed rights and competing public interests is dependent upon an assumption that the core values that underlie any claimed individual right and any competing public interest in question are, in fact, determinable to some workable degree. Particular values—such as autonomy[10]—may be subject to different understandings. In addition, as was discussed above, the content and reasons that are validly deemed to underlie a particular right or a particular public interest may be a matter of dispute. For instance, whether the public interest in the suppression of hate speech validly includes 'silencing' concerns is a matter of intense debate.

It is also obvious that any core values—even if determinable at this moment—are not cast in stone. Our understandings of the content and reasons that are

---

[8] The claim that pornography or hate speech is not a form of speech that the 'right to free speech' encompasses must be distinguished from a different claim: that, while the right to free speech provides strong *prima facie* reasons to protect pornography or hate speech (as speech), there are powerful reasons to override these speech-based concerns and justify its regulation. See, e.g., Catharine A. MacKinnon, *Only Words* (Cambridge, Mass.: Harvard University Press, 1993), 71–110 (arguing that the values embodied in the Fourteenth Amendment compete with and override those of the First Amendment in this context). Such arguments assume the existence of a Tier One case: that the right to free speech is opposed by unrelated public-interest concerns. They assume the use of the traditional, trumping relationship between rights and public interests—an assumption which makes regulation of the speech in question much more difficult to justify.

[9] See, e.g., David Kretzmer, 'Freedom of Speech and Racism' (1987) 8 *Cardozo Law Review* 445, 456. For a general discussion of this theory, see Massey, n. 6 above, 155– 158.

[10] See, e.g., John Christman (ed.), *The Inner Citadel: Essays on Individual Autonomy* (New York: Oxford University Press, 1989).

validly deemed to underlie particular rights or public interests are the products of shifting and evolving political, social, and legal understandings. Indeed, it is through consideration of concrete cases that the implications of general or abstract rights are explored, and their refined meanings determined.[11] For instance, in a recent doctrinal shift, the Supreme Court has held that equal treatment of religious believers and others is a paramount concern in cases involving the right to free religious exercise and, as a consequence, free-exercise claims (as a class) will generally lose to public interests expressed as a part of 'religiously neutral' state laws.[12] Some commentators have agreed, arguing that free-exercise rights should not mean that religious exercise be privileged, but that it simply be treated with the same regard as citizens' other concerns.[13] If this understanding of the core meaning of the right to religious exercise takes hold, it will obviously affect the presumptive power of this right *vis-à-vis* other, conflicting community interests. As our understandings of rights and public interests change, so will our understandings of the relations that govern their conflicts.

Although these problems in application exist, they are not peculiar to the application of our model of rights/public interests conflicts. Indeed, such problems are involved in every attempted application or articulation of law. What concerns do we—as a society—believe to underlie the right to free speech? What concerns do we—as a society—believe to underlie the public interest in national security? There are no simple, uncontroverted, or final answers to these questions. Despite such problems, the individual rights and public interests that our legal system articulates serve distinct and critical social functions. Joseph Raz has observed, for instance, that rights are a kind of shorthand, 'intermediate conclusions in arguments from ultimate values to duties'.[14] They 'enable a common culture to be formed round shared intermediate conclusions, in spite of a great degree of haziness and disagreement concerning ultimate values'.[15] Determinations of the core values that underlie claimed rights and competing public interests must be made with reference to prevailing understandings, and with knowledge of the limitations that those understandings necessarily imply. Within that dynamic framework, we can apply the principles of our model in a meaningful way.

---

[11] See Joseph Raz, 'On the Nature of Rights' (1984) 93 *Mind* 194, 211–212. As Andrew Halpin has observed, arguments that may be maintained 'for the establishment of an ideal abstract right in . . . an ideal society . . . [may be] absurdly inapplicable to working through the realities of the actual society encountered, in which the right is to be established'. Andrew Halpin, *Rights and Law Analysis and Theory* (Oxford: Hart Publishing, 1997), 173. Such refinements in meaning could be the products of external (Tier One) or internal (Tier Two) conflicts.

[12] See *Lyng* v. *Northwest Indian Cemetery Protective Association*, 485 US 439 (1988) and *Employment Division* v. *Smith*, 494 US 872 (1990) (if a state law simply prohibits religious conduct, that—in the absence of evidence of intent to discriminate against the religious—creates no cognizable claim under the First Amendment's Free Exercise Clause).

[13] See, e.g., Christopher L. Eisgruber and Lawrence G. Sager, 'The Vulnerability of Conscience: The Constitutional Basis for Protecting Religious Conduct' (1994) 61 *University of Chicago Law Review* 1245, 1283.

[14] Raz, n. 11 above, 208.　　　[15] *Ibid.*

One final—and related—objection must also be noted. One could argue that in any case, the core values that underlie the claimed right and the competing public interest *may be* of the same kind, if those values are framed more abstractly. For instance, the state of affairs that a public-interest claim of national security attempts to achieve—i.e., the physical security of its citizens—may be understood, at some level, to include the preservation of citizens' rights to free speech. Or—in an even broader vein— it could be argued that all traditional human rights and competing public interests are grounded in concern for human well-being, rendering the values that underlie those conflicting claims similar in every case. If this approach is used, all cases are Tier Two cases, and the usefulness of the model—as something which predicts and explains the *relative* power of rights in law—fails.

The values that undergird any claimed right and the values that undergird any competing public interest can always be expanded (through greater and greater abstraction) until those values 'merge'. Particular rights and public interests are, however, obviously more than these generic articulations capture: they are grounded in values which have particular content, and which give them (in turn) distinctive identity and character.[16] Our concern is not with rights and public interests *as they might be conceived*, but rather with rights and public interests *as they are used and understood* in legal discourse. To have useful legal meaning, rights and the values that they protect—and public interests and the values that they protect—must be substantively constrained. Indeed, when we think of the 'right to confrontation', 'the right to free speech', 'the public interest in national security', 'the public interest in environmental protection', and so on, specific, substantive concerns come immediately to mind. It is those commonly understood and real constraints that provide the 'great common ground' for societal understandings of the nature of claimed rights and competing public interests, and that are necessary for a meaningful discussion about them. And it is those constraints that determine the presumptive power of claimed rights and competing public interests in the ways described here.

Thus far, we have set forth a two-tiered relational model which predicts when a claimed right will—and should—have presumptive power over a competing public interest, and when it will—and should—not. When we examine particular rights/public interests relations that we find in law, we find that this model accurately describes existing legal relations. For example:

- *The claimed right to distribute religious literature (as an incident of free religious exercise) vs. the competing public interest in preventing solicitation.* In cases of this type, the claimed right has been accorded presumptive power.[17]

---

[16] See J. E. Penner, *The Idea of Property in Law* (Oxford: Clarendon Press, 1997), 54 ('[re]conceiving all interests [that rights protect] as mere manifestations of an interest in autonomy or some such general interest may be wrong-headed in principle', since the variety of interests found in law reflects—in fact—the variety of societally recognized values).

[17] See *Murdock* v. *Pennsylvania*, 319 US 105 (1943); *Cantwell* v. *Connecticut*, 310 US 296 (1940).

The model predicts this result, since the core values that underlie the claimed right (protection of religious activity, for reasons of freedom of conscience) and the core values that underlie the competing public interest (freedom from solicitation, for reasons of the need for peace or privacy) are not the same. This is a Tier One case, in which the claimed right has presumptive power.

- *The claimed right to free religious exercise vs. the competing public interest in compulsory childhood education.* In this case, the claimed right was accorded presumptive power.[18] The model predicts this result, since the core values that underlie the claimed right (protection of religious expression, for reasons of freedom of conscience) and the core values that underlie the competing public interest (the attendance of children at school, for reasons of fostering an educated citizenry) are not the same. This is a Tier One case, in which the claimed right has presumptive power.

- *The claimed right of women to attend an all-male, state-funded academy (as an incident of equal protection) vs. the competing public interest in providing single-sex, male education.* In this case, the claimed right was accorded presumptive power.[19] The model predicts this result, since the core values that underlie the claimed right (the achievement of equal educational opportunity, for reasons of equality) and the core values that underlie the competing public interest (the ability of males to attend single-sex state-funded schools, for reasons of providing pedagogically diverse, single-sex educational opportunities) are not the same. This is a Tier One case, in which the claimed right has presumptive power.

- *The claimed right of men to attend an all-female, state-funded school (as an incident of equal protection) vs. the competing public interest in providing single-sex, female education for women.* In this case, the Supreme Court has indicated that the claimed right may well be subordinate to the state's competing public interest.[20] Although this result may seem peculiar at first blush (particularly in light of the preceding example), it is explained by the core values that the Court understands—in this case—to underlie the asserted public interest. If single-sex, female education is understood *not* as a simple manifestation of a public interest in pedagogical diversity, *but rather* as a vehicle created to overcome past discrimination against women (and to provide them with equal educational opportunity), the claimed right would be unable (in the Court's view) to prevail over this competing public interest.[21] This result is, in fact, in accordance with our model. In the case that the Court posits, *both* of the competing claims are concerned with the achievement of equal educational opportunity, for reasons of gender equality. The claimed right and the competing public interest are integrally related, both presenting (in effect) internal, defining interpretations of what the nature of the

---

[18] See *Wisconsin* v. *Yoder*, 406 US 205 (1972).
[19] See *United States* v. *Virginia*, 518 US 515 (1996).
[20] See *Mississippi University for Women* v. *Hogan*, 458 US 718, 728–730 (1982).   [21] *Ibid.*

foundational right of equality should be. As a result, this is a Tier Two case, and the claimed right and the competing public interest are of equal presumptive power.

- *The claimed right to the exercise of political speech (through the giving of corporate campaign contributions) vs. the competing public interest in restricting corporate giving 'to avoid corruption or the appearance of corruption'.*[22] In this case, the claimed right was afforded presumptive power, as a formal matter, but was nonetheless defeated by ' "the compelling government . . . interest in preventing corruption" '.[23] This result is perhaps more satisfactorily predicted and explained by the application of our model. The core values that underlie the claimed right were described by the Court as the protection of (corporate) expressive activity, for reasons of the need for (and right of) all to participate in the political process; those that underlie the competing public interest were described by the Court as the prevention of the massive infusion of corporate money into election campaigns, in order to protect the political process from 'corros[ion] and distort[ion]'.[24] Since this public interest involved (at its core) the protection of the ability *of all citizens* to engage in effective political speech,[25] this is—in fact—a Tier Two case, in which the same core values infused both the claimed right and the competing public interest. As a result, the claimed right in fact possesses no normative superiority, and—as a result—should be afforded no presumptive power.

* * *

We have now established when, and why, claimed rights—as a general proposition—enjoy presumptive power over competing public interests. We shall now see how these rules can explain, and guide, our treatment of property claims in law.

---

[22] *Austin* v. *Michigan Chamber of Commerce*, 494 US 652, 658 (1990).

[23] *Ibid.* (quoting *FEC* v. *National Conservative Political Action Committee*, 470 US 480, 500–501 (1985)).

[24] *Ibid.* 660.

[25] *Ibid.* 659 (quoting *FEC* v. *Massachusetts Citizens for Life, Inc.*, 479 US 238, 257 (1986)) (goal of statute is to prevent corporations from obtaining ' "an unfair advantage in the political marketplace" ').

7

The Variable Power of Property Rights: Explaining the (Otherwise) Inexplicable in Law

Generally, property rights—like all legal rights—are deemed to have presumptive power when opposed by non-rights (public) interests. If an individual asserts a legally cognizable property right regarding land, chattels, ideas, reputation, or other identifiable subject, we expect—and the law generally recognizes—that this right will have presumptive or *prima facie* power against competing public interests. In any particular case, the public interest may ultimately prevail; but to do so, it must be of a particularly compelling nature, not simply the assertion of an ordinary or routine goal of government.

We have seen, however, that this expectation is not borne out in the legal treatment of a significant number of property claims. In land-use and environmental cases, for instance, the Supreme Court has routinely afforded far less protection to individuals' claims of property rights than the 'right to property' (as a general principle) seems to require. By using what we have called the operative conception of property, the Court has afforded claimed property rights far less presumptive power than we would otherwise expect; indeed, it has seemed to assume that collective power to change existing rights is somehow 'a part' of the very idea of property.

We are now in a position to explain what would otherwise be seen as the aberrational treatment of claimed property rights in these cases. Using the conceptual framework set forth in the last chapter, we can explain why some claimed property rights lack—*and should lack*—presumptive power.

(i) The presumptive power of property: a two-tiered model

In the preceding chapter, we constructed a two-tiered model which generally predicts when claimed rights will enjoy presumptive power in law. We can now restate this model in terms of the particular right to property. Thus:

- **In a Tier One case**, the claimed property right and the competing public interest have the traditional relation associated with rights. In this case, the core values that underlie the claimed right and the competing public interest are *different in kind*; as a result, the claimed right and the opposing public interest are distinct and unrelated entities. The claimed property right—in this case—enjoys presumptive power.

• **In a Tier Two case,** the claimed property right and the competing public interest have a very different relation. In this case, the claimed property right and the competing public interest involve core values that are *the same in kind*; the claimed right and the competing public interest are seen, most accurately, as presenting internal, competing interpretations about the nature of the foundational right ('the right to property') that both, in fact, involve. In this case, the claimed property right and the competing public interest are of presumptively equal power, with neither favoured—as a threshold matter— over the other.

These possible relations between claimed property rights and competing public interests can be schematically illustrated as shown in Figure 3, below:

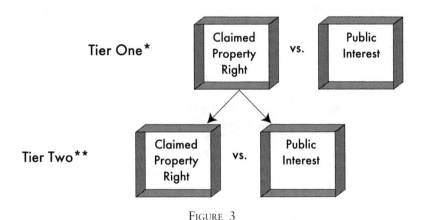

FIGURE 3

* claimed property right and competing public interest involve *different* core values; claimed property right has presumptive power
** claimed property right and competing public interest involve *the same* core values; conflict presents an internal question of what the foundational right (in Tier One) is; claimed property right and the competing public interest are of presumptively equal power

The reason for the greater presumptive power of property rights in Tier One cases is provided by the normative hypothesis, explained in Chapter 5, which our model incorporates. The presumptive power of property rights—like all rights—is rooted in the assumption that the values that property rights involve are—as a *prima facie* matter, at least—more important or more worthy (as a societally determined matter) than those involved in competing public interests. If this is determined in a particular case *not* to be true—if the values that underlie the claimed property right *are shared*, in fact, by the competing public inter-est—then the normative reason for the right's presumptive power fails. There is no basis for assuming the normative superiority of the values protected by the claimed property right, and no basis for affording the claimed right presumptive power.

Does our model in fact accurately predict, and explain, the presumptive power (or lack thereof) of property-rights claims that we find in law? Furthermore, can it provide guidance on how difficult and unsettled conflicts involving property-rights claims and competing public interests *should be* resolved in law? We will now proceed to consider these questions.

(ii) SETTINGS FOR TRADITIONALLY POWERFUL PROPERTY CLAIMS: CASES INVOLVING LAND TITLES, EXCLUSION, PATENTS, AND SIMILAR INDIVIDUAL INTERESTS

To explore the explanatory power of our model, let us begin with consideration of the following example: an individual's claimed right to title to her land, and the opposing public interest in taking that land for a public highway project. Our general understanding of how this conflict is resolved in law is clear. The holder of title to land possesses a claimed property right which carries signif-icant presumptive power. Although the building of a highway may serve many laudable public interests, we assume that those interests cannot be vindicated without a direct—and expensive—reckoning with the competing rights of the title holder of that land. Title to land can be subordinated to this public project, through the power of eminent domain, but only if just compensation for the loss of the owner's right to title is paid.

The question for us is whether this result is predicted and explained by our model. In this case, the individual's claim is clearly one that we traditionally associate with property rights. The state of affairs that it attempts to achieve or protect—that of individual title (and control) of validly acquired land—is within just about anyone's central notions of property interests. The reasons why we, as a society, protect land titles are also among those commonly associ-ated with property rights. We protect land titles to encourage individual invest-ment, reward individual labour, promote community stability, and so on. We also protect land titles because of our strong belief in the human need for secu-rity which devices such as land titles provide.[1] All of these reasons—whether the product of general economic theories or individually based considerations—are among those traditionally associated with individual property rights.

Consider, now, the competing public interest. It is immediately apparent that the core values that underlie the public interest in this case are of a very different

---

[1] Whether the protection of particular titles is justified—on distributive justice or other grounds—is, of course, a different question. See Ch. 12, below.

character. The state of affairs that the public interest attempts to achieve—the use of land for public transportation—is something quite different from what the property claim attempts to achieve. In addition, the reasons that are usually believed to ground the public interest—such as achieving the efficient movement of goods and services, the prevention of accidents, the reduction of pollution from cars stopped in traffic, and so on—have nothing to do with the reasons why we, as a society, have chosen to recognize the competing property claim.

From this analysis, it is apparent that this is a Tier One case under our model. Since the claimed right and the competing public interest involve different core values, they are simply opposing and unrelated entities. The values that underlie the claimed right, and which are the basis for its powerful normative appeal, stand unchallenged by the competing public interest. As a consequence, our model predicts that this Tier One case will—and should—involve a claimed right with presumptive power. This is, in fact, the relation that one finds in law. Indeed, the idea that the state could simply take individual land for a public road without legal consequence is quite unthinkable to us.

Before we move on, we need to address an objection that was briefly discussed in the preceding chapter, in connection with the presentation of the general model. This objection asserts that the claimed right and the competing public interest in this case involve—in fact—the *same* core values, since both involve (at least at some level) the promotion of general (collective) economic interests. One could argue, for instance, that the protection of title to land promotes individual security and initiative, which in turn produce useful development of land, which in turn contributes to economic growth; and that this state of affairs—economic growth—is what the highway project also seeks to accomplish, for very similar reasons.

This objection raises the question of the degree of immediacy or abstraction with which we understand the core values that claimed rights and competing public interests involve.[2] As we previously observed, the values that undergird any claimed right and any competing public interest can always be expanded, through greater and greater abstraction, until those values 'merge'—even if that merger is in some general notion of societal or human well-being. Indeed, we can safely assume that collective interests of *some* kind are always promoted by legal rights, since those rights are social and political creations. Although such insights are certainly interesting and (in some senses) true, they do not have much relevance to our inquiry. Our concern is with rights as they are used and understood *in law*—and the current treatment of individual rights in law does not dissolve the *individually* oriented and *individually* beneficial states of affairs that these rights protect into general or societal interests. The core values that these rights protect in law are understood in much different terms, i.e., as involving the protection of the interests of the claimed-rights holders.[3] In our

---

[2] See Ch. 6, above.
[3] If we were to abandon this understanding of claimed rights in law, then the outcome of any particular right/public interest conflict might well, of course, be different.

case, for instance, title to land is seen very much in individually protective terms—terms that abstract statements about collective economic interests do not capture. If we are to examine the operation of this claimed right in law, it is with these specific, substantive, and limiting understandings that we must grapple.

The presumptive power that the claimed right commands in our claim-of-title/highway-construction case is a common feature of cases involving title claims to land or chattels. The taking of title to land or chattels—for instance, the state's confiscation of a citizen's land, automobiles, furniture, or books—instantly bears, in the American mind, a heavy presumption of invalidity. Indeed, the fact that we would view such actions in 'confiscatory' terms captures prevailing common and legal attitudes toward them. These attitudes are grounded in the fact that it would be very unusual for the core values (and the normative judgements) that the title claims present to be matched, in kind, by the competing public interests. In particular, the values of human security and human identity with objects that title claims involve will almost never be matched by the interests that oppose them. We may *overcome* the power of title claims—for instance, when an individual's land or chattels are used in the commission of crime[4]—with public interests of unusual urgency. However, such instances are very controversial in law, and remain (most certainly) rarities.

Cases involving title claims are not the only ones where claimed property rights enjoy presumptive power in law—there are, of course, many others. Let us take, for instance, the ability of an owner to exclude strangers from her land. In *Loretto* v. *Teleprompter Manhattan CATV Corporation*,[5] an apartment building owner challenged a New York statute that required landlords to permit the installation of cable television transmission lines to service the building's tenants. Loretto challenged this law on takings grounds, claiming that it impaired her right to exclude whom she wanted from her property. The United States Supreme Court upheld Loretto's claim, citing Loretto's 'special' injury.[6] 'The power to exclude has traditionally been considered one of the most treasured strands in an owner's bundle of property rights',[7] and is entitled to special protection. When—as in this case—there is a permanent, physical occupation authorized by government, there is a compensatable taking of property. This is true, despite the government action's obvious public benefit.[8]

This treatment of the ability of an owner to exclude others from his land is echoed in other decisions.[9] Indeed, the deferential approach that the Court has taken to this right in *Loretto* and other cases is predicted by our model of

---

[4] See, e.g., *Bennis* v. *Michigan*, 516 US 442 (1996) (upholding forfeiture of automobile used in crime).

[5] 458 US 419 (1982).   [6] *Ibid*. 436.   [7] *Ibid*. 435 (footnote omitted).

[8] *Ibid*. 434–435.

[9] See, e.g., *Dolan* v. *City of Tigard*, 512 US 374 (1994); *Nollan* v. *California Coastal Commission*, 483 US 825 (1987).

rights/public interests conflicts. The core values that the ability to exclude is generally believed to involve—the ability of a landowner to preclude the permanent, physical invasion of land by strangers, for psychological and economically rooted reasons[10]—are not matched by the core values involved in cable television service,[11] public recreational access,[12] and the promotion of bicycle and pedestrian traffic.[13] Unless these competing claims are somehow reconceived, there is little mystery to the claimed rights' presumptive power in these and similar cases.

A broadly similar case—pitting an individual's claim of control over a valuable commodity against an asserted public interest in access, use, or ultimate control—is presented by the 'presidential papers' case of former President Richard Nixon.[14] In this case, Nixon asserted title to the mass of documents, tape recordings, and other materials that he had compiled during his years as President of the United States, with all of the rights of disposition and control that title of chattels (usually) conveys. The federal government—although conceding Nixon's title—asserted the right to the papers' 'complete possession and control', under the terms of the Presidential Recordings and Materials Preservation Act of 1974, which was passed by Congress shortly after Nixon's resignation.[15] In this case, Nixon's claim involved core values—individual use and control of chattels for reasons of protecting individual security, autonomy, and the products of labour—which are traditionally associated with the right to property. The competing public interest—which asserted public control, for reasons of protecting the integrity of the judicial process and advancing historical research[16]—involved core values of an entirely different kind. As a result, the values which underlay the claimed right stood, unchallenged, by the competing public interest. The presumptive power that Nixon's claim was afforded was therefore quite predictable when the court adjudicated this Tier One case.[17]

As a final example of a presumptively power property claim, let us consider an individual's claimed right to the exclusive use and control of her patented pharmaceutical invention, and the opposing public interest in making that invention available for the treatment of the largest number of citizens possible. Our general understanding of how this conflict is resolved in law is clear. If a patent has been validly granted, the claimed right that it creates is a claimed property right, and has clear presumptive power. If an individual holds valid

---

[10] See, e.g., *Loretto*, n. 5 above, 435–436 (the permanent, physical occupation of land by strangers denies the owner's essential rights to control, use, and dispose of that property).

[11] See *ibid.*   [12] See *Nollan*, n. 9 above.   [13] See *Dolan*, n. 9 above.

[14] See *Nixon v. United States*, 978 F 2d 1269 (D.C. Cir. 1992) (U.S.).

[15] See Pub. L. 93–526, Title I, §§101–106, 88 Stat. 1695–1698 (1974) (U.S.).

[16] See *ibid.* § 104(a).

[17] See *Nixon*, n. 14 above, 1285–1287. Indeed, the only real question—in the Court's view—was whether, on the basis of history, custom, and practice, Nixon was the owner or legal title holder of the materials in question. See *ibid.* 1275–1284. Once that question was resolved in Nixon's favour, the result—that compensation was owed for the public 'taking' of his rights—was (in the Court's view) an easy one. See *ibid.* 1284–1287.

patent rights, those rights cannot simply be abrogated, without legal consequence, in favour of the ordinary or routine goals of government. Although previously conferred patent rights might be overcome by a competing public interest, it would take a public interest of an extremely compelling kind—indeed, a national crisis of some sort—for this to be justified.

This understanding of the presumptive power of patent claims is evident in the treatment of a very recent instance of the collision of patent rights with a potentially catastrophic public-health crisis. Recently, several countries have considered or passed laws declaring health emergencies in order to justify their purchases of anti-AIDS drugs from suppliers who manufacture generic drugs in violation of US patent laws.[18] These actions were met by expressions of outrage and lawsuits by drug companies, who claimed the protection of their patents under Article 31 of the World Trade Organization's TRIPS Agreement.[19] Article 31 incorporates the idea of strong patent protection, authorizing the use of a patented drug without authorization of the patent-right holder in cases of 'national emergency or other circumstances of extreme urgency or in cases of public non-commercial use'.[20] Even in these circumstances, however, the patent-right holder must be paid 'adequate remuneration in the circumstances of each case'.[21] President Clinton eventually issued an executive order declaring that the United States government would not seek to interfere with countries in sub-Saharan Africa that may violate American patent laws in order to procure AIDS drugs at lower prices.[22] Even then, Clinton's order was carefully limited in scope—it stressed the extraordinary nature of the AIDS public-health crisis and authorized only those initiatives that provide 'adequate and effective intellectual property protection consistent with' the TRIPS Agreement.[23]

The question for us is whether the treatment of a patent claim in a case such as this is predicted and explained by our model. The patent claim in this case involves core values that we associate with property rights. The state of affairs that it attempts to achieve or protect—that of individual use and control of a valuable commodity—is something that we clearly associate with the right to property. In addition, the reasons that are traditionally cited for this protection—such as the encouragement of individual initiative, the rewarding of investment, the need to protect individual reliance and security, and so on—are among those associated with property rights.

Consider, now, the competing public interest. The state of affairs that this interest attempts to achieve is the widespread use of the pharmaceutical invention

[18] See Donald G. McNeil Jr., 'As Devastating Epidemics Increase, Nations Take on Drug Companies', *New York Times*, 9 July 2000, A8; Donald G. McNeil Jr., 'Patent Holders Fight Proposal on Generic AIDS Drugs for Poor', *New York Times*, 18 May 2000, A5.

[19] See *ibid*.

[20] Agreement on Trade-Related Aspects of Intellectual Property Rights (Marrakesh, 15 April 1994), Agreement Establishing the World Trade Organization, Annex 1C, art. 31, Legal Instruments—Results of the Uruguay Round vol. 31, 33 ILM 1125, 1209–1210 (1994).

[21] *Ibid.*   [22] See Executive Order No. 13155, 65 Federal Register 30521 (2000) (U.S.).

[23] *Ibid.*

to meet public-health needs. It is immediately apparent that this state of affairs has no similarity to the individual use and control that the patent claim attempts to achieve.

The question of the similarity or dissimilarity of the *reasons* that ground societal recognition of these conflicting claims is more complex, and requires careful evaluation. When we think of the reasons why we—as a society—may seek the widespread use of a patented pharmaceutical invention, and why we—as a society—choose to grant individuals patents for invented drugs, the advancement of public health objectives comes immediately to mind in both cases. Indeed, the general societal objectives that individual patent rights serve are much more likely to be immediately identified than are the general societal objectives that (arguably) are served by other individual property rights. For this reason, it is possible for these general societal goals to be readily seen as essential reasons for the protection of individual patent claims in a way that—for instance—general economic growth (as a reason for the protection of individual title claims) is not.

Even if patent claims are seen in this way, however, there are clearly *other* values and other reasons that we associate with patent claims that general societal objectives do not capture. Patents for drugs are granted because of our belief that the patent system will encourage the inventions necessary for public-health objectives. They are also granted, and subsequently protected, because of our belief that we—as a society—have agreed, in an explicit bargain, to protect the individual interests in investment, labour, and reliance that patents represent. In short, although some of the reasons that underlie an individual's patent claim and that underlie competing public-health objectives are very similar in kind, others clearly are not.

With very different states of affairs advanced by the conflicting claims, and different reasons—at least in part—grounding them, the reason for the claimed right's presumptive power in this case is apparent. Since the claimed right and the competing public interest involve different core values, they are opposing and unrelated entities. The essential values that underlie the claimed right, and which are the basis for its particularly powerful normative appeal, stand unchallenged by the competing public interest. As a consequence, this is a Tier One case under our model, in which the claimed right will, and should—on the basis of societally determined core values—enjoy presumptive power. This is, in fact, the relation that one finds in the international agreement previously discussed, and in domestic law. Patent claims can be overcome by competing public interests, but only if those public interests are of a particularly compelling nature.

* * *

Before we leave our examples of cases that involve traditionally powerful property claims, there is an important caveat that inheres in our analysis and that must be underscored. Throughout our analysis, we have used 'existing' or 'current' or 'traditional' understandings of particular claims and the values that underlie them. We have used these because of our interest in determining how *these* claims operate—and should operate—in law. Our analysis has established that *if* claims and their underlying values are understood in particular ('traditional') ways, *then* particular relations between those claims and competing public interests will follow.

Our analysis of 'existing' or 'current' or 'traditional' understandings does not deny, in any way, the possibility that all of these claims or their underlying values could—as a societal matter—be otherwise understood. All individual and public claims are subject to dispute, discard, evolution, and change, as societally constructed understandings. For instance, the values that underlie individual claims to protection of title to land—which are rarely questioned in the United States[24]—are undergoing radical reevaluation in South Africa, Zimbabwe, Venezuela, and elsewhere.[25] There is also, in Anglo-American case law and commentary, recent recognition of an erosion of the power of arbitrary exclusion that traditionally has been afforded to private landowners.[26] As two prominent commentators have recently observed, '[t]he notion is slowly beginning to infiltrate the common law concept of property that the relative size or character of the territory and the social merit or virtue of competing uses imposes an inevitable qualification on the workability of the trespassory concept.'[27] The advent of the personal income tax, the ascendence or decline of particular welfare programmes, the evolution of environmental standards, and other political initiatives illustrate the continually changing social attitudes about the nature of government and the claims that it can legitimately make. As our understandings of the values that underlie individual and public claims change, so will our analyses under our model. Our discussion of 'existing' or 'current' or 'traditional' claims or values is not meant to ignore these contingencies, or to somehow enshrine (as a normative matter) particular existing understandings.

---

[24] Although contemporary understandings about the protection of land title are well entrenched in the United States, they are, in fact, of relatively recent vintage. Even into the nineteenth century, state governments often took property for roads and other public projects with no payment of compensation. See Morton J. Horwitz, *The Transformation of American Law 1780–1860* (Cambridge, Mass.: Harvard University Press, 1977), 63–64; William Michael Treanor, 'The Origins and Original Significance of the Just Compensation Clause of the Fifth Amendment' (1985) 94 *Yale Law Journal* 694, 695. In 1802, a Pennsylvania court observed that it could not 'consider the legislature[']s applying a certain portion of every man's land for the purposes of laying out public roads and highways, without compensation, as any infringement of the constitution; such compensation having been originally made in each purchaser's original grant'. *M'Clenachan* v. *Curwin*, 3 Yeates 362, 373 (Pa. 1802) (U.S.).

[25] For instance, the need for land redistribution is an accepted part of the South African political and economic landscape. See A. J. van der Walt, *Constitutional Property Clauses: A Comparative Analysis* (Cape Town: Juta and Company, Ltd., 1999), 328.

[26] See Kevin Gray, 'Property in Thin Air' (1991) 50 *Cambridge Law Journal* 252, 290.

[27] Kevin Gray and Susan Francis Gray, 'The Idea of Property in Land', in Susan Bright and John Dewar (eds.), *Land Law: Themes and Perspectives* (Oxford: Oxford University Press, 1998), 15, 38 (footnote omitted). 'In a crowded urban environment, where recreational, associational, and expressional space is increasingly at a premium, an unanalysed, monolithic privilege of . . . exclusion is no longer tenable.') *Ibid.* 38–39.

Acknowledgment of the potentially fluid nature of claims and their values may sometimes complicate our application of our model of rights/public interest conflicts. Such problems are, however, not unique to our model—they are involved in every attempted articulation or application of existing law, as socially constructed relations. No discussion of existing law can ignore the contingent judgements in which the law is moored, or avoid the limitations that those contingencies necessarily imply. Indeed, it is the great strength of our model that it can establish the relative power of competing claims, *whatever* their nature, and *whatever* their changing formulations.

* * *

So far, we have examined cases in which claimed property rights enjoy presumptive power—cases in which they are afforded the power that rights, *qua* rights, are expected to enjoy. Far more intriguing are those cases in which claimed property rights—although clearly recognized as such in law—are denied presumptive power. We will now proceed to examine those cases.

(iii) SETTINGS FOR TRADITIONALLY WEAK PROPERTY CLAIMS:
CASES INVOLVING ENVIRONMENTAL LAWS, ZONING CONTROLS,
AND SIMILAR PUBLIC INTERESTS

We have previously seen how, in many cases involving individual/state conflicts over physical resources, individual property claims are often not afforded the presumptive power that we would otherwise expect in law.[28] In cases involving environmental or other land-use controls, in particular, individuals' claimed property rights seem to be routinely subordinated to routine government interests. As Richard Epstein has observed, under current court interpretations, 'any legitimate public function of conceivable merit justifies government restriction on land use. . . . Aesthetics, popular sentiments, and environmental objectives all become appropriate pegs on which to hang legal justification for land use restrictions.'[29]

Can this disregard of property rights be justified? To begin our exploration of this question, we will consider the familiar facts of the *Lucas* case. In that case, Lucas demanded that he be permitted to develop his land in a way that was permissible when the land was purchased. The State demanded that its newly enacted regulations, which prohibited the development of Lucas's land and other shoreline areas, be implemented. Lucas contended that his demand asserted a constitutionally protected property right; the State contended that the

---

[28] See Ch. 3, above.
[29] Richard A. Epstein, 'Property, Speech, and the Politics of Distrust' (1992) 59 *University of Chicago Law Review* 41, 76.

public interests which its demand involved—the prevention of erosion, the preservation of the existing beach/dune system, and other ecological concerns— justified the denial of Lucas's claim.[30]

Lucas's demand falls squarely within traditional property rights notions. Legally cognizable rights in land are universally recognized to include the rights to possess, use, transfer, and exclude, and Lucas's demand—that he be permitted to use his land in a way that was permitted at the time of his purchase—falls well within usually accepted notions of property rights.[31] The State's demand that development be prohibited for ecological reasons is (on the other hand) the assertion of what would generally be regarded as a routine or ordinary government interest. Although ecological concerns are important, they are generally not considered to be as compelling (for instance) as public health or safety. Because of the particular natures of these claims, we would expect that Lucas's demand would—under the traditional view of rights—'trump' or presumptively best the State's asserted interest.

The answer that the law yields is, in fact, quite different. Although the Court held that Lucas's land use claim was—because of the severity of the impairment involved—possibly of a 'categorically compensable' nature,[32] Lucas's claim must be assessed, the Court wrote, in light of the 'background principles of the State's law of property and nuisance' that were 'part of his title to begin with'.[33] These principles include consideration of the degree to which his activities may harm other private or public land and the social value of his activities.[34]

The extent to which the Court intended to permit states—through expansive interpretations of 'background principles'—to defeat takings claims under this test is unclear.[35] It is clear, however, that the acceptance of at least some *later-recognized* common-law restrictions is contemplated—a surprising result, when we think of the presumptive power that property rights are supposed (in theory, at least) to have. Are the complaints by property-rights advocates about such restrictions justified?

To answer this question, we must consider the nature of the competing claims. In the *Lucas* case, the individual claim involved core values that are associated with traditional understandings of property rights. Protection of the ability to build or otherwise to use one's land is something that we generally associate with property rights. Furthermore, the reasons that such abilities are

---

[30] *Lucas v. South Carolina Coastal Council*, 505 US 1003, 1008–1009 (1992).
[31] See, e.g., *Loretto*, n. 5 above, 435.   [32] *Lucas*, n. 30 above, 1015.
[33] *Ibid.* 1027, 1029.   [34] *Ibid.* 1030–1031.
[35] See, e.g., Frank I. Michelman, 'Property, Federalism, and Jurisprudence: A Comment on Lucas and Judicial Conservatism' (1993) 35 *William and Mary Law Review* 301, 317–318 ('It could well be that a significant number of state judiciaries, dealing with regulatory taking claims in the aftermath of the *Lucas* decision, honestly will see their States' background laws of property and nuisance in the light of a jurisprudence of adaptive and evolving principles including expansive principles of public trust and social responsibility'. If this does occur, 'then the regulatory-taking project—the *Lucas* Court's apparent drive to put some muscle back into constitutional protection for property against costly regulation—is at the mercy of state judiciaries'.).

protected by law—for instance, to protect individual investments and expectations—are those that we associate strongly with the protection of property.

What about the competing public interest? When we analyse it, we find that it
asserts—in fact—property-based values of a very similar kind. In *Lucas*, the State
was concerned that additional shoreline development would destroy the existing
beach/dune system, accelerate erosion, and precipitate other damage to private
and public land. These concerns involve the protection of the ability of others
(public or private landowners) to use, preserve, and enjoy *their* land—abilities
that we traditionally associate with property rights. Furthermore, the reasons that
underlie such concerns—such as the protection of the investments and expectations of other shoreline users and owners whose land-based interests are affected
by development activities—are within core notions of property rights.

Since the core values that underlie the claimed right and those that underlie
the competing public interest in this case are the same or a very similar kind,[36]
this a Tier Two case under our model. This is not a case in which the 'right
to property' opposes an unrelated—and, presumably, normatively less
compelling—public interest; rather, this is a case in which the claimed right and
the competing public interest are, in fact, different interpretations of *what a
foundational right—the 'right to property'—should be*. Does the right to use
one's land include the right to act in ways that cause erosion or other ecological
consequences to land of adjacent or nearby landowners? Put more broadly, does
the right to property protection, claimed by one individual, include the right to
act in ways that are, in fact, detrimental to the same property interests held by
others? In such situations, the normative powers of the interests that the claimed
right protects *are equalled by* the normative powers of the interests that the public demand asserts. As a consequence, there is no reason to afford the claimed
right presumptive power.[37]

---

[36] One could argue that the content of the claimed right and the content of the opposing public
interest in this case are in fact *different* in nature, on the following ground: the claimed right seeks
individual control of the land in question, and the competing public interest seeks to deny that control. Seen in this way, the content of the claimed right and the content of the competing public interest are of diametrically opposing natures.

This analysis of the public-interest demand is, however, of a very superficial nature. All public-
interest demands that compete with claimed rights seek to deny the state of affairs that the claimed
rights assert; it is that opposition which makes the public interests 'competing' claims. However,
characterizing the public interest's content as simply 'opposition to what the right demands' tells us
little about what truly motivates and informs this public-interest demand.

In fact, this public interest—like all others—is *more* than the mere negation of the rights
claimant's proposed agenda; it is also the advancement of the positive interests of other individuals,
or members of the public, whom the state (as surrogate) represents. In this positive function, the
public interest in this case involves very specific content. It seeks to prevent a particular kind of land
use, in order to preserve the land held by others. Seen this way, it is apparent that the claimed right
and the competing public interest actually involve content of the very same kind: both are concerned
with the preservation, use, and enjoyment of land.

[37] Compare Joseph L. Sax, 'Takings, Private Property and Public Rights' (1971) 81 *Yale Law
Journal* 149, 161 (when conflicting uses—although framed in 'individual' and 'public' terms—essentially involve the claims of competing resource users, 'neither is *a priori* entitled to prevail, because
neither claimant has any more right to impose on his neighbor than his neighbor does on him').

Indeed, to afford the claimed rights presumptive power in such cases would create a very peculiar situation in our law. To grant the claimed rights in these cases such power *simply because they are 'rights'* would mean that the legal protection afforded to particular interests would depend solely upon the happenstance of whether they are asserted under an 'individual' or 'collective' label. There is no reason why the property interests of one person should be presumptively superior to the property interests of many persons, simply because the interests of the many are asserted 'publicly' or 'collectively'. *It is the nature of the interests and the values that they assert—not the identities or numbers of the holders—that should determine normative (and presumptive) power.* If the claimed property right and the competing public interest involve interests and values of the same kind—if, for instance, the land-use or preservation claims of one landowner are opposed by the collectively asserted land-use or preservation claims of others—there is no reason to give the individual claim presumptive power.

The situation that we find in the *Lucas* case is replicated in other land-use cases in which the proposed use of land by one owner would severely and directly affect the use or enjoyment of identifiable land owned by others. The reason that the claimed property rights lack presumptive power in such cases is perhaps fairly easily seen, since we are all familiar with the 'nuisance paradigm'—the idea that the use of land by one person cannot impair the land use or enjoyment of others. Indeed, even those who would vigorously champion property rights acknowledge that nuisance law constrains the freedom with which landowners might otherwise act.[38] The theoretical underpinning of this principle is simple: since all landowners (presumably) have equal rights in the use and enjoyment of their land, there is no basis for presumptively favouring the claim of one over that of another.[39] What must be realized, however, is that nuisance is *not*—as some have argued—some kind of 'exception' to the otherwise broad and unassailable power of property rights.[40] Rather, it is simply one manifestation of a very basic principle: that the normative basis for the presumed superiority of a property right—or any right—fails when it is opposed by a public interest that involves values of a similar kind.

This principle explains, in fact, the lack of presumptive power afforded to a wide range of land-use claims. Let us take, for instance, the imposition of zoning controls—a practice which has been explicitly approved by the Supreme Court[41]

---

[38] See Epstein, n. 29 above, 58. The nuisance limitation on land use is of such importance that its abrogation has been held to be a 'taking' of 'property' for which compensation must be paid. *Bormann v. Board of Supervisors in and for Kossuth County*, 584 NW 2d 309 (Iowa 1998) (U.S.).

[39] Ultimately, of course, the claim of one *must* be favoured over the claim of another—since, in the resolution of this conflict, only one of the claimed entitlements must (and will) prevail. This, however, is not a function of presumptive power, but of decisions on other bases that we (as a society) make.

[40] See, e.g., *Keystone Bituminous Coal Association v. DeBenedictis*, 480 US 470, 511–512 (1987) (Rehnquist, J., dissenting) (discussing the 'nuisance exception' to the Takings Clause).

[41] See *Agins v. Tiburon*, 447 US 255 (1980); *Euclid v. Ambler Realty Company*, 272 US 365 (1926).

and, indeed, enjoys widespread public acceptance.[42] In the typical zoning case, zoning is imposed to prevent the use of land in ways that are deemed (by local government) to be deleterious to the existing character of an area, or to the kind of community that the public (through elected representatives) has expressed a desire to become. If the imposition of a zoning scheme is opposed by a landowner whose use is curtailed, the ensuing conflict pits the property-rights claim of that owner against the property-based interests of other owners, asserted through the public-interest control. Since the core values that underlie the claimed right and the conflicting public interest are the same in kind, this is a Tier Two case: there is no basis for assuming the normative superiority of the claimed right's concerns, and the claimed right—for that reason—lacks presumptive power.

The cases that *Lucas*, zoning, and similar land-use conflicts represent are, in a sense, the easy ones. The existence of a Tier Two case can be readily recognized when the conflict involves claims of the kind that we have thus far considered—that is, when the claimed property right and the competing public interest assert traditional property claims of physical use or economic protection of contiguous or other nearby landowners. What about the broader run of land-use cases, in which the interests asserted by the collective entity are not the simple assertions of the claims of other (individual) landowners?

Let us consider, for instance, a broad ecological measure, such as the preservation of wetlands and the marine life that they spawn. Let us assume, further, that this measure is opposed by landowners whose previously permitted uses are now curtailed. How should this conflict be resolved? *With what notions of presumptive power* should we approach this conflict?

Popular notions about the presumptive powers of individual and collective claims in this context are mixed. While there is generally broad public support for environmental laws, some have targeted them as examples of unjustified assaults on citizens' property rights.[43] Legal treatment of these cases in the United States has, however, been remarkably uniform. Few courts have accepted the 'trumping' model of individual property rights over environmental laws that property-rights advocates have demanded. In fact, in the nearly twenty-five years since the National Environmental Policy Act,[44] the Federal Water Pollution Control Act,[45] and the Federal Clean Air Act[46] were enacted, no legal challenge to the fundamental validity of these laws has been seriously entertained.[47] As one property-rights advocate has lamented, '[t]he federal

---

[42] This acceptance is, of course, not universal; in the view of Richard Epstein, for instance, zoning is only one of many regulatory schemes that are pursued by 'activist government . . . [to] alter . . . the distribution of property holdings among the citizenry'. Epstein, n. 29 above, 67.

[43] See, e.g., Epstein, n. 29 above; James V. DeLong, *Property Matters: How Property Rights Are Under Assault—And Why You Should Care* (New York: The Free Press, 1997).

[44] 42 U.S.C. §§ 4321–4370d (1994).   [45] 33 U.S.C. §§ 1251–1376 (1999).

[46] 42 U.S.C. §§ 7401–7671q (1994).

[47] See, e.g., *United States Trust Company* v. *New Jersey*, 431 US 1, 50 (1977) (Brennan, J., dissenting) ('[A]ll private rights of property, even if acquired through contract with the State, are subordinated to reasonable exercises of the State's lawmaking powers in the areas of . . . environmental protection'.).

courts have withdrawn from protection of property [in these cases], except for occasional unpredictable interventions in some of the most egregious situations.'[48] Why is this so? Why—despite the bitterness generated in some quarters by, for instance, wetlands-preservation laws—has the essential parity of these control initiatives with private property rights been so broadly assumed?

If we examine these cases in light of the principles that we have previously established, we find that there are deeply rooted reasons why private property claims lack presumptive power when opposed by environmental laws. Those who lament the courts' treatment of these cases make a crucial assumption: that the private property claims involved invoke concerns of a uniquely powerful and compelling character, which deserve presumptive power *vis-à-vis* competing public claims. In fact, even a cursory examination of the competing values that underlie these claims reveals this assumption to be untrue.

Let us take, for instance, the restriction of private land use to preserve coastal wetlands. This conflict pits the claimed property right of the landowner to use his land against the public interest in the wetlands' protection. The core values that underlie the claimed right are ones with which we are very familiar. The ability to build, or to use, is something that we generally associate with property rights in land. Furthermore, the reasons that such abilities are generally protected by law—for instance, to protect individual investments and expectations—are those which we associate with property rights.

What about the competing public interest? The state of affairs that it seeks to accomplish is, one may argue, very simple and straightforward: it seeks to preserve particular wetlands from change or degradation. Although this content is (on one level) of the same kind as that asserted by the conflicting right—both involving land-based values, of a traditional kind—there is a twist in this case. While—in our previous land-use cases—the public interests in question asserted the preservation claims of the affected land's owner, in this cases it does not. Here, the preservation claim—asserted by the public interest—is not to preserve one's *own* wetlands, but to preserve the wetlands *of others*. As a consequence, the values that underlie this public interest (as so far understood) are quite different from those that underlie the claimed right. Whether the public demands preservation for aesthetic, cultural, psychological, or other reasons, it is apparent that these values (arguably, at least) are quite different from those generally associated with property rights.

If this were all that this story involved, we would (it seems) have a Tier One case on our hands, with the claimed right enjoying traditional, presumptive power. However, the values that the public interest asserts cannot be understood so narrowly. Because of the physical and biological interdependence of wetlands, other shoreline lands, and the oceans that border them—because the filling or pollution of wetlands destroys the animal life, plant life, and physical integrity of other land and bodies of water in ways that transcend the boundaries

---

[48] DeLong, n. 43 above, 88.

of particular parcels—the landowner's desired actions affect not only his own property interests, but the property interests of others as well. Those who want to maintain the physical and biological integrity of coastal areas for shellfish harvesting, tourism, recreation, or other purposes clearly have property interests of their own at stake that are as real as those of the thwarted landowner. As Joseph Sax has written, '[a] pristine example of the inextricability of property interests is marine life that breeds along the shallow wetlands shorelines, depending upon maintenance of the shoreline habitat. The wetlands owner thus does not use only his own tract, but demands, as a condition of developing his property, that ocean users tolerate a change in their use of the ocean.'[49] We recognize, in such environmental laws, that protectable property interests in physical resources go far beyond the narrow concern of simple freedom to use one's land. We recognize, in such laws, that the interests asserted by the claimed right and the interests asserted by the public interest *are—by their very nature—inextricably and unalterably interdependent.*

This *interdependent* nature of property interests—the fact that protection of one person's property interest so often affects the property interests of others—explains why property rights so often lack, *and should lack*, presumptive power in land-use cases. When understood in this way, it is apparent that the claimed right and the competing public interest involved in this case are not entirely different and unrelated entities; rather, they are *deeply and equally* rooted in property-based concerns. Both demands involve the claimants' use and enjoyment of physical resources, content that we associate with property claims; and both involve reasons—such as the protection of 'legitimate', 'investment-backed', or other expectations—that property, as commonly understood, involves. The question that this dispute presents is not whether the 'right to property' has been impaired by an asserted, unrelated public interest, but what the foundational 'right to property'—which both involve—should mean. The heightened normative value that we ascribe to property interests does not distinguish the claimed right in this case; it is involved in *both* competing claims. This is a Tier Two case under our model: the claimed right and the competing public interest involve core values of the same kind, and—as a result—neither is favoured (as a threshold matter) over the other.

Environmental laws may, of course, be grounded in many different values. They may, for instance, be motivated by the belief that the preservation of the environment is an intrinsically valuable objective, apart from human needs or desires—a grounding that is not generally associated (under current understandings) with how or why we protect individual property rights. *If* environmental laws are understood in a way that strips them of any assertion of competing, property-based claims, and *if* the claimed property rights that oppose them retain traditional understandings, then the presumptive power

[49] Sax, n. 37 above, 159.

that property-rights advocates claim for those rights would, in fact, follow.[50] It is very rare, however, for public environmental claims to fail to assert core values that are deeply rooted in ideas of the preservation and conservation of resources for human enjoyment and use. Indeed, the presence of property-based claims on both sides of the dispute is a very common characteristic of environmental and other physical-resource cases.

Our model explains why, in law, property rights lack trumping power when opposed by zoning controls, clean-air restrictions, ecological concerns, and so on. When an industry owner's claimed right to engage in polluting activities is opposed by a public interest in clean air; when a landowner's claimed right to erect a building is opposed by a public interest in the preservation of the character of a community; when a landowner's claimed right to use his land destroys, in the process, a species of flora or fauna that is a valued and integral part of a larger biological system—in all of these cases, and others like them, the asserted individual right and the competing public interest may be grounded in competing property-based concerns. If so, the vindication of the individual's claimed property right to use his land as he (alone) sees fit necessarily and inevitably denies the property-based claims of others (for clean air, community character, or ecological preservation) that are asserted by the competing public interest. The assumed normative superiority of the values that the claimed right protects—the assumption that drives the presumptive power of rights—is absent in these cases. In these cases, there is no normative basis—grounded in the assumed normative superiority of property rights, as rights—presumptively to privilege the individuals' claims. The fact that the individual demands in these cases fall within our understanding of the 'right to property' does not mean that these demands are presumed to be superior to the public-interest demands that compete with them. The individual demands may—in the end—prevail, on some other basis; but that result is not driven by the usual power that we associate with rights. We must evaluate the merits of the conflicting claims in these cases apart from ideas of presumptive power. The traditional, 'trumping' idea of rights simply does not apply in these cases.

---

[50] Indeed, those who make the most eloquent and powerful arguments for grounding public environmental claims in non-human-centric values implicitly recognize that if public environmental claims are to be reconceived in this way—*and if those claims are to retain the parity in presumptive power which they currently enjoy*—opposing individual property rights must be reconceived along the same lines as well. As Eric Freyfogle has written, if we are to implement a new environmental ethic—one that is grounded in the belief that nature is intrinsically valuable in its own right—we must also reconceive our understanding of the nature of private property. We must abandon current beliefs that land has only instrumentalist value, and require landowners 'to live in right relation to the land—. . . to live in harmonious partnership with it, working to make the land fruitful while respecting its limits and residing always in awe of its inscrutable power.' Eric T. Freyfogle, 'Ethics, Community, and Private Land' (1996) 23 *Ecology Law Quarterly* 631, 652. See also Koen Raes, 'Individualist Subjectivism and the World as Property; On the Interrelations Between Concepts of Value and Concepts of Ownership', in G. E. van Maanen and A. J. van der Walt (eds.), *Property Law on the Threshold of the 21st Century* (Antwerp: Maklu, 1996), 91, 108–114 (challenging the establishment of property rights on the basis of a 'subjectivist and instrumentalist account of nature', in which 'the subjective preferences of human beings [are] . . . the sole yardstick of value').

In explaining the power of property-rights claims in land-use cases, it is important, of course, that we keep in mind what we are saying and what we are not. We are not saying that in every case in which (for instance) the land-use claims of one landowner are asserted against public interests which assert property interests of others, the individual claimant will lose; indeed, there are many situations, in law, in which the opposite is true. For instance, when zoning is at issue—perhaps the most ubiquitous form of land-use control—individual claimants will tend to lose cases involving the zoning of raw land, but will tend to win cases involving the attempted elimination through zoning of pre-existing uses. The point is not that individual claims will always (or *should* always) lose, but rather that they will lack (and *should* lack) the presumptive power which—as asserted rights—we might otherwise expect.

Richard Epstein, a prominent advocate for property rights, has criticized the recognition of dependencies in nature in land-use cases on the ground that it will erode, too far, individual control and land-use rights. He argues that if wetlands are protected, under this theory, so may uplands be as well—extending and expanding the erosion of land-use rights.[51] The obvious problem with this argument is that we must have a *reason* for the privileging of individual claims—something which sheer iteration of those claims does not, of itself, supply. As Epstein himself acknowledges, our recognition of natural dependencies in law is 'more pervasive today than before, not because the world has changed but because our perception of the world has changed'.[52] As we increasingly recognize the dependencies that exist in nature, a case which seemed to require simple protection of the landowner a hundred years ago may well be seen as something considerably more complex. We may decide that the interests asserted by the individual property owner are particularly compelling and thus are, on balance, deserving of protection; but this conclusion will be consciously driven by what we, as a society, decide (under these circumstances) property rights *should be*, not by an application of the idea of the presumed superiority of 'rights'.

---

[51] Richard A. Epstein, 'Life in No Trump: Property and Speech Under the Constitution' (2001) 53 *Maine Law Review* 23, 26–27.
[52] *Ibid.*

8

Moving into More Uncharted and Controversial Waters: The Body as Property, Personal Information as Property, Cultural Property, and State Redistributive Claims

So far, we have used our two-tiered model to explain why property-rights claims are granted or denied presumptive power in existing law. In this chapter, we will consider how property-rights claims *should* be treated, in cases in which the law is emerging or unsettled. If we (as a society) determine that 'the body' is property, that 'personal information' is property, or that 'cultural claims' are property, what power should such claims have? Does our model of rights/public interests relations provide any guidance in these cases?

(i) THE BODY AS PROPERTY

Whether individuals should be afforded property rights in their own bodies or body parts is the subject of sharp current debate. Some argue that since the ability to control is the core idea of property, and since control of one's body is also at the core of our understandings of physical integrity and human personality, there is no logical reason why 'body rights' should not have the status of 'property rights'.[1] Others oppose this conclusion, arguing, for instance, that societally imposed restrictions on what can be done with body parts—

---

[1] See, e.g., Lori B. Andrews, 'My Body, My Property', originally published in (1986) 16 *Hastings Center Report* 28, reprinted in Elizabeth Mensch and Alan Freeman (eds.), *Property Law: International Library of Essays in Law and Legal Theory* (New York: New York University Press, 1992), bk. ii, 27; William Boulier, 'Sperm, Spleens, and Other Valuables: The Need to Recognize Property Rights in Human Body Parts' (1995) 23 *Hofstra Law Review* 693; Susan E. Looper-Friedman, '"Keep Your Laws Off My Body": Abortion Regulation and the Takings Clause' (1995) 29 *New England Law Review* 253. See also Stephen R. Munzer, *A Theory of Property* (Cambridge: Cambridge University Press, 1990), 41–56 (arguing that at least some property rights in the body should be recognized).

such as general prohibitions on sale[2]—are fatal to the idea of 'the body as property', or that property includes the idea of severability, a characteristic which body parts lack.[3] There is also concern that the extension of property rights to body parts would erode the fundamental distinction between human beings and non-human entities, with undesirable results.[4] Whatever the merits of the positions in this debate, they are not (strictly speaking) our concern. We will assume, for our purposes, that the individual's right to control her own body and the disposition of its parts is a legally cognizable property right, with whatever upsides and downsides the recognition of this right entails. The question that we will consider is this: *if* individuals are afforded property rights in their own bodies or body parts, what should the presumptive power of such rights be?

Disputes in which the human body, body parts, or body products have been asserted to be property have generally involved disputes between private parties rather than individual/state conflicts. Efforts by the state to obtain body parts or substances from citizens in the pursuit of important public goals is not, however, unimaginable. For instance, citizens could be required to give samples of blood or other bodily fluids in order to track the progression of certain diseases or otherwise to safeguard public health. Or body parts or substances could be removed in the course of treatment at state-owned hospitals and used—over the later objection of the person from whom they were taken—for medical research with public health objectives.[5] There have also been reported cases in which state officials removed organs for transplant from the bodies of deceased per-

---

[2] Prohibitions on disposition include those found in the National Organ Transplant Act, 42 U.S.C. § 274e (1994) (prohibiting the sale of human organs used in transplantation) and various state laws. See, e.g., Md. Code Ann., Health § 5–408 (a)(2) (2000) (U.S.) ('A person other than a nonprofit organization . . . may not sell, buy or act as a broker for a profit in a transfer of any human organ that . . . [i]s removed from a human body that is alive or dead at the time of removal'.).

The idea that such statutes reflect a societal consensus that the body or its parts cannot be property is undermined by the simultaneous existence of many situations in which the sale or other 'property'-like treatment of bodily substances and body parts is permitted by law. See, e.g., *United States* v. *Garber*, 607 F 2d 92, 97 (5th Cir. 1979) (U.S.) ('[B]lood plasma, . . . like any salable part of the human body, is tangible property'.); *Hecht* v. *Superior Court*, 20 Cal Rptr 2d 275, 283 (Ct. App. 1993) (U.S.) (deceased's frozen semen was 'property' under state probate code); *In re Moyer*, 577 P 2d 108, 110 n. 4 (Utah 1978) (U.S.) (property rights of a person in her body and organs is assumed by state anatomical gift act). Indeed, reproductive gametes are becoming a very hot subject of competitive bidding. See Gina Kolata, '$50,000 Offered to Tall, Smart Egg Donor', *New York Times*, 3 March 1999, A10.

[3] See, e.g., J. E. Penner, *The Idea of Property in Law* (Oxford: Clarendon Press, 1997), 113–117 (arguing that '[t]o be conceived of as an object of property a thing must first be considered as separable and distinct from any person who might hold it'—and that most body parts lack this character).

[4] See, e.g., Michael D. Rivard, 'Toward a General Theory of Constitutional Personhood: A Theory of Constitutional Personhood for Transgenic Humanoid Species' (1992) 39 *University of California Los Angeles Law Review* 1425.

[5] See, e.g., *Moore* v. *Regents of the University of California*, 793 P 2d 479 (Cal. 1990), cert. denied, 499 US 936 (1991) (spleen and other bodily substances, removed from patient during the course of treatment, used for creation of cell line without patient's knowledge or consent).

sons,[6] or conducted medical experiments on the bodies of deceased persons,[7] over the objections and property claims of the deceased person's relatives.

The instinctive repugnance that we feel from the mention of such state actions is very real and very powerful—and is rooted in the fact that in each instance, this is a Tier One case. The core values that underlie a claim of 'the body (or its parts) as property' are unanswered by the asserted public interest, *even if* that public interest is recognized as an important or particularly sympathetic one. The state of affairs that the individual's property claim attempts to achieve in such cases is that of individual control over the human body and its substances, in order to protect personal freedom and autonomy. In cases involving claims of property rights over one's own body, the interests in freedom and autonomy involve dispositional control over oneself; in cases involving claims of property rights over the bodies of relatives or partners, the interests in freedom and autonomy involve dispositional control over those close to us. In both cases, however, the vindication of personal decisionmaking over human bodies or their substances is the core interest asserted.

The competing public interests in these cases, on the other hand, seek to achieve states of affairs in which the body or its substances are publicly controlled or publicly used, in order to safeguard public health, or to enable others (through research or transplants) to live. As laudable as such public interests may be, they do not share the core values that the individual claims assert. The individual claims—grounded, as they are, in outraged losses of autonomy and control— assert, as rights, normative judgements which are not matched by the competing public claims. The claimed rights and the competing public interests are entirely different and distinct entities, and occupy the opposing relation that we generally expect claimed rights and competing public interests to occupy. *If* (as we have posed) the individual claims are property rights, they will clearly enjoy presumptive power. Interests in medical research, public health, or other public objectives might overcome these individual claims, but they would have to be of an extraordinarily compelling nature to do so.

Indeed, because of the particular nature of 'body as property' claims, it is difficult to imagine situations in which such claims—if recognized as property rights—will *not* enjoy presumptive power over competing public interests. The particularly clear values of personal freedom and personal autonomy that such claims represent will almost never be shared by the public interests which oppose them. It is difficult to imagine a public interest which opposes individual

---

[6] See, e.g., *Whaley v. County of Tuscola*, 58 F 3d 1111 (6th Cir. 1995), cert. denied, 516 US 975 (1995); *Brotherton v. Cleveland*, 923 F 2d 477 (6th Cir. 1991) (U.S.); *State v. Powell*, 497 So 2d 1188 (Fla. 1986), cert. denied, 481 US 1059 (1987). In *Whaley* and *Brotherton*, the relatives of the deceased persons were held to have constitutionally cognizable property interests which were impaired by state actors; in *Powell*, they were not.

[7] See, e.g., *Arnaud v. Odom*, 870 F 2d 304 (5th Cir. 1989), cert. denied, 493 US 855 (1989) (state coroner conducted medical experiments upon the corpses of two infant children without relatives' consent).

bodily control and which simultaneously has, at its core, the protection of personal individual freedom and individual bodily autonomy. Perhaps the only examples can be found in those cases in which the public interest involves 'inalienability' rules, or rules which are based on the belief that particular claimed exercises of individual autonomy under the 'body as property' rubric serve, in fact, to *undermine* the personal autonomy of those who assert them.[8] This theory has been used, for instance, in opposing the claimed right of women to engage in 'surrogacy contracts', in which they agree (for a fee) to bear a child for others.[9] In such cases, opposition to the claimed right is based on the belief that the public's assessment of the individual's best (or 'autonomy-enhancing') interests is superior to the assessment of such interests by the individual herself. Apart from the difficult question of whether one can enhance someone's autonomy by restricting that autonomy, the public interest in such cases shares (at least arguably) the same values as the claimed right.[10] Absent such a situation, it is difficult to imagine when the normative values—and resulting presumptive power—of a claimed right that 'the body is property' would be equalled by a competing public interest. In deciding whether such claims are—indeed—cognizable 'property rights', we must be aware of the very powerful protection that such categorization will confer.

(ii) Personal information as property

The idea that the human body (or a part of it) is property may challenge the boundaries of what we, as a society, believe an acceptable 'property' claim to be. Far more conventional—but still controversial—is a claim that information that the human body yields, or other kinds of personal information, is property which the individual can protect from state collection or control.

Let us take, for instance, an effort by the state to obtain DNA samples from individuals for identification purposes, and the resistance by those individuals to the state's collective efforts. This is an area of intense current controversy. Currently, all fifty states in the United States require persons convicted of crimes

---

[8] See Guido Calabresi and A. Douglas Melamed, 'Property Rules, Liability Rules, and Inalienability: One View of the Cathedral' (1972) 85 *Harvard Law Review* 1089; Margaret Jane Radin, 'Market-Inalienability' (1987) 100 *Harvard Law Review* 1849.

[9] See, e.g., *In the Matter of Baby M*, 537 A 2d 1227, 1250 (N.J. 1988) (U.S.) (describing the 'potential degradation' of women which results from surrogacy contracts); Richard John Neuhaus, 'Renting Women, Buying Babies and Class Struggles', originally published in *Society*, March/April 1988, 8, reprinted in Mensch and Freeman (eds.), n. 1 above, 17.

[10] Of course, such public policies can also be grounded in very different values, such as concern about the effects on third parties that such exercises of autonomy create. See, e.g., Calabresi and Melamed, n. 8 above, 1112 ('If [X] . . . is allowed to sell himself into slavery, or to take undue risks of becoming penniless, or to sell a kidney, [Y] . . . may be harmed, simply because [Y] . . . is a sensitive man who is made unhappy by [such actions]'.).

to provide DNA samples[11] under the apparent rationale that entanglement with the criminal justice system constitutes a waiver of the individual's right to object, or that the state's interest in identifying persons who have committed or may commit crimes overrides any ground for objection.[12] Some states, in addition, take samples from those who have simply been arrested for an otherwise covered offence,[13] and the executive branch of the federal government is seeking Congressional approval for the creation of a DNA databank of profiles taken from 'detainees in a war or conflict', including some 7,600 prisoners from the conflict in Afghanistan.[14] The legality of such efforts is, however, far from clear. For although the courts have agreed that persons accused of serious crimes may be compelled to submit to bodily invasion when potentially probative of their guilt or innocence,[15] the idea of wholesale sampling of individuals' DNA for the purpose of compiling identification data banks remains controversial and has been addressed by few courts.[16]

Furthermore, the issue of individual control over information contained in encoded genetic material will undoubtedly become more pressing for the general population as scientists race to determine the function of every gene in the human genome. The accomplishment of this project carries tremendous potential for the identification and treatment of genetically based disease. It also carries distinct risks. As the result of such advances in scientific knowledge, delineation of an individual's genetic information could become a routine part of private and public decisionmaking processes, with dangers of discrimination

[11] See C. J. Chivers, 'Proposal to Increase Use of DNA', *New York Times*, 24 February 2000, A23. Under a recent proposal sponsored by the Governor of New York, every person convicted of any crime in the State of New York would be required to provide a biological sample for a state database. This would force approximately 126,000 people each year to submit DNA, including those convicted of minor offences such as subway fare-beating or charges resulting from political demonstrations. *Ibid.*

[12] See, e.g., *Gaines* v. *Nevada*, 998 P 2d 166, 171–175 (Nev. 2000), cert. denied, 531 US 856 (2000); *Landry* v. *Attorney General*, 709 NE 2d 1085 (Mass. 1999), cert. denied, 528 US 1073 (2000); *Doles* v. *State*, 994 P 2d 315 (Wyo. 1999) (U.S.).

[13] See Jean E. McEwen, 'DNA Sampling and Banking: Practices and Procedures in the United States', in Bartha Maria Knoppers (ed.), *Human DNA: Law and Policy—International and Comparative Perspectives* (The Hague: Kluwer Law International, 1997), 407. See also Francis X. Clines, 'Virginia May Get DNA From Felony Suspects', *New York Times*, 17 February 2002, A16 ('Virginia is on the verge of making a quantum leap in amassing DNA evidence by requiring that everyone arrested on suspicion of a violent crime yield genetic samples for possible matches in unsolved cases.').

[14] See David Johnston, 'Law Change Sought to Set Up DNA Databank for Captured Qaeda Fighters', *New York Times*, 6 March 2002, A13.

[15] See, e.g., *Schmerber* v. *California*, 384 US 757 (1966). Even this power is limited to relatively minor and non-invasive procedures. See *ibid.* 771–772 (intrusions into an individual's body must be minor, must be a reasonable and effective means to obtain probative evidence, and must impose virtually no physical risk, trauma, or pain).

[16] Wholesale DNA testing has been occasionally conducted in other countries in attempts to solve crimes. In Germany, for instance, 16,400 men were tested in 1998 in an effort to identify the perpetrator of a particularly heinous murder, and suggestions have recently been made that the country's entire adult male population of 41 million persons be tested in an attempt to solve the murder of a 12-year-old child. Geir Moulson, 'Mass DNA Test Urged in German Sex Slaying', *Philadelphia Inquirer*, 13 March 2001, A6.

against persons whose genetic information shows characteristics such as susceptibility to cancer, predisposition to alcoholism, predisposition toward risk-taking, or other 'undesirable' physical or psychological traits.[17] Indeed, use of genetic information by public or private actors could proceed, in many instances, with little in the way of intrusive collection efforts: since all people leave cells containing DNA on almost everything that they touch, assessing an individual's genetic profile would be a relatively easy—and, from the individual's point of view, an often invisible—task. In addition, blood samples routinely taken from all military inductees and all newborn babies offer large, inchoate DNA 'banks' in the United States.[18]

The collection or use of individuals' DNA profiles in pursuit of public safety, public health, or other collective objectives could be challenged on several grounds. For instance, it could be argued that the state's gathering or use of this information is an invasion of privacy, in violation of federal or state constitutional guarantees. Additionally, opponents of such programmes could argue that such samples or the information that they contain are property, with the presumption of individual control which that assertion involves. Indeed, federal legislation was recently proposed which would establish an individually identifiable DNA sample as the 'property' of its 'source'.[19] The question that arises is this: if the right to control DNA sampling and DNA information is a property right, what would the power of this claimed right—*vis-à-vis* competing public interests—be?

It is apparent, upon even cursory reflection, that the core values that underlie a claim of DNA or the information that it contains as one's property, and the core values that underlie the state's use of DNA profiles for criminal-identification programmes, public-health profiles, employment profiles, or other such purposes, are of radically different natures. The state of affairs that the individual claim attempts to achieve or protect in these cases is that of individual control of a particular substance and the information that it contains, in order to protect personal freedom and autonomy—in particular, the extent to which one's identity, health, or other characteristics are presented to the world. The competing public interests seek to achieve states of affairs in which this substance and its information

---

[17] On 9 February 2000, President Clinton issued an Executive Order which prohibits federal agencies from using genetic information in any decision to hire, promote, or dismiss workers. This order was in response, in part, to an allegation that the Lawrence Berkeley Laboratory, a research institution jointly operated by state and federal agencies, conducted tests on employees' blood and urine for syphilis, sickle cell trait, and pregnancy without their knowledge or consent. See Robert Pear, 'Clinton Bans Use of Genetic Makeup in Federal Employment', *New York Times*, 9 February 2000, A18; *Norman-Bloodsaw* v. *Lawrence Berkeley Laboratory*, 135 F 3d 1260 (9th Cir. 1998) (U.S.).

[18] See McEwen, n. 13 above, 410–411, 415.

[19] Genetic Confidentiality and Nondiscrimination Act of 1996, S. 1898, 104th Cong. §§ 3(12), 104 (1996) (U.S.). See also Patricia Roche, '*Caveat Venditor:* Protecting Privacy and Ownership Interests in DNA,' in Knoppers (ed.), n. 13 above, 33. In Colorado, Florida, Georgia, Louisiana, and Oregon, genetic information is now declared—by statute—to be the personal property of its source, and other states are considering similar legislation. See Thomas Fitzgerald, 'Two Pennsylvania Bills Would Protect Genetic Data', *Philadelphia Inquirer*, 28 March 2001, A-1.

are publicly accessible and publicly usable, in order to promote public safety or public health, and to *prevent* (in many cases) the very kind of autonomous behaviour and decisionmaking that the individuals in question want to protect. In these situations, the competing values that are involved are not only unrelated—they are, in critical ways, directly oppositional in nature.

Because of the natures of the different core values of the competing interests in these cases, these are Tier One cases under our model. The claimed rights and the competing public interests are entirely different and unrelated entities, in the kind of opposing relation that we generally expect claimed rights and competing public interests to occupy. Because the core values that underlie the claimed rights are not shared in any way by the competing public interests—because the powerful normative reasons that ground our decision to recognize individuals' claims to DNA protection as 'property rights' are left unchallenged by the public interests that ground the ideas of compelled DNA production or free public DNA use—the claimed rights should, in this case, enjoy clear presumptive power. Interests in public health or public safety might overcome these private claims, but they would have to be of a particularly compelling nature to do so.

The presumptive power which individuals' claimed property rights in their genetic information should enjoy when opposed by most imaginable public interests is replicated when other kinds of personal information as property are considered. Whether one considers medical records as property,[20] employment records as property,[21] addresses and phone numbers as property,[22] or cyberspace transactions as property,[23] it is highly unlikely that the core values that underlie these claims—that the interests in personal freedom and autonomous decisionmaking that these claims involve—will be any part of competing public interests to collect, use, and disseminate this information.[24] As a result, the legal protection that should be given to such claims is clear. If the right to control personal information is a cognizable property right, it should—in such cases—be afforded strong presumptive power.

---

[20] See Beverly Woodward, 'The Computer-Based Patient Record and Confidentiality' (1995) 333 *New England Journal of Medicine* 1419; Anne Wells Branscomb, *Who Owns Information?* (New York: Basic Books, 1994), 54–72.

[21] See, e.g., 'California to Sell Confidential Wage Data', *New York Times*, 4 June 1999, A20.

[22] A debate currently rages about states' sale of drivers' licence information, including drivers' names, addresses, and telephone numbers, to private information brokers. See Jan Crawford Greenburg, 'Court Upholds Drivers' Privacy; Justices Back Congress in Restricting States' Sale of Personal Data', *Chicago Tribune*, 13 January 2000, N9 (New York garnered revenue of $17 million in one year of such sales; Wisconsin, $8 million).

[23] For a discussion about how cyberspace transactions are—under current practice—treated as a marketable commodity by those who have access to such data see Jerry Kang, 'Information Privacy in Cyberspace Transactions' (1998) 50 *Stanford Law Review* 1193.

[24] For instance, it has been argued that the public collection and dissemination of individuals' health data will 'help consumers make informed choices among health plans and providers, . . . provide more effective clinical care, . . . [help the monitoring of] fraud and abuse, [help] to track and evaluate access to health services . . ., . . . [and assist in research of] the determinants, prevention, and treatment of disease'. Lawrence O. Gostin, 'Health Information Privacy' (1995) 80 *Cornell Law Review* 451, 453.

(iii) CULTURAL PROPERTY CLAIMS

In recent years, the public's assertion of distinct public claims regarding land, buildings, and chattels because of their historical, archeological, aesthetic, or other cultural value has gained momentum both nationally and internationally. As Joseph Sax has observed, '[p]ublic responsibility for the conservation of artifacts of historic or aesthetic value is now acknowledged everywhere. One way or another the state will ensure preservation of a Stonehenge or a Grand Canyon as well as a great many lesser cultural icons.'[25] Historic buildings, places of natural wonder, religious objects, battlefields, national documents, works of art, archeological finds, and other places and objects are routinely asserted to be the subjects of distinct public interests, to be recognized and enforced through law.

The idea that unifies all of these initiatives is that defined groups of people—such as the residents of a town, the citizens of a state, the members of a tribe, or the citizens of a nation—have identifiable interests in particular kinds of tangible or intangible property which are legally cognizable and which should be protected for the benefit of those groups, even if those interests are (at the same time) inconsistent with the bundle of rights that title holders traditionally enjoy. The reasons for legal recognition of such group interests are diverse, but have coalesced around the idea of 'cultural property': that there are certain tangible or intangible things which are of such importance to a defined cultural group that they should be subject to that group's claims to disposition and control. The idea that there are collective interests of this sort is a relatively recent innovation in Anglo-American law; as one writer has observed, only a century ago the private owner of Stonehenge threatened to dismantle and sell it.[26] The group that is recognized to have such a claim may be defined with reference to political boundaries (such as a nation's claims) or may be defined by traits such as ethnicity, language, religion, or history.[27] The things that are subject to the claim may embody some aspect of the group's cultural identity, or may inculcate and reinforce the group's shared norms or values.[28] Although cultural property often involves human artifacts, it may involve natural objects and

[25] Joseph L. Sax, 'Heritage Preservation as a Public Duty: The Abbe Gregoire and the Origins of an Idea' (1990) 88 *Michigan Law Review* 1142, 1142.

[26] See Wayland Kennet, *Preservation* (London: Maurice Temple Smith Ltd., 1972), 37.

[27] See Patty Gerstenblith, 'Identity and Cultural Property: The Protection of Cultural Property in the United States' (1995) 75 *Boston University Law Review* 559, 567; Jonathan Drimmer, 'Hate Property: A Substantive Limitation for America's Cultural Property Laws' (1998) 65 *Tennessee Law Review* 691, 698–699.

[28] See Rosemary J. Coombe, 'The Properties of Culture and the Politics of Possessing Identity: Native Claims in the Cultural Appropriation Controversy', in Dan Danielsen and Karen Engle (eds.), *After Identity: A Reader in Law and Culture* (New York: Routledge, 1995), 251, 262; Roger W. Mastalir, 'A Proposal for Protecting the "Cultural" and "Property" Aspects of Cultural Property Under International Law' (1992–1993) 16 *Fordham International Law Journal* 1033, 1039.

places as well.[29] As John Merryman has written, cultural property responds to '[t]he need for cultural identity, for a sense of significance, for reassurance about one's place in the scheme of things, for a "legible past", for answers to the great existential questions about our nature and our fate'.[30]

On the international level, the protection of cultural property has taken the forms, most prominently, of the protection of identified land, buildings, and other property in the event of armed conflict,[31] and of the prohibition of the import, export, or transfer of chattels identified to be cultural property without the cultural group's permission.[32] In the United States, the earliest efforts to protect cultural property involved the preservation of national historic sites such as Independence Hall in Philadelphia and the Gettysburg Battlefield in Pennsylvania.[33] In the twentieth century, a series of national laws extended protection to sites, buildings, and objects of historic, scientific, aesthetic, or other perceived national interest.[34] Although these laws deal primarily with land or objects that are—for other reasons—federally owned or federally controlled, their protection has been extended, in some instances, to privately owned land

---

[29] See Sax, n. 25 above, 1142; J. H. Merryman, 'The Public Interest in Cultural Property' (1989) 77 *California Law Review* 339, 341–342. See also Convention on the Means of Prohibiting and Preventing the Illicit Import, Export and Transfer of Ownership of Cultural Property (Paris, 14 November 1970), 823 UNTS 231, 234, 236 (cultural property includes '[r]are collections and specimens of fauna, flora, minerals, and anatomy, and objects of palaeontological interest; . . . property relating to history . . .; . . . products of archeological excavations . . .; . . . elements of artistic or historical monuments or archeological sites . . .; . . . objects of ethnological interest; . . . property of artistic interest . . .;' and so on). In an interesting recent case, the Confederated Tribes of the Grand Ronde of Oregon have asserted a cultural property claim to the Willamette Meteorite, the centrepiece of the new Planetarium of the American Museum of Natural History in New York City. See Robert D. McFadden, 'Meteorite Dispute Greets Opening of Planetarium', *New York Times*, 19 February 2000, A1.

[30] Merryman, n. 29 above, 349. See also Sherry Hutt and C. Timothy McKeown, 'Control of Cultural Property as Human Rights Law' (1999) 31 *Arizona State Law Journal* 363.

[31] See, e.g., Convention for the Protection of Cultural Property in the Event of Armed Conflict (The Hague, 14 May 1954), 249 UNTS 240.

[32] See, e.g., Convention on the Means of Prohibiting and Preventing the Illicit Import, Export and Transfer of Ownership of Cultural Property, n. 29 above; UNIDROIT Convention on Stolen or Illegally Exported Cultural Objects (Rome, 24 June 1995), 34 ILM 1330.

[33] See Gerstenblith, n. 27 above, 574–577.

[34] See, e.g., Antiquities Act of 1906, 16 U.S.C. §§ 431–433 (2000) (setting aside as national monuments 'historic landmarks, historic and prehistoric structures, and other objects of historic or scientific interest' located on federal land); Historic Sites, Buildings, and Antiquities Act, 16 U.S.C. §§ 461–467 (2000) (declaring a national policy of 'preserv[ing] for public use historic sites, buildings, and objects of national significance for the inspiration and benefit of the people of the United States'); National Historic Preservation Act, 16 U.S.C. § 470 *et seq.* (2000) (establishing the National Register of Historic Places); Archeological Resources Protection Act of 1979, 16 U.S.C. § 470aa *et seq.* (2000) (criminalizing the excavation, destruction, unauthorized removal, sale, and purchase of archeological resources from federal land); Abandoned Shipwreck Act of 1987, 43 U.S.C. §§ 2101–2106 (1994) (transferring title to abandoned and embedded shipwrecks to state governments and abrogating the law of finds and salvage); Native American Graves Protection and Repatriation Act, 25 U.S.C. §§ 3001–3013 (2000) (requiring federal agencies to consult with Native American tribes before undertaking excavations of Native American human remains or cultural items on federal land, and criminalizing the trafficking in such items).

and objects as well.[35] In addition, some states and local governments have enacted laws that mandate public control of what would otherwise be privately owned or controlled cultural property. For instance, New York City prevents the substantial alteration of designated historic structures, even if privately owned,[36] and the State of Alabama has declared the State to be the owner of all archeological objects unearthed, even if found on private land.[37]

When cultural property notions are applied to land or chattels that are privately owned, the idea of public control which cultural property entails—and traditional notions of the rights that private ownership confers—are often on a collision course.[38] Indeed, many private landowners and commentators have strenuously opposed what are seen as unjustified (and uncompensated) public incursions under cultural property theories upon private property rights. In some states, private-property activists have pushed for the enactment of 'property protection' laws which they threaten to use against public efforts to protect historic buildings or other cultural property.[39]

The courts have exhibited remarkable receptiveness to public efforts to protect cultural property, even when those efforts have conflicted with private property rights of a previously well established and traditional nature. The ability of states and localities to prevent the destruction of historic structures is—after the Supreme Court's endorsement[40]—a generally assumed public power,[41] and the ability of government to protect other cultural property, such as archeological sites and Native American burial grounds, has largely been assumed as well.[42] In

---

[35] See, e.g., *Landmarks Preservation Council* v. *City of Chicago*, 531 NE 2d 9 (Ill. 1988) (U.S.) (holding that the National Trust for Historic Preservation has standing to challenge the destruction of private buildings not yet declared to be 'national landmarks').

[36] New York City's historic preservation laws were the subject of a famous Supreme Court case, in which they were upheld against a 'takings' challenge. See *Penn Central Transportation Company* v. *New York City*, 438 US 104 (1978).

[37] See Ala. Code § 41–3–1 (2000) (U.S.).

[38] There has been a spirited debate on whether the root idea of collective identity which cultural property presents is at odds with the primacy that Western liberal democracies place upon the liberty and autonomy of the individual. See Joseph L. Sax, *Playing Darts with a Rembrandt: Public and Private Rights in Cultural Treasures* (Ann Arbor, Mich.: University of Michigan Press, 1999).

[39] See, e.g., Peter Mitchell, 'New Property-Rights Law Sends City Planners Scrambling for Cover', *Wall Street Journal*, 25 October 1995 (describing new Florida property-rights legislation and its dampening effect on municipal historic-preservation efforts).

[40] See *Penn Central Transportation Company*, n. 36 above.

[41] Cases in which this power has been upheld include *United Artists' Theater Circuit, Inc.* v. *City of Philadelphia*, 635 A 2d 612 (Pa. 1993) (U.S.); *W.W.W. Associates, Inc.* v. *Rettaliata*, 572 NYS 2d 22 (N.Y. App. Div. 1991) (U.S.); *Shubert Organizations, Inc.* v. *Landmarks Preservation Commission*, 570 NYS 2d 504 (N.Y. App. Div. 1991), cert. denied, 504 US 946 (1992). The Supreme Court of Pennsylvania has recently observed that 'in fifteen years since *Penn Central*, no other state has rejected the notion that no taking occurs when a state designates a building as historic'. *United Artists' Theater Circuit, Inc.*, above, 619. See Daniel T. Cavarello, 'From Penn Central to United Artists' I & II: The Rise to Immunity of Historic Preservation Designation From Successful Takings Challenges' (1995) 22 *Boston College Environmental Affairs Law Review* 593.

[42] See, e.g., *Hunziker* v. *State*, 519 NW 2d 367 (Ia. 1994), cert. denied, 514 US 1003 (1995) (upholding state prohibition of disinterment of Native American burial mounds found on private land); *People* v. *Van Horn*, 267 Cal Rptr 804 (Ct. App. 1990) (U.S.) (upholding state prohibition of possession of certain Native American artifacts or human remains taken from Native American graves).

Whitacre v. *State*,[43] for instance, Native American artifacts were found on privately owned land. When the land was purchased, the State of Indiana exercised no control over archaeological investigations and excavations on private property; this changed when Indiana's Historic Preservation and Archeology Act was amended several years later. The control that the State asserted under the amended Act over the excavation and disposition of artifacts was clearly in conflict with the traditional prerogatives of landowners under the common law of finds. An appellate court nonetheless broadly held, with apparent ease, that the State had power to regulate 'activities on private property that affect . . . historical and archeological cultur[al] [resources]'.[44]

In reaching such results, courts often reason that cultural-property laws do not impair property rights because cultural-property laws simply confirm limitations that are inherent in the property owners' titles.[45] Under the 'theory of the public trust', for instance, the public generally (or a particular cultural group) is deemed to have pre-existing and inviolable rights in certain natural or man-made resources.[46] To put the matter in terms that we have previously described, the rights that a property owner is denied are simply not a part of the theory of rights that is recognized (by law) as the theoretical dimension of the property owner's title.[47] Although this approach may seem quite satisfactory in some cases—for instance, those in which the cultural property law seeks to confirm established historical practice or widespread cultural understanding[48]—it is much less satisfactory in others. It is quite difficult, for instance, to claim that a newly enacted law that designates ordinary homes as historic sites, or prohibits the harvesting of ancient redwood trees, simply confirms restrictions that were a part of title to begin with.

Indeed, in its most prominent decision of this type, the Supreme Court acknowledged that the cultural-property law in issue—an historic-preservation ordinance—impaired previously established and previously protected private property rights.[49] The Court nonetheless upheld the ordinance, on the ground

---

[43] 619 NE 2d 605 (Ind. App. 1993) (U.S.).   [44] *Ibid*. 608.

[45] See, e.g., *Charrier* v. *Bell*, 496 So 2d 601 (La. App. 1986) (U.S.); *Hunziker*, n. 42 above, 371.

[46] See, e.g., Richard J. Lazarus, 'Changing Conceptions of Property and Sovereignty in Natural Resources: Questioning the Public Trust Doctrine' (1986) 71 *Iowa Law Review* 631; Jan S. Stevens, 'The Public Trust: A Sovereign's Ancient Prerogative Becomes the People's Environmental Right' (1980) 14 *University of California Davis Law Review* 195.

[47] As one court stated, 'parties acquiring rights in trust property generally hold those rights subject to the trust, and can assert no vested right to use those rights in a manner harmful to the trust'. *National Audubon Society* v. *Superior Court*, 658 P 2d 709, 721 (Cal.), cert. denied, 464 US 977 (1983).

[48] See, e.g., *Illinois Central Railroad Company* v. *Illinois*, 146 US 387 (1892) (public rights regarding navigable waters); *City of Los Angeles* v. *Venice Peninsula Properties*, 644 P 2d 792 (Cal. 1982), rev'd on other grounds, 466 US 198 (1984) (public rights regarding tidelands). Joseph Sax has described such cases as 'preventing the destabilizing disappointment of expectations held in common but without formal recognition such as title'. Joseph Sax, 'Liberating the Public Trust Doctrine from Its Historical Shackles' (1980) 14 *University of California Davis Law Review* 185, 188 (footnote omitted).

[49] See *Penn Central Transportation Company*, n. 36 above, 136 (ordinance 'restricted . . . the exploitation of property interests, . . . to a greater extent than provided for under applicable zoning laws').

that this impairment lacked constitutional significance. Regulations designating landmarks and prohibiting contrary modifications and uses are not unconstitutional takings if they 'are substantially related to the promotion of the general welfare and . . . permit reasonable beneficial use of the landmark site'.[50]

Is there a way to explain the apparent weakness of property-rights claims when opposed by cultural-property laws? Indeed, if we consult our model, we find that there are very real reasons why claimed private property rights often fail—and *should fail*—in these cases.

Let us take, for instance, a building owner's claimed right to destroy or alter a historic building, and the competing public interest in the building's preservation. In this case, the claimed right seeks to protect individual use and control of a valuable resource, in order to protect the investment and expectations of the building owner. These core values are clearly within traditional notions of property rights and what their reasons and objectives should be.

What about the competing public interest? We might understand the public interest in historic preservation in the terms that neighbouring property owners might employ: that is, that the preservation of historic structures is important because of the role that those structures play in restoring or maintaining the vitality of the community of which they are a part.[51] Under this understanding, historic preservation functions much like zoning: it protects the investments and expectations of *all* landowners whose property values are—unavoidably—intertwined. In the City of Charleston, South Carolina, for instance, the charm and character of each person's land in the historic peninsula area is dependent upon the charm and character of the land of others—making the public interest in historic preservation the assertion, in fact, of the property interests of others. In this situation, the relative power of the public interest *vis-à-vis* the claimed right is easy to see. Like zoning, the public interest in this case is grounded in core values that are of the same or a very similar kind to those that ground the claimed right. Both competing claims involve the protection of traditionally recognized property interests in land; both simply assert—as an essential matter—different interpretations of what, in this context, the foundational right to property protection should be. As a consequence, the claimed right in this Tier Two case can legitimately claim no normative superiority; it can claim no presumptive power.

Cultural-property cases that involve the conflict of traditional, land-based claims are, however, the easy ones; in many cases involving cultural property, the interests that the public asserts are of an entirely different character. For instance, the public may wish to protect a historic structure which is isolated, and has—of itself—little effect on surrounding land values; or the cultural-property interest may be asserted in a natural place or chattel whose value lies

---

[50] See *Penn Central Transportation Company*, n. 36 above, 138.

[51] See, e.g., Carol M. Rose, 'Preservation and Community: New Directions in the Law of Historic Preservation' (1981) 33 *Stanford Law Review* 473, 504–517.

in its unique character. In such cases, the cultural-property claim is most deeply rooted in intellectual or emotional or psychological interests, rather than economic ones. How can these cases be analysed under our model? Is there any way to explain—and justify—the frequent and apparent weakness of private-property claims in such cases?

Let us take, for instance, a landowner's assertion of ownership and control of an ancient artifact found on her land, and the competing public claim to title or control over this object. The landowner's claimed right in this case is rooted in the theory of constructive possession of the fruits of the land as an incident of ownership of the land itself. Under general principles of the common law, chattels that are found in an embedded state in private land are ordinarily believed to be in the constructive possession of the land's owner and, thus, awarded to her.[52] The state of affairs that the claimed right attempts to achieve is the protection of individual power to control a valuable object—a power clearly associated with traditional understandings of the scope and nature of property rights.

The core values that any claimed right involves are determined, however, not only by the protection of a particular state of affairs, but by the protection of that state of affairs for particular reasons. In the case of found, embedded chattels, the landowner's claimed right to ownership and control is honoured for complex reasons. In part, we honour such claims for the reasons that we generally afford property rights in land: to protect expectations, encourage investment, reward labour, and so on. However, these are not the only reasons that we honour such claims—one need only think of the old adage of 'finders keepers' to realize that there is more. The finder of a lost dollar on the street would generally have no expectations, would have made no investment, and would have expended little labour in making his find; yet, as against all comers (except the true owner), we strongly protect his claim. It is the fact of possession itself that creates reasons for the claimed right's protection. Those reasons are practical in nature, such as the simplicity of the rule of first possession and the 'signalling' function that first possession communicates to the world.[53] They are also deeply psychological—they recognize the natural human tendency to bond with objects that are in one's physical possession, and which become, as the result of that possession, a part of one's history and identity.[54]

We have identified the core values that underlie the claimed right in our found-artifact case. What about the competing public interest? In fact, we find

---

[52] See, e.g., *Bishop* v. *Ellsworth*, 234 NE 2d 49, 52 (Ill. App. Ct. 1968) (U.S.) (embedded property found on private land 'is and always has been in the constructive possession of the owner of said premises and in a legal sense the property can be neither mislaid nor lost'). See generally Gerstenblith, n. 27 above, 587–595 (discussing the common law of finds).

[53] See Carol M. Rose, 'Possession as the Origin of Property' (1985) 52 *University of Chicago Law Review* 73.

[54] See Margaret Radin, 'Property and Personhood' (1982) 34 *Stanford Law Review* 957 (describing the role of object attachment in human life). Cf. Jack L. Knetsch, 'The Endowment Effect and Evidence of Nonreversible Indifference Curves' (1989) 79 *American Economic Review* 1277.

that the core values that ground the public interest in this case are of the same or a very similar kind. The public interest in an ancient artifact asserts the claim of the public generally—or of a particular cultural group—to title and/or control over the artifact in question. The state of affairs that the public interest asserts is, thus, of a kind that we readily associate with property rights. The reasons that cultural-property claims are asserted as public interests are diverse, but they coalesce around what we would traditionally call 'personality theories' of property: the recognition that physical objects and other resources can be critical to human attempts to construct cultures, preserve memories, inspire wonder, embody aspirations, and ultimately understand—in some way—the place of individuals in the human and natural worlds. Although such reasons for honouring claims for possession and control may be more subtle than purely material ones, they have long been traditionally associated with property claims and property rights.

The extent to which we (as a society) are willing to recognize such claims, and grant them legally cognizable status, is an evolving and uncertain one. Although the United States government has willingly participated in international efforts to protect cultural property of other nations, federal and state governments have only begun to extend the same protection to cultural property in private hands at home.[55] However, to the extent that such recognition is afforded, it is clear that public interests in cultural property will—and should—have presumptive power that equals the claimed individual rights to property protection with which they conflict. The core values that underlie cultural-property claims—the states of affairs that they seek to protect, and the reasons for that protection—are as rooted in traditional property notions as are the core values that underlie the opposing individual claims. There is no reason, in these Tier Two cases, presumptively to privilege a landowner's claim to an ancient artifact over the claim of an originating native group, or presumptively to privilege the claim of an owner of ancient redwood trees over the public claim of preservation. In each case, the idea of the protection of property *and the reasons for the protection of property* speak powerfully for both private and public claims. The resolution of such conflicts should depend upon what we, as a society, determine that property rights should be, in the particular case at hand. It should not be influenced by any idea that the private claim—by definition—asserts values of a particularly worthy character, or deserves—by definition—*prima facie* or trumping power.

---

[55] See, e.g., James A. R. Nafziger, 'The Underlying Constitutionalism of the Law Governing Archeological and Other Cultural Heritage' (1994) 30 *Willamette Law Review* 581, 581–589. For a powerful argument in favour of increased protection see Sax, n. 38 above.

(iv) STATE REDISTRIBUTIVE CLAIMS

Our apparent toleration of government schemes to redistribute property is a chronic source of irritation and perplexity to those who advocate the presumptive power of property rights. There is no more definitive interference with property rights than the taking of title; yet we find, for instance, casual (if any) constitutional concern about what are simply redistributive transfers. The apparent ease with which wealth can be taken from one citizen and transferred (through taxation and the mechanisms of welfare programmes) to other citizens is inexplicable under traditional notions of property rights. In most of these transfers, the monetary benefits received by the recipients far outweigh the monetary benefits received by the parties taxed; yet these transfers do not generate the kind of outrage that one would expect from such marked and widespread disregard of property rights.[56]

The transfer of wealth in this country through the taxation of one and the giving to another is not uncontroversial; indeed, many have strongly opposed state welfare programmes, leading (in recent years) to their curtailment in some ways. The objections that are raised to such programmes are, however, more often that these programmes are ineffectual or detrimental as a matter of social policy, than that they violate property rights. Indeed, even those who oppose the idea of redistribution for redistribution's sake 'must come to grips with the common perception [that] . . . charitable assistance to the poor' is a desirable and historically accepted part of our political landscape.[57]

Why are these transfers not 'takings', as some have argued?[58] Why do the courts—and seemingly most citizens—see these transfers as 'exceptions' to the legal protection of property? Many answers to this question have been offered—for instance, that taxpayers see such transfers as 'insurance' for themselves in their own times of need, or that they receive value in exchange for these transfers in the form of the prevention of civil unrest or other public goods. There is undoubtedly some truth in these explanations. In the discussion that follows, however, I will advance another explanation for our widespread tolerance of these transfers—one that is rooted in the particular nature of the rights and public interests that conflict in these cases.

---

[56] See, e.g., Jan Narveson, *The Libertarian Idea* (Philadelphia, Pa.: Temple University Press, 1988), 232, 250. Perhaps most famous is Robert Nozick's polemic against redistributive taxation as 'forced labor'. Robert Nozick, *Anarchy, State, and Utopia* (New York: Basic Books, Inc., 1974), 169.

[57] Richard A. Epstein, 'Property, Speech, and the Politics of Distrust' (1992) 59 *University of Chicago Law Review* 41, 87. As Carol Rose has observed, '[h]istoric views about property certainly assumed that the haves should give to the have-nots.'. Carol M. Rose, 'What Government Can Do for Property (and Vice Versa),' in Nicholas Mercuro and Warren J. Samuels (eds.), *The Fundamental Interrelationships Between Government and Property* (Stamford, Conn.: JAI Press, 1999), 209, 218.

[58] See, e.g., Richard A. Epstein, *Takings: Private Property and the Power of Eminent Domain* (Cambridge, Mass.: Harvard University Press, 1985), 95, 200, 306–329.

Let us take, for instance, an individual's claimed right to retain title to the money that she has earned, and the competing public demand that this money be taken through taxation for the payment of welfare benefits to others. In this case, the core values that underlie the taxpayer's claim are among those most clearly associated with property rights. The protection of an individual's money is a state of affairs which property, as an idea, is commonly believed to exemplify. Moreover, the reasons that money is protected—to reward industry, provide security, protect expectations, and so on—are among those traditionally associated with property rights. It is these core values, and the presumed normative superiority of these core values, that the claimed right asserts.

What about the competing public interest? At first blush, the core values that are asserted by the competing public interest seem to be very different. The claimed right seeks to protect the taxpayer's control of the money in question, and the competing public interest seeks to deny that control. Seen in this way, the states of affairs that the different claims seek to achieve are of diametrically opposing natures.

This analysis of the public-interest demand is, however, a very superficial one. All public-interest demands that compete with claimed rights seek to deny the states of affairs that the claimed rights assert: it is that opposition that make the public interests 'competing' claims. Characterizing the public interest's content as simply 'opposition to what the taxpayer demands' tells us little about the nature of the public interest, or why it is asserted.

In fact, the public interest in this case is *more* than the mere negation of the rights claimant's agenda; it is also the advancement of positive interests, positive goals. By implementing a programme of public welfare, the state seeks to take money from citizens who are better-off, and to give it to the poor. Through this action, the state seeks to achieve a particular state of affairs: the meeting of poor citizens' acquisitive desires. Seen in this way, it is apparent that the claimed right and the competing public interest actually involve content of the very same kind: the assuaging of the human desire for material goods.

What about the *reasons* that underlie the competing claims? Are these of the same kind, as well? The reasons for the implementation of a state welfare programme could be many: they could range from a desire to purchase social peace to an altruistic desire to feed the hungry. If the welfare programme is implemented by the better-off for purely manipulative or self-interested reasons, then the reasons—and the resulting core values—that underlie the competing claims seems to be quite different. If the claimed property right rewards acquisitive desires in order to assure the security of the taxpayer, this is quite different from the rewarding of acquisitive desires in order to prevent the recipient from engaging in theft or engaging in bloodshed. If, however, the welfare programme is implemented because it is believed (by society) that the needs of the poor for food, clothing, and other necessities of life should be met—if it is implemented from a desire to meet the needs of material well-being, shared by all persons—

then the core values that underlie the competing claims would be, on many levels, remarkably similar.

The fact that welfare programmes are so widely accepted, and so weakly challenged on takings grounds, suggests that the reasons for their existence are, in fact, largely of the more altruistic kind.[59] Because welfare programmes address, and are intended to address, the acquisitive desires of recipients for reasons of their well-being—because they involve, in short, core values that underlie the recognition and protection of all human acquisitive desires—the presumed normative superiority of the values that the claimed right asserts is, in fact, untrue in these cases.[60] When wealth is transferred under such programmes, the claimed right and the competing public interest involve recognition of the same human needs, the same human desires. There is no reason, in these Tier Two cases, presumptively to privilege the taxpayer's claim. In such cases, the idea of property and the reasons for the protection of property speak powerfully for both private *and* public claims. The normative power of the interests that the claimed right protects *are equalled by* the normative power of the interests that the public demand asserts. As a consequence, there is no reason to assume that the claimed right asserts values of a particularly worthy character, or deserves—for that reason—*prima facie* or trumping power.

Indeed, it is because property rights are so often *allocative* in nature—it is because they so often involve honouring the acquisitive interests of some, to the detriment of the identical interests of others—that we so often accept redistributive schemes. The claimed right of a property holder against a redistributive action is grounded—if at all—in the normative superiority of the values that his claim (presumably) involves. If, however, the claimed right and the competing public interest are grounded in the *same* values—if, for instance, the need for security of those with wealth is opposed by a public interest which asserts (through welfare programmes, medicare programmes, or other means) the security interests of others—then the reason for the presumed superiority of the claimed right is severely undermined. There is no obvious reason why we should

---

[59] Indeed, the fact that we, as a society, place great value in the protection of property does not mean that we care nothing for the plights of others. As Joseph Singer has written:

> Contrary to what some believe and others fear, the protection of property rights does not commit us to the view that gross inequality is a necessary fact of life or that individuals have no legitimate claim to lean on other people. Property is not merely an individual right, it is not based solely on the notion of self-interest or self-reliance. It is, in fact, an intensely social institution. It implicates social relationships that combine individualism with a large amount of communal responsibility. We value self-reliance, but we also value looking out for others. We praise those who are not selfish, who look beyond themselves. We are committed, not to indifference, but to compassion, empathy, fellow feeling. Those commitments are present in popular culture, in a variety of religious traditions, and even in American law.

Joseph William Singer, *The Edges of the Field: Lessons on the Obligations of Ownership* (Boston, Mass.: Beacon Press, 2000), 3 (footnote omitted).

[60] Cf. Paul Jones, 'Freedom and the Redistribution of Resources' (1982) 11 *Journal of Social Policy* 217, 222–223 (if one person loses freedom when his property is redistributed, another gains freedom when the property is received).

privilege the need for human security or the need to appropriate the necessities of life of one individual over the identical needs of another. There is no reason to believe (on this basis, at least) that the claimed right protects more important values, or—as a consequence—deserves presumptive power.

Indeed, this truth is implicitly acknowledged by libertarian writers who profess hostility to the idea of redistribution for redistribution's sake. In what often seems like an anomalous afterthought, libertarians who forcefully oppose state redistributive programmes often acknowledge, on moral grounds, the need for charity or other poor relief.[61] This strain of libertarianism is explained when we combine an important principle of libertarianism with the insights of our model. As Stephen Perry has illuminated, basic principles of libertarian thought stress not only that people are entitled to the fruits of their labours, but also that they are responsible for the harms that their actions cause.[62] Because the same human desires—and the same core values—are involved in the acquisitive claims of all people, *and* because granting the acquisitive claims of some people (to physical, finite, non-shareable goods) necessarily means denying the acquisitive claims of others, the conclusion that existing distributions of wealth 'harm' those who possess little is undeniable.[63] The libertarian acknowledgment that charity or some other social response is necessary is an implicit recognition of this truth.

The conclusion that claimed property rights lack presumptive power when they are confronted by state redistributive claims could be seen as a deeply unsettling or improbable one. Does this mean that property protection has no meaning in this context—that titles to land, chattels, money, and other wealth are completely insecure? If so, this does not seem to describe our legal system or our intuitive notions about the relative power of state redistributive claims.

The answers to this objection are several. First, the question that we have addressed is whether claimed property rights, when opposed by state redistributive demands, *deserve presumptive power*. We have found that when the same

---

[61] See, e.g., Epstein, n. 57 above, 42–43; Epstein, n. 58 above, 319–320, 324.

[62] See Stephen R. Perry, 'Libertarianism, Entitlement, and Responsibility' (1997) 26 *Philosophy and Public Affairs* 351, 363–373. In classic formulations of libertarian theory, these principles are 'two sides of the same coin'; they are unified in the idea 'that people "own" the effects, both good and bad, that causally flow from their actions'. *Ibid.* 352. See, e.g., Richard A. Epstein, 'A Theory of Strict Liability' (1973) 2 *Journal of Legal Studies* 151, 159 (when one acts, he should 'bear all the costs and enjoy all the benefits of that decision'). Cf. Nozick, n. 56 above, 33 (libertarian theory 'prohibits aggression against another').

[63] Indeed, one could say, it is impossible—in the case of claims to such goods—simultaneously to fulfil the libertarian self-ownership thesis, that 'each is free (morally speaking) to use [his] powers as he wishes', and also to meet the injunction that these powers must not be 'deploy[ed] . . . aggressively against others'. G. A. Cohen, *Self-Ownership, Freedom, and Equality* (Cambridge: Cambridge University Press, 1995), 67. It is perhaps for this reason that libertarians so often focus on 'created' resources, those in which—by acting in the world—the actor personally produces a commodity or asset of some sort which did not previously exist. See, e.g., Nozick, n. 56 above, 225–226. In such cases, at least arguably, (pre-existing) goods are not wrested from one and given to another, avoiding the aggression that distribution of physical, finite, non-shareable goods involves. The problem, of course, is that in the real world, this is—apart, perhaps, from intellectual property claims—largely an empty set.

human interests underlie both claims, there is no reason to afford such power to the individual's protective claim. This does not mean that the individual claim will always (or *should* always) lose—it means that the individual claim will lack (and *should* lack) the presumptive power which, as an asserted right, we might otherwise expect. We may ultimately decide that the individual claim should, on balance, prevail; however, that conclusion must be justified by what we (as a society) have consciously evaluated the relative merits of the conflicting claims to be, not by a presumption of the superiority of the individual's protective claim.

In addition, we must recognize the social and political controls that inhibit the assertion of public-interest claims of a redistributive kind. The redistributive claims that we (as a society) choose to assert are the results of complex and volatile social and political factors. For instance, we are (as a society) apparently far more willing to assert redistributive claims to money, or other forms of fungible wealth, than we are to land; and we are more willing to press redistributive claims against those with greater wealth than against those with lesser.[64] There may be excellent reasons for these differences—for instance, there are different degrees of human attachment to fungible and non-fungible property,[65] and even private-property advocates recognize that it is likely true that 'a dollar of income is worth more to a poor person than to a rich one'.[66] The acceptability of the assertion of state redistributive claims of any particular kind will depend upon the historical, social, economic, and other factors that prevail in a particular society at that moment.

The implementation of state redistributive schemes is also inhibited by the *idea* of property, which exerts very powerful social and political influence. Property is both an *idea* and an *institution*; it is how people envision it—'that is, what concept they have of it'[67]—and also how it is, as a social, political, and legal institution, implemented to resolve particular conflicts in society. The idea of property as protection from the predations of others is a powerful and enduring one.[68] It is difficult to imagine any person who has no interest, no psychological investment of any kind, in the *idea* of property protection. The desire to

---

[64] See Laura S. Underkuffler, 'The Perfidy of Property' (1991) 70 *Texas Law Review* 293, 308 (property is commonly envisioned as having a highly protected core, with less stringent protection as the size of one's holdings increase).

[65] See Radin, n. 54 above.

[66] Epstein, n. 57 above, 87. See also Richard A. Posner, *Economic Analysis of Law* (4th edn., Boston, Mass.: Little, Brown and Company, 1992), 458.

[67] C. B. Macpherson, 'The Meaning of Property', in C. B. Macpherson (ed.), *Property: Mainstream and Critical Positions* (Toronto: University of Toronto Press, 1978), 1, 1.

[68] See, e.g., Robert W. Gordon, 'Paradoxical Property', in John Brewer and Susan Staves (eds.), *Early Modern Conceptions of Property* (London: Routledge, 1996), 95, 108 (Despite threats to the idea of property as 'absolute dominion', the idea persists; its 'core image . . ., [with] the owner in undisturbed enjoyment of his physical things, is too compelling. It still offers something to everyone: security, autonomy, expressive freedom, protection from arbitrary encroachment or restraint, participation as an equal in economic and civic life, both apology for the status quo and a promise of emancipation from it.').

protect one's property transcends the boundaries of rich and poor; indeed, those who have little may have a greater stake in (and greater moral claim to) the protection of what little they do have. In recent debates in South Africa, for instance, the experiences of formerly oppressed and disadvantaged groups with discriminatory dispossessions during the apartheid years led to their support for the inclusion of property in the new Constitution's list of personal guarantees. This was true even though the constitutionalization of property secures fruits garnered by others through the workings of the apartheid system.[69]

When we, as a society, consider taking from one person and giving to another, the *idea* of property as protection restrains, very powerfully, the making of this choice.[70] The greater risk—all things considered—is not that redistributive claims will be asserted too easily, but that they will not be asserted when—as a matter of justice or good social policy—they should be.

There is, in short, an array of forces—practical, political, and theoretical—which resist the assertion of state redistributive claims. Our discussion, thus far, does not determine whether state redistributive claims will (or should) be asserted.[71] It determines only what the *power* of those claims—if asserted—will (and should) be.

[69] See A. J. van der Walt, 'The Constitutional Property Clause: Striking a Balance Between Guarantee and Limitation', in Janet McLean (ed.), *Property and the Constitution* (Oxford: Hart Publishing, 1999), 109, 112.

[70] See Jennifer Nedelsky, 'American Constitutionalism and the Paradox of Private Property', in Jon Elster and Rune Slagstad (eds.), *Constitutionalism and Democracy* (Cambridge: Cambridge University Press, 1988), 241, 263 (the popular idea of property as protections serves, in important ways, as a limit to the legitimate powers of government).

[71] The further argument that state redistributive claims *must* or *should* be asserted (under certain circumstances) as a part of the constitutional protection of property is made in Ch. 12, below.

9

Property, Speech, and the Politics of Presumptive Power

In the preceding chapters, we have examined a variety of cases in which claimed individual rights to property protection conflict with public interests. We have found that whether the claimed property rights enjoy presumptive power will depend upon the core values that underlie the claimed right and the competing public interest in each case. When a claimed property right and the competing public interest involve core values that are different in kind, the assumed normative superiority of the claimed right—as a *prima facie* matter, at least—stands unchallenged, and the right enjoys and deserves presumptive power. If (on the other hand) the claimed property right and the competing public interest involve core values of the same or a very similar kind, the normative power of the values that the claimed right protects is equalled by the normative power of the values that the public interest asserts. In this situation, there is no reason to afford the claimed right presumptive power.

If we further analyse our findings, we observe that the cases in which the claimed right lacks presumptive power tend—in the property context—to be one of the following kinds:

—cases in which there is a *physical interdependence or other interconnectedness* (of an ecological, biological, economic, or other nature) between the interests protected by the claimed property right and the interests protected by the competing public interest (for instance, conflicts between claimed rights to use land, and public interests—such as environmental controls, zoning controls, or historic-preservation laws—which assert the land-based interests of others that will be harmed by the proposed use); and

—cases in which the conflicting claims involve *competition over the same resource, for similar property-based reasons* (for instance, conflicts between a landowner's claim and public cultural-property claims, or conflicts between a taxpayer's claim and public-welfare programmes). In cases of this kind, the resolution of the conflict has an *overtly and unavoidably allocative* aspect: our resolution of the conflicting claims determines whose 'property', in the end, the object or resource will be.

The fact that claimed rights to property protection sometimes lack presumptive power, under the conditions which we have described, does not make them

124   *The Idea of Property*

unique; indeed, as we earlier discussed,[1] all rights lack—and should lack—presumptive power in similar circumstances (i.e., when opposed by competing public interests that involve core values of the same or a similar kind). However, the wide range of cases in which property rights have this characteristic has unique effects on the way in which we regard this right. In order to explore this further, we will consider an argument made by Richard Epstein regarding property and speech.

(i) A CLAIM TO EQUALITY: THE EPSTEINIAN CHALLENGE

In his well known article, 'Property, Speech, and the Politics of Distrust',[2] Richard Epstein makes a simple but compelling argument. There has been, he argues, a mistake in 'the dominant mode of thinking about property rights during the past fifty years [that] has been . . . of constitutional dimensions'.[3] This mistake, in Epstein's view, is the refusal of the American courts to accord to individual property rights the same kind of protection from government regulation that is accorded to other constitutional rights. Using free speech as his example, Epstein argues that the 'attitude of distrust' with which courts approach government regulation of speech should animate—in equal measure—their approach to government regulation of property.[4] Both are constitutional rights, of equal stature; both are of critical importance to the freedom of individuals; both should, as a matter of law and policy, be afforded the same protection, the same presumptive power.

The constitutional scheme of individual rights is premised, Epstein argues, upon the idea of well defined rights which protect individuals against the oppressive exercise of government power.[5] By guaranteeing freedom of speech, for instance, we (as a society) can resist government actions and government misconduct.[6] The protection of property is similarly crucial. The Takings Clause is motivated by 'a fear that the legislature has imperfect knowledge, imperfect motives, or both'.[7] By ensuring that compensation is paid when property is taken, the Clause protects the property holder against what would otherwise be the dangers of unchecked majoritarian power.[8]

The implementation of these principles does not, of course, require a scheme in which rights are absolute under all circumstances. It does not, for instance, require a total ban on government regulation of speech or property. Rather, it requires a strong presumption that speech and property are protected, and that this protection can be overridden only by a government interest of a particularly

---

[1] See Ch. 6, above.
[2] Richard A. Epstein, 'Property, Speech, and the Politics of Distrust' (1992) 59 *University of Chicago Law Review* 41.
[3] *Ibid*. 41.   [4] See *ibid*. 48–49.   [5] See *ibid*. 49–59.   [6] See *ibid*. 49–50.
[7] *Ibid*. 52.   [8] See *ibid*.

urgent or compelling nature.[9] In other words, there is every reason, in this context, to treat these rights as '*rights*'.

The model that Epstein sketches is a familiar and compelling one. Speech and property are constitutionally protected because we, as a society, have decided to protect them against the pressures of majoritarian government. They are—as a matter of constitutional text and constitutional theory—of apparently equal standing and equal power. Just as the right to free speech is deemed to be presumptively more powerful than competing public interests, as expressed through ordinary legislation, so must the right to property. To argue otherwise is to contradict the principles of limited government and the understandings of rights which undergird the American system of government.

Having made that observation, however, we are left with an odd paradox. For, as Epstein readily acknowledges—indeed, it is the core fact of which he complains—the courts have repeatedly failed to treat these rights with equal deference. 'The modern insistence', he writes, is 'that speech is a fundamental liberty, while property is the creature of legislation and subject to its whims'.[10] Although we seem to assume (as a matter of approach) that speech should be protected, we do not extend this assumption to property.

In challenging the different levels of presumptive protection afforded to property and speech, Epstein is, of course, not alone. An array of academic and political commentators has lamented the courts' apparent failure to protect property rights with the vigour extended to other rights.

Have the courts, as Epstein and other critics argue, simply 'gone . . . astray'[11] in their differing approaches to property and speech? Have they simply failed to appreciate the fundamental nature of the values that property involves?

Different answers have been advanced to this challenge. For instance, it has been argued that property rights—to the extent that they anchor economic rights—protect freedoms that are less essential to central understandings of constitutionally protected liberty.[12] In this chapter, I shall suggest a different explanation: one grounded in the nature of property rights, the nature of competing public interests, and the resulting relations between them.

(ii) Property and speech: explaining difference

In prior chapters, we explained how the presumptive power that we traditionally associate with legal rights is a function of the identity, or lack of identity, between the core values that underlie the claimed right and competing public interest in each case. If these values are different in kind, the normative power that the claimed right asserts stands unchallenged, and the claimed right enjoys

---

[9] See *ibid*. 45.   [10] *Ibid*. 46.   [11] *Ibid*. 59.
[12] See C. Edwin Baker, 'Property and Its Relation to Constitutionally Protected Liberty' (1986) 134 *University of Pennsylvania Law Review* 741.

presumptive power. If (on the other hand) these values are of the same or a very similar kind, there is no basis for a conclusion that the claimed right involves normatively superior values, and no basis for affording it presumptive power.

When we consider the right to free speech in light of these principles, we quickly observe the following pattern. In the typical free speech/public interest conflict—when free-speech rights are opposed, for instance, by interests in national security, public decency, public order, public safety, and so on—the values that underlie the claimed right and those that underlie the competing public interest are not the same. Whatever values are involved in these competing public interests, they are not those that are generally associated with the right to free speech. As a result, the claimed right to free speech will—in all of these cases—enjoy presumptive power.

Indeed, the general lack of identity between the values that underlie claimed rights to free speech and those that underlie competing public interests explains the presumptive power that free-speech rights seem so ubiquitously to enjoy in law. *Almost never* are the values that undergird free-speech claims answered by the public interests that oppose them. Although one can think of instances in which free-speech values are also a part of the public-interest claim—for instance, when pornographic or hate speech is opposed on the ground that it 'silences' women or members of minority groups[13]—those instances are very rare. As a result, we tend to believe—and rightly so—that free-speech rights will (always) enjoy presumptive power in law.

What about property? In some cases—for instance, when a patent claim is opposed by a public-health demand, or when title to land is opposed by a public road-building project—the values that underlie the competing claims are very different in kind, and the claimed right enjoys presumptive power. In such cases, the assumption that property rights enjoy presumptive power is justified.

Such cases are, however, a small minority of those involving property claims with which the courts deal. Far more often, property cases involve the claimed rights to use, enjoy, or exclude from land, or other disputes over physical resources. In such cases, the claimed right and the competing public interest generally assert—as an essential matter—*competing* property values, *competing* property interests.

Indeed, when disputes involve questions of use or control of physical resources, the conditions that we have identified with property claims that lack (and should lack) presumptive power are very often present. When conflicting claims involve use or control of physical resources—when they involve use or control of physical *things*—those claims will often share a physical interdependence or other connectedness, or will determine whose 'property' the object or resource (in the end) will be. In all such cases, the claimed rights involved do not have a monopoly on the values that we associate with the protection of prop-

---

[13] See Ch. 6, above.

erty. As a result, they assert no uniquely powerful normative claims, and (as a result) are afforded no presumptive power.

The critical point that Epstein and similar critics miss is that *because* property claims so often involve disputes of these kinds—*because* they so often involve *interdependent* claims or *allocational* claims—the normative power of the values that these claimed rights assert is much more frequently matched by the normative power of the competing public interests than is true in other contexts.[14] The claim by Epstein and others that speech and property should be equally powerful and equally protected ignores the fact that speech and property are critically different in this regard. Although the normative superiority of the claimed right fails only rarely in free-speech cases, this is a *routine occurrence* in property cases, particularly those that involve disputes over physical resources. Property, as a general matter, is 'protected less' because it *should be* 'protected less'—it involves, far less often, the uniquely powerful normative claims that justify the 'trumping' or presumptive power of rights.

(iii) PROPERTY, SPEECH, AND THE POLITICS OF OUTRAGE

The presence or absence of presumptive power has important doctrinal consequences in law. If the claimed right to property protection legitimately claims presumptive power, it asserts a very strong claim to indemnity for loss, and places the burden upon the one who would deny that right to justify that denial. When opposing collective interests, such a presumptively powerful right has a 'certain threshold weight';[15] it can be overridden (without legal consequence) only by public interests of an unusually compelling character. When one considers the different protection afforded in the aggregate to property and speech by law, the practical effects of these doctrinal tests are obvious.

The idea of the presumptive power of rights is tremendously important as a doctrinal matter. It is also important for the powerful social, political, and psychological claims which it can bring to bear on critical social issues. The 'politics of outrage' with which Epstein's article is infused is an example of this power. For instance, Epstein argues that the failure of the courts to afford property rights the presumptive power that is afforded to the right of free speech is 'a mistake of constitutional dimensions'.[16] 'The current laws', he writes, 'make it

---

[14] In a recent article in which Epstein responds to my arguments, he indicates that he is aware of the frequent interdependence of property claims and competing public interests but simply discounts it. In his view, individual claims—*because* they are individual claims—are inherently superior to public claims, even when identically grounded. See Richard A. Epstein, 'Life in No Trump: Property and Speech Under the Constitution' (2001) 53 *Maine Law Review* 23, 26–28. In my view, it is the nature of competing interests and the values that they assert that should determine presumptive power—not the fortuitous identities or numbers of their holders.

[15] Ronald Dworkin, *Taking Rights Seriously* (Cambridge, Mass.: Harvard University Press, 1977), 92.

[16] Epstein, n. 2 above, 41.

impossible to have well-defined property rights in anything. . . . [V]irtually any
asset is fair game for obstruction by the political process, whether through taxation or regulation.'[17] The 'presumption of legislative knowledge and probity'
that has characterized the courts' regulation of property 'has led to a continuous
judicial horror show with respect to economic liberties and private property'.[18]

A declaration of outrage from the denial of rights may be an appropriate force
to bring to bear on some social and political issues. We must be careful, however, lest it blind us to the actual social choices that rights, and the claims that
oppose them, involve. Claimed entitlements to use land—or to destroy buildings—or to control wealth—assert interests that compete with other interests,
expectations that compete with the expectations of others. If building on shoreline land accelerates erosion or destroys marine biological systems—if the
destruction of an historic building damages the value of adjacent land or
destroys evidence of our common history—if the control of wealth by one
person denies the most basic acquisitive needs of others—there is no way to
simplify the deeply conflicting and equally compelling claims that these cases
present by invoking 'outrage' at the claims that the public presents. The deep
issues that these conflicts assert are not answered by the simple claim that property, as a right, must be protected.

Whether rights have the presumptive power that is claimed for them is a
tremendously important issue. It is important not only as a doctrinal matter—
in determining, for instance, whether there is a violation of the right to free
speech or a violation of the right to property protection in a given case—but also
for the role that it plays in shaping the social and political debates that, in turn,
shape our society and our laws. The outrage that a publisher feels when his
speech is curtailed—or the outrage that a landowner feels when her ability to
drain wetlands is denied—depends, deeply and psychologically, on the idea of
the presumptive power of rights. If we persist in the simplistic idea that property
is (and should be) an invariably powerful right—if we refuse to acknowledge the
interconnected and distributive qualities of property rights and property systems—we will encourage false beliefs of entitlement, strife, and resulting alien-
ation from political and social institutions. We will also mask the critical
societal choices that property necessarily and inevitably involves.

[17] Epstein, n. 2 above, 56.   [18] *Ibid.* 59.

10

Reimagining Public Interests: A Cautionary Note

In prior chapters, we discussed how claimed rights and competing public interests must be seen in terms of the core values that they actually involve if the relation between them in law is to be accurately assessed. In particular, we determined that whether claimed rights should enjoy presumptive power should depend not on the simple fact of their classification as 'rights', but rather on the core values that those rights and their competitors actually involve. To put the matter another way, it is the nature of the interests involved that should determine presumptive power, not the identity or numbers of their holders.

There is, for instance, no obvious reason why the property-based concerns of one person should presumptively best the property-based concerns of many people, simply because the concerns of the many are asserted under a 'public' or 'collective' label. If a claimed property right to build on urban land is opposed by a public interest in retaining the character of a neighbourhood—or if a claimed property right to drain wetlands is opposed by a public interest in preserving shellfish beds—we must recognize that the normative values that we ascribe to the individual property-rights claims in these cases are matched by the property-based claims of other individuals that the public interests, as surrogates, represent.

This method of analysis—in which we 'pierce the public interest veil' and recognize public interests, essentially, as aggregations of individual concerns—has the immediate and practical effect of enhancing the presumptive power that these public interests would otherwise enjoy. By reconceptualizing public interests in this way, we recognize the individually protective functions of these interests and, as a result, their normative parity with the claimed rights that oppose them. They are, as a result, as deserving of presumptive power.

The idea that public interests in these cases should be 'seen for what they are'—that they should be seen as comprised of the many individual interests that they (in fact) represent—seems, at first blush, to be a simple net gain for public interests and their champions. Any method of analysis that renders public interests in a broad class of cases as powerful as claimed individual rights seems to be one that champions of the 'idea of the public interest' would support. Is, however, the situation quite so simple?

In fact, the way in which we have reconceptualized public interests in these cases raises a subtle but important question. Whether 'the idea of the public interest' exists as something apart from simple aggregations of individual claims

and preferences is a matter of intense debate.[1] Some have argued that public
interests are (or can be) no more, in the end, than the sums of the claims and
preferences of individuals.[2] Others argue that this 'aggregative' view of public
interests fails to capture important characteristics of public interests, such as
their transcendence of the immediate self-interests of social- or polity-group
members in favour of long-term goals and moral commitments.[3] By advocating
an approach in which ostensibly 'public' interests are reimagined in 'individual'
terms, have we intentionally—or inadvertently—subscribed to the former view?
Have we (in the view of many critics) rejected a potentially rich view of 'public
interests', for a quite impoverished one?

In fact, our analysis has little or no relation to the 'aggregative' theory of public interests and to the debate which surrounds it. Our analysis simply requires
that when public interests are rooted in what are (essentially) individual,
property-based concerns, that fact must be recognized. This is not to say that
this is all that they *can* encompass, as a practical matter, or that it is all that they
should encompass, as a normative matter. Indeed, we have—thus far—maintained an entirely formal approach to the public interests that we have
analysed.[4] We have not speculated about how particular public interests were
derived, or what their content should be. We have simply taken examples of
articulated public interests commonly found in Anglo-American law, and pro-
ceeded to determine what the relative power of those public interests—when
their precise nature is analysed—should be.

* * *

The articulation of public interests serves a particular function in diverse, plu-
ralistic societies such as our own. Public interests provide a means for people
with different value systems, political ideas, religious convictions, and other
interests to articulate a common ground for determining and promoting that

---

[1] See, e.g., Edgar Bodenheimer, 'Prolegomena to a Theory of the Public Interest', in Carl J.
Friedrich (ed.), *Nomos V: The Public Interest* (New York: Atherton Press, 1962), 205; Gerhard
Colm, 'The Public Interest: Essential Key to Public Policy', in *ibid.* 115; Gerhart Niemeyer, 'Public
Interest and Private Utility', in *ibid.* 1; J. Roland Pennock, 'The One and the Many: A Note on the
Concept', in *ibid.* 177.

[2] The roots for this view are often traced to the ideas of Jeremy Bentham. See, e.g., Jeremy
Bentham, *An Introduction to the Principles of Morals and Legislation* (J. H. Burns and H.L.A. Hart
(eds.), London: University of London—Athlone Press, 1970), 12 (the interest of the community is
identical with 'the sum of the interests of the several members who compose it').

[3] See Bodenheimer, n. 1 above, 206–208; Colm, n. 1 above, 117–119. Much of this debate turns,
of course, on whether one understands 'individual self-interests' to include egotistical and altruistic
concerns: see, e.g., C. W. Cassinelli, 'Some Reflections on the Concept of the Public Interest' (1958)
69 *Ethics* 48; whether the 'public interest' is viewed as 'an ethical imperative . . ., some superior standard of rational and "right" political wisdom, or the goals or consensus of a large portion of the elec-
torate': Frank J. Sorauf, 'The Conceptual Muddle', in Friedrich (ed.), n. 1 above, 183, 184; and so
on.

[4] This 'hands off' approach toward public interests is abandoned only in later chapters, where I
argue that the particular nature of property requires the assertion of public redistributive claims in
some cases. See Chs. 12–14, below.

society's ultimate values.[5] Public interests that are ultimately identified by government may involve particular constitutive qualities that are unique to public-interest claims.[6] They may also be rooted in individual concerns, of a nature that is no different from those asserted by the individual rights that oppose them. Our approach does not assume that particular public interests are of one kind or the other. It simply requires that we recognize the *actual values* that these socially constructed claims assert, in our assessment of their presumptive power.

[5] Colm, n. 1 above, 120.
[6] See Jeremy Waldron, 'Can Communal Goods Be Human Rights?' (1987) 28 *Archives Européennes de Sociologie* 296, 301, 302.

11

Reprise: Two Conceptions of Property—When and Why They are Used in Law

In earlier chapters, we described the four dimensions involved in any legally cognizable conception of property: theory, space, stringency, and time. We also saw how they are assembled, in law, to create two very different conceptions of property. We are now in a position to explain when and why conceptions of property with these characteristics are used in particular cases.

Let us take, first, the common conception of property. Under this conception of property, property rights afford the individual tremendous protection against competing public interests. 'Property' represents defined individual interests, which are protected—as rights—against collective power. When this relation is captured in conventional legal terms, it is expressed by the principle that property rights, as 'rights', are presumptively superior to the public interests that oppose them. They may be overridden without legal consequence by public interests of a particularly dire or compelling nature, but only by interests of that nature. They cannot be overridden by the simple or routine goals of government.

The key ideas involved in this conception of property are that property rights offer *protection;* that they *oppose* competing public interests; and that they are, as 'rights', *presumptively superior* to the public interests that oppose them. It is readily apparent, when understood this way, that the common conception of property is simply a recasting of what we have described, under our model, as a Tier One case. The common conception of property simply captures, in concrete form, our intuitive understanding that when property rights are opposed by public interests of an unrelated character, their presumed normative superiority will remain unchallenged, and they will enjoy presumptive power. Indeed, if one considers the situations in which the common conception of property is used in law—for instance, in the protection of titles to land or chattels against government taking, or in the protection of patents or copyrights against government abrogation—these are invariably Tier One cases, in which the core values that underlie the claimed rights and the core values that underlie the competing public interests are of different natures altogether. The common conception of property—with its image of property as something which *opposes* public interests—captures this relation and its truth.

What about the second, or operative, conception of property? Here, the understanding of property and its protection is very different. Under this conception, property describes how particular individual/collective tensions have been resolved, at the moment, but the rights thus established may be established and re-established (without legal consequence) as new circumstances justify. Although there is an ostensible relation of resistance and conflict between property rights and the public interests that oppose them, the true relation in these cases is one in which the boundaries and protections of property rights are modified, with little effort, with the ebb and flow of collective pressures. When this conception is captured in conventional legal terms, it is expressed by the principle that property rights, although (ostensibly) 'rights', lack the presumptive power that we expect. Indeed, collective power to change these rights without impairment of these rights *seems to be a part of* the very idea of property.

The individual/collective relation that the operative conception of property seeks to articulate—one in which the claimed property right and the competing public interest have apparently equal influence in determining what property shall be—is what we have described, under our model, as a Tier Two case. In cases of this kind, the values that we identify with property ground the claimed right *and* the competing public interest; as a result, the competing forces have equal normative appeal and equal presumptive power. If we consider the cases in which we found the operative conception of property to be used in law—such as those involving zoning, environmental controls, or other land-use issues—we realize that all of them were cases of this type. In these cases, property did not 'oppose' unrelated interests. Rather, the struggle between individually asserted property values and collectively asserted property values determined—in each case—what the 'right to property' would be.

* * *

It is often remarked that property 'has different meaning in different contexts'. The strength of property claims pertaining to land is, for instance, so different when one considers the legal protection afforded to title and the legal protection afforded to use that the legal meaning of property rights seems (on the surface) quite incoherent. The way to achieve coherent understanding is not, however, to demand that all property rights in all settings be granted great presumptive power, or that all property rights in all settings be granted none. Rather, we must understand that the presumptive power of property rights—like the presumptive power of all rights—depends upon the nature of the public interests that oppose them. It is only when we understand the opposing claims' core values, and their resulting relation, that we can predict or understand the power of property claims in law.

This understanding of property is, admittedly, not always an easy one. The idea that property's presumptive power depends upon the context in which it is asserted is often neither simple nor tidy. As we have stressed above, our understandings of the core values that underlie any claimed property right or opposing public interest are socially constructed, changeable, and often contentious.

The understandings of core values that we have employed are those that are believed to be consonant with common (social and legal) understandings—but we have openly acknowledged that those understandings are subject to disputation and change, and that if they change, the analysis that follows will change as well.

This acknowledgment of the fluidity of our understandings of property rights and their presumptive power conflicts with our natural desire for certainty or simplicity in law. However, its central role in our analysis identifies a central mission of this book. 'Property' is not a preordained or acontextual concept— it is a socially constructed concept, with all of the flux and change which that involves. There is a temptation, in analysing the power of property, either to ignore the socially constructed (and volatile) nature of property, or to acknowledge this nature of property and then—effectively—end the inquiry. Our analysis offers a third choice. We can—through the use of our analysis—both embrace the socially constructed nature of property *and* proceed to determine whether it deserves presumptive power.

PART III
PROPERTY AS A
CONSTITUTIONAL RIGHT:
NEW DIRECTIONS

12

The Justice Content of Property: Constitutional Implications

In earlier chapters, we discussed how claimed property rights often lack—and should lack—presumptive power because the core values that underlie the claimed right and the core values that underlie the competing public interest are, in fact, of the same or very similar character. We saw that this pattern is particularly true in cases in which the competing claims are of a physically interdependent or other interconnected nature, or in which the conflict has an overtly allocative aspect—such that our resolution of the conflicting claims determines whose 'property', in the end, the object or resource will be.[1]

In this chapter, we shall consider what this last, 'allocative' characteristic of property claims—what has been called the 'justice content' of property claims[2]—means for the protection of property as a constitutional right. Thus far, our inquiry has been limited to the relative power of property rights when the state chooses to assert, as a public interest, the property claims of others. We have not argued that the state *must* or *should* assert such claims; indeed, one could conclude from our discussion thus far that the assertion of such claims is an entirely optional or discretionary matter. In this chapter, we shall see that where rights to external, physical, finite resources are concerned, claimed property rights differ from other constitutional rights—and must be governed by very different principles. We shall also see how the establishment of a property regime in such cases *requires* that the interests of others not be ignored.

(i) THE TRADITIONAL MODEL OF CONSTITUTIONAL RIGHTS: PROTECTING
INDIVIDUALS FROM GOVERNMENT POWER

The traditional view of constitutional rights begins with a simple premise. Because those in positions of power are human beings, there is a continual danger that they will act in ways that are personally self-serving or otherwise undesirable from a societal point of view. Human frailties and other problems mean that we cannot assume that those in power will be enlightened statesmen who

---

[1] See Chs. 7 and 8, above.

[2] See J. W. Harris, 'Is Property a Human Right?', in Janet McLean (ed.), *Property and the Constitution* (Oxford: Hart Publishing, 1999), 64, 87 ('[T]he [property] holdings vested in any particular person at any particular time are stamped, morally, with a contestable and mutable mix of property-specific justice reasons.').

will adjust clashing interests and render them subservient to the public good. Rather, we must keep in mind the potentially oppressive power of government, and protect the most basic rights of citizens through the enactment of entrenched constitutional guarantees.[3]

In the American array of constitutional rights, it is widely claimed that the right to the protection of property is an important—indeed, some would say, the *most* important—right conferred.[4] Although the equality of property rights with other constitutionally protected rights occasionally has been questioned, most assume that property rights enjoy bedrock status in our constitutional scheme. Property rights, it is argued, provide individual security and (in the process) diffuse political power. They create and protect material wealth and prosperity, necessary preconditions for social civility, social stability, and the maintenance of democratic governance.

Based upon the (perhaps too) familiar image of Lockean entitlements,[5] the constitutional protection of property in the United States Constitution is seen as a classic example of a 'negative'[6] or 'first-generation'[7] right: it provides individual protection from the claims of others, in particular, others operating under the mantle of collective power. Property protects what is ours—our possessions, even our liberty—from majoritarian tyranny. As one South African scholar has written, the American Takings Clause, in particular, 'is a classic example of a property clause cast in . . . [the liberal] mould', with the constitutional protection of property as a guarantor of personal freedom and security.[8]

---

[3] See, e.g., Richard A. Epstein, 'Property, Speech, and the Politics of Distrust' (1992) 59 *University of Chicago Law Review* 41, 48–50.

[4] See, e.g., James W. Ely, Jr., *The Guardian of Every Other Right: A Constitutional History of Property Rights* (New York: Oxford University Press, 1992).

[5] See John Locke, 'Second Treatise of Government,' in his *Two Treatises of Government* (Peter Laslett (ed.), 2nd edn., Cambridge: Cambridge University Press, 1960 (1698)), § 193 (property as that which 'without a Man's own consent . . . cannot be taken from him'). Elsewhere, I have argued that Locke's understanding of property was in fact much broader than generally believed: it encompassed a broad range of individual rights, liberties, powers, and immunities, exercised within a collective context of support and restraint. See Laura S. Underkuffler, 'On Property: An Essay,' originally published in (1990) 100 *Yale Law Journal* 127, reprinted in Elizabeth Mensch and Alan Freeman (eds.), *Property Law: International Library of Essays in Law and Legal Theory* (New York: New York University Press, 1992), bk. i, 403, 414–417.

[6] The common division of rights into 'positive' rights (those that require state action) and 'negative' rights (those that protect individuals from state action) is generally traced to Isaiah Berlin, 'Two Concepts of Liberty', in his *Four Essays on Liberty* (New York: Oxford University Press, 1970), 118.

[7] The categorization of constitutional rights into 'first-generation rights' (those that refer to traditional liberal, civil, and political rights), 'second-generation rights' (those that refer to social, cultural, and economic rights), and 'third-generation rights' (those that refer to rights such as self-determination, peace, development, and a protected environment) seems to be a part of common parlance in just about all of the world's constitutional systems other than the United States. See, e.g., Bertus de Villiers, 'Social and Economic Rights', in Dawid van Wyk, John Dugard, Bertus de Villiers, and Dennis Davis (eds.), *Rights and Constitutionalism: The New South African Legal Order* (Oxford: Clarendon Press, 1996) 599, 603; Lourens du Plessis and Hugh Corder, *Understanding South Africa's Transitional Bill of Rights* (Kenwyn: Juta and Company, Ltd., 1994), 24.

[8] A. J. van der Walt, 'Property Rights, Land Rights, and Environmental Rights', in van Wyk, Dugard, de Villiers, and Davis (eds.), n. 7 above, 455, 461.

The depth of our commitment to this idea of constitutional property protection is perhaps most evident when we attempt to convince others of its wisdom. For instance, in an article addressed to those who were drafting constitutions for countries in post-communist Eastern Europe, Cass Sunstein describes the kind of '[f]irm . . . protection' that constitutional rights in a liberal democratic regime should provide.[9] Under this model, a constitution, with its prohibitions upon government action, is intended to emphasize and entrench the foundational principle that private actions must be distinguished from—and protected from—public ones.[10] And critical among private interests and actions that need protection are those associated with the ownership of property.[11]

Advocates of this model acknowledge that it is never, in practice, absolute; even purely negative, 'private' rights require state action for enforcement,[12] and there are times when a system of liberal constitutional rights should be accompanied by other, presumably legislative social strategies.[13] The fundamental purpose and operation of such constitutional rights are, however, very clear. Constitutional rights—including the right to the protection of property—are intended to protect individuals from the predations of government. By protecting property rights, we believe that we can protect free enterprise, political liberty, and the general right of personal freedom from tyrannical exercises of government power.

This idea of the Constitution as a charter of negative rights—and of the right to the protection of property as simply one of those rights—is an entrenched feature of American political and legal discourse.[14] Indeed, few would deny that property—and the constitutional protection of property—perform many of the functions claimed. 'Property' describes, on its most elemental level, what we have, and that it cannot be forcibly taken from us. The importance of this idea in constructing societies and governments is obvious and undeniable. The constitutional protection of property is, in turn, simply an extension of that function.

---

[9] Cass R. Sunstein, 'On Property and Constitutionalism' (1993) 14 *Cardozo Law Review* 907, 907–909.

[10] See *ibid*. 921–922.   [11] See *ibid*.

[12] See *ibid*. 918–919 ('It is, of course, misleading to think of these as genuinely negative rights. They depend for their existence on governmental institutions willing to recognize, create, and protect them.').

[13] See *ibid*. 917. Such strategies may include redistributive programmes of a limited nature, such as those designed to bring about 'equality of opportunity and . . . freedom from desperate conditions'. *Ibid*.

[14] For instance, Judge Richard Posner has argued that the American Constitution 'is a charter of negative rather than positive liberties. . . . The men who wrote the Bill of Rights were not concerned that government might do too little for the people but that it might do too much to them.' *Jackson* v. *City of Joliet*, 715 F 2d 1200, 1203 (7th Cir. 1983), cert. denied, 465 US 1049 (1984). For instance, proposals to interpret the Fourteenth Amendment 'to guarantee the provision of basic services such as education, poor relief, and . . . police protection' would 'turn the [Amendment] . . . on its head. It would change it from a protection against coercion by state government to a command that the state use its taxing power to coerce some of its citizens to provide services to others.' *Ibid*. 1203–1204.

Is this, however, *all* that the protection of property—as a constitutional matter—involves? Is the constitutional protection of property simply another negative right, another individual guarantee?

(ii) THE RIGHT TO PROPERTY: A DIFFERENT RIGHT

Let us consider, in more depth, the traditional model of individual/state relations that constitutional rights of the American kind are assumed to involve. This model is one in which human freedoms exist, and the state must be prevented from destroying these freedoms. It assumes that previously existing, 'fundamental' freedoms must be protected from government power.

When one considers many constitutionally protected rights, this model seems to be very true. We seek—through freedom of speech, freedom of religion, freedom from cruel and unusual punishment, and so on—to protect ourselves from the dangers of government. The state's role is at best protecting, and at worst oppressing, but whatever its stance, it is—essentially—an external one. The state does not create these freedoms, nor allocate them to us. It simply protects—or destroys—what we, as human beings, would otherwise freely, naturally, and equally enjoy.

In fact, when we consider freedom of conscience, freedom of speech, due process of law, and other constitutional rights, we are concerned with what may be called, in a sense, constitutional 'public goods'.[15] Because these rights involve the exercise of freedoms which individuals freely, naturally, and equally enjoy, there is no additional cost necessarily entailed—to society or to other individuals—if another person believes freely, or speaks freely, or is offered the protection of the laws. The extension and protection of these rights is, indeed, very 'cheap' in societal terms:[16] upon granting one person the right to speak, there is no *necessary* taking of that same right from another.[17]

[15] See Dennis C. Mueller, *Public Choice II* (Cambridge: Cambridge University Press, 1989), 11 (public goods have two salient characteristics: first, if such goods are consumed by one person, this does not detract from the benefits enjoyed by others; and secondly, no one can easily be precluded from enjoying such goods, once they have been produced). See also Joseph Raz, 'Rights and Individual Well-Being', in his *Ethics in the Public Domain: Essays in the Morality of Law and Politics* (Oxford: Clarendon Press, 1994), 29, 37 (public goods are those 'which . . . serve the interest of people generally in a conflict-free, non-exclusive, and non-excludable way').

[16] One could argue that the addition of rights-holders always involves some additional cost, in the form of additional societal resources necessary for additional protection. In this limited sense, of course, all rights recognized by law are 'positive' rights which impose burdens upon others for their protection.

[17] There may exist, of course, be situations in which the exercise of the right to speak by one person will infringe upon the exercise of the right to speak by others. See, e.g., Ch. 6, above (discussing 'silencing' claims); Alon Harel, 'The Boundaries of Justifiable Tolerance: A Liberal Perspective', in David Heyd (ed.), *Toleration: An Elusive Virtue* (Princeton, N.J.: Princeton University Press, 1996), 114. While such situations can be imagined, it is rare—in the free-speech context—that there is a *necessary and inevitable correlation* between the granting of the right to free speech to one person and the infringement of the same right of another. If such allocational issues do exist, in a particular case, the principles that are suggested for allocational rights (see sect. (iii) below) presumably exist.

What about property? Property rights are (in the main) quite different. When property involves external, physical, finite resources, it deals with goods of a reverse, or 'private' kind. If the enjoyment of a particular resource by one person is protected, then the enjoyment of that same resource by another is denied. If my right to possess this land is upheld, your claim to possess that land is denied. If my right to clear timber, deplete species, or strip mine land is upheld, your claim to control those resources is denied. The very nature of these resources, and of individual property claims to them, means that the extension of property protection in such resources to one person *necessarily and inevitably* denies the same rights to others.[18]

Indeed, when we consider property rights in such resources, the state's role is completely and essentially different from that which it occupies regarding freedom of conscience, freedom of speech, due process of law, or other such rights. Where rights to external, physical, finite resources are concerned, the establishment of a property regime *itself* is a necessarily and unavoidably allocative act.[19] The state—in creating and enforcing such rights—makes deliberate, binding, and final choices about who shall enjoy and who shall not. It *necessarily and affirmatively* grants the acquisitive claims of some people, and denies the same claims of others. A property regime, which implements such rights, does not involve the simple protection of natural and pre-existing human freedoms; it involves the enforcement of *positive* rights, *allocative* rights.

What does all of this mean for the constitutional right to property protection? It is to this question that we now turn.

(iii) THE MEANING OF DIFFERENCE

As we have noted, it is often argued that property rights are the most important rights in a liberal democratic order. Those arguments carry an obvious corollary: that with 'most important' status comes 'most protected' status, as well. If the protection of private property makes individuals independent and, thus,

---

[18] See Frank I. Michelman, 'Liberties, Fair Values, and Constitutional Method' (1992) 59 *University of Chicago Law Review* 91, 97–105 (discussing the intrinsic interdependence of claims of proprietary liberty). Cf. Guido Calabresi and A. Douglas Melamed, 'Property Rules, Liability Rules, and Inalienability: One View of the Cathedral' (1972) 85 *Harvard Law Review* 1089, 1105–1110 (when 'property rules' are applied to claims of conflicting entitlements, one claim is entirely vindicated, and the other claim is entirely denied). This preclusive nature of property rules 'lies at the core of the notions of "ownership" and "property"'. Louis Kaplow and Steven Shavell, 'Property Rules Versus Liability Rules: An Economic Analysis' (1996) 109 *Harvard Law Review* 713, 716.

[19] Contexts in which property arguably lacks this allocative nature include non-external 'goods' as property (e.g. ideas, personal information, and so on) and other legal rights as property (e.g., the enforceability of contracts, the right to be left alone, the right to one's good name, the right to self-defence, and so on). See, e.g., Jeremy Waldron, 'Property Law', in Dennis Patterson (ed.), *A Companion to Philosophy of Law and Legal Theory* (Cambridge, Mass.: Blackwell Publishers, 1996), 3, 5 (distinguishing physical resources whose use involves the exclusion of others, and forms of intellectual property whose use involves no such limitations).

capable of self-government; if it diffuses political power; if it creates wealth and prosperity, necessary preconditions for social civility, stability, and the maintenance of democratic governance—then the strongest protection of private property, in our foundational document, would seem to be justified.

We have found, however, that property as a right is not so simple. Although individual property holdings may serve all of these functions, the creation of a property regime—to enforce rights in external, physical, finite resources—will necessarily protect the interests of some at the expense of the identical interests of others. Through other constitutional rights, we seek to protect what we all freely, equally, and naturally enjoy; through property rights in resources, we seek to protect what we have, to the derogation, exclusion, and injury of others. This nature of property—this 'specialness' of property—should make it *less protected* as a right, not more.

If property rights are to be less protected, *how much* less protected should they be? We have already established, in prior chapters, that when property rights are opposed by public interests that are grounded in the same core values—for instance, when individual claims to wealth or physical resources are opposed by state redistributive claims—these rights lack, and *should* lack, presumptive power. More than this, however, is needed to interpret this right. The fact that claimed property rights and opposing public interests are 'equally matched' in presumptive power does not tell us much about what principles we should use—as a constitutional matter—to resolve these conflicts, or whether we, as a society, have an obligation to assert—in any circumstance—state redistributive claims.

The necessarily allocative nature of property rights in finite, private goods demands that we adopt a more complex approach to this constitutional right. That approach, I suggest, should include the principles that follow.

- *Property must be explicitly recognized as both idea and institution; and the roles of both idea and institution must be acknowledged in the interpretation of this right.*

Property, as we have previously observed,[20] is both *idea* and *institution*; it is both the general idea or concept of property protection which individuals hold, and the separate question of the protection afforded to particular persons and their objects of property by social, legal, and political institutions. In practice, this distinction is often obscured. When we speak of the 'constitutional protection of property', for instance, we tend to slur these together. We tend to assume that 'property protection', in the constitutional sense, means the idea of property *as reflected in* existing institutional arrangements.

Property, as an American constitutional idea, is envisioned as a bulwark surrounding a sphere of individual liberty; it is an absolute and inalienable right, which provides security and protection. Property, as a social, legal, and polit-

---

[20] See Ch. 8, sect. (iv), above.

ical institution, is, of course, wholly (and necessarily) different. It is, in its institutional form, the resolution of conflicting claims and conflicting desires for what are often external, physical, finite goods. In this process, some will win and some will lose; it is impossible to protect the claims and security of all.

This dual nature that property exhibits does not, of itself, distinguish this right from other rights. All traditional (liberal) constitutional rights involve the clash between the absoluteness of their statements, as ideas, and the compromises of the institutions that implement them. In this simple characteristic, the right to property protection is certainly not unique. The protection of property is, however—by virtue of its allocative nature—the most paradoxical and extreme of these. It is the idea whose absoluteness we cherish, perhaps, most deeply; yet it is also the institution which, in most circumstances, must be the most questioned and the least protected.

Because of this deeply paradoxical nature of property, it is particularly important that the separate roles of idea and institution in the functioning of this right be recognized. The idea of property as 'a right', bounded and protected, is a deeply ingrained and enduring one. This idea can be acknowledged as powerful and important; indeed, it may often usefully constrain (through its psychological and rhetorical force) those changes to existing or presumed entitlements that we might otherwise make. However, property—as a constitutional matter—must ultimately be seen for what it is. It must be recognized as the adjustment and compromise of *conflicting* claims through the operation of a legal institution.

Explicit recognition of the dual nature of property would accomplish an important goal. No longer would we attempt to implement, as an institutional matter, an idea of property protection that is impossible, in fact, to realize. We would be free of the dangerous and naïve illusion that the protection of property is 'impartial' in nature and that we can, through the simple protection of existing entitlements, protect the interests and expectations of all. We would recognize, explicitly and unequivocally, that the 'idea' of property protection does not answer institutional questions; and that we must—*for other articulated reasons*—make decisions about the implementation of this right.

- *Social aspirations and social goals must be seen as inherent and unavoidable parts of the constitutional right to property protection.*

The interpretation of particular constitutional rights in light of social aspirations and social goals is a common approach in many of the world's constitutional systems. In India, for instance, the Supreme Court has developed an interpretative approach which evaluates particular constitutional rights in light of broader goals of social justice, substantive equality, and human dignity.[21] In

[21] See, e.g., *Hussainara Khatoon* v. *State of Bihar*, AIR 1979 S.C. 1360, 1363–1367 (India); *Francis Coralie Mullin* v.*Union Territory of Delhi*, AIR 1981 S.C. 746, 752–754 (India). See also Dennis Davis, Matthew Chaskalson, and Johan de Waal, 'Democracy and Constitutionalism: The Role of

Germany, the Federal Constitutional Court has repeatedly stated that the fundamental individual rights guaranteed by the country's Basic Law (*Grundgesetz*) establish an 'objective order of values' for the interpretation of rights.[22] This 'objective value order' has as its centre the 'free development of the human personality in the social community'.[23]

The judicial approach to many constitutional rights in the United States is, in fact, quite similar. Courts routinely speak, for instance, of the purposes of free speech, the goals of equal protection, and the justice afforded by due process of law. In so doing, they recognize that these rights, although 'individual' in nature, must be understood and informed by the social context and social aspirations within which these rights are embedded.

The exemption of property rights from this approach is striking. Although consideration of the 'purposes' of free speech is a routine part of the courts' treatment of this right, there is no similar, routine discussion of the 'purposes' of property.[24] Indeed, consideration of social aspirations or goals seems to be distinctly inconsistent with the conventional judicial view of the nature of this right. The fundamental purpose of property, it is argued, is the protection of the individual from the state; how, then, can *collective* aspirations or *collective* goals be a part of the interpretation of this right?

Indeed, it is precisely because of the widespread nature of this conventional view that we have resisted the practice—common in other Western constitutional systems[25]—of including social and economic rights in our foundational

Constitutional Interpretation', in van Wyk, Dugard, de Villiers, and Davis (eds.), n. 7 above, 1, 48–52, 62–64. This has been called a 'purposive' approach to constitutional rights. See *ibid.* 62.

    The adoption of this approach has been vigorously advocated for interpretative questions under the new South African Constitution. Commentators have urged 'a purposive approach . . . [under] which the adjudicating court attempts to develop a theory as to the nature of the fundamental principles contained in a Bill of Rights, which in turn makes the most sense of the purpose of a Bill of Rights within the context of a society proclaiming democratic aspirations'. *Ibid.* 123. It appears that this approach has been adopted by the South African Supreme Court. See, e.g., *S. v. Zuma and Two Others* 1995 (2) SALR 642 (CC) [13]–[18] (S. Afr.); *S. v. Makwanyane and Another* 1995 (3) SALR 391 (CC) [9] (S. Afr.).

    [22] See, e.g., 7 BVerfGE 198, 205 (1958) (F.R.G.). Property rights are, for instance, to be interpreted in a manner which balances individual and social interests with the common good as a basic, referential, and limiting principle. See, e.g., 52 BVerfGE 1, 29 (1979) (F.R.G.) 25 BVerfGE 112, 118 (1969) (F.R.G.).

    [23] 7 BVerfGE 198, 205 (1958) (F.R.G.). The core of German constitutionalism has been described as 'both contractarian and communitarian'. 'The Basic Law . . . reflects a conscious ordering of individual freedoms and public interests. It resounds with the language of human freedom, but a freedom restrained by certain political values, community norms, and ethical principles.' Donald P. Kommers, 'The Jurisprudence of Free Speech in the United States and the Federal Republic of Germany' (1980) 53 *Southern California Law Review* 657, 677. See also Donald P. Kommers, 'German Constitutionalism: A Prolegomenon' (1991) 40 *Emory Law Journal* 837, 855–873.

    [24] It has been suggested that this is attributable both to the absence of any mention in the Constitution of the obligations of ownership, and to the courts' apparent reluctance to acknowledge such obligations in their abstract statements of this right. See Gregory S. Alexander, 'Civic Property' (1997) 6 *Social and Legal Studies* 217, 225–226.

    [25] Examples include the right to free primary education (Constitution of Ireland); the right to work and protection of workers (Constitution of the Netherlands and Constitution of Greece); the

document. The purpose of the Constitution, in the words of Justice Rehnquist, is 'to protect the people from the State, not to ensure that the State protect[s] them from each other'.[26] In this view, claims of one citizen against another should be left to the political process, not made the subject of constitutional guarantees.[27]

This conventional view, when applied to the right to property protection, is unworkable—indeed, it is deeply ironic—on several grounds. First, the idea that questions of property distribution or *re*distribution should be left to the polit- ical process makes no sense if the point of the constitutional protection of prop- erty is to immunize it from legislative change. The conventional view does not attempt to shift such decisions from the constitutional to the legislative (or other political) level—it attempts, in actuality, to preclude them altogether.

In addition, the attempt to separate the 'protective' nature of property from the 'social' nature of property ignores the essential nature of this right. Property rights are, *by nature*, social rights;[28] they embody how we, *as a society*, have chosen to reward the claims of some to external, physical, and finite goods, and to deny the same claims of others. Try as we may to separate this right from choice, conflict, and vexing social questions, it cannot be done. Why do we reward this claim, and not that one? What is our *purpose* for protecting the acquisitive desires of one person, and for denying the protection of the acquisi- tive desires of another? To deny the relevance of such questions to the interpre- tation of this right is to treat the most contextualized right without mention of context, the most conflicted right without mention of conflict.

In a series of opinions, the recently established Hungarian Constitutional Court has addressed the fundamental question of how the constitutional guar- antee of property protection can be reconciled with the fact that property is a social institution and must, as a result, be subordinate to evolving public needs. The Hungarian Court's consideration of this question is particularly trenchant since it occurred in the context of a contemporary society's complete rethinking of the idea of property and the idea of law in the course of its transformation from a communist political system to a market-oriented, liberal democratic one. Faced with the vast possibilities that this situation presented, the Court chose to

---

right to health services (Constitution of Greece and Constitution of Portugal); and the right to pro- tection of the environment (Constitution of Greece). See De Villiers, n. 7 above, 613.

[26] *DeShaney* v. *Winnebago County Department of Social Services*, 489 US 189, 196 (1989).

[27] See *ibid*.

[28] As Joseph Singer has written, '[i]f "property is a set of social relations among human beings", the legal definition of those relationships confers—or withholds—power over others. The grant of a property right to one person leaves others vulnerable to the will of the owner. Conversely, the refusal to grant a property right leaves the claimant [as the] vulnerable [one]'. Joseph William Singer, 'Sovereignty and Property' (1991) 86 *Northwestern University Law Review* 1, 41 (quoting Felix S. Cohen, 'Dialogue on Private Property' (1954) 9 *Rutgers Law Review* 357, 365). See also Frank I. Michelman, 'Possession vs. Distribution in the Constitutional Idea of Property' (1987) 72 *Iowa Law Review* 1319, 1335 ('[P]rivate power is power no less constituted by public law than is governmental power itself, specifically, if ironically, the very law that secures private property against encroachment.').

locate the constitutional right to the protection of property[29] at the figurative bottom of the Constitution's hierarchy of fundamental rights.[30] Of all of the individual rights that the Hungarian Constitution guarantees—such as rights to life, human dignity, freedom of expression, freedom of religion, due process of law, and so on—the right to the protection of property has been recognized as that which depends, most fundamentally, upon social context, and which must, as a result, be most readily compromised. '[T]he scope of the constitutional protection of property', the Court wrote, 'may not be identified with the protection of . . . abstract civil law property . . . nor with its determination as a negative and absolute right.' Rather, it must be considered 'within the framework of (constitutional) public and private law restrictions', and its enforcement must take into account—in each case—the 'subject, object and function' of competing private and public claims.[31]

Our interpretation of the constitutional right to property protection must, in short, explicitly acknowledge what this right necessarily and essentially involves. When property rights concern external, physical, finite resources—when they concern honouring the claims of some, to the detriment of the identical claims of others—they are not simply private interests with which the state neutrally coexists. Property rights of this kind are collective, enforced, even violent decisions about who shall enjoy the privileges and resources which this society allocates among its citizens. Questions about the kind of society that we are, and the kind of society that we wish to become, must be recognized as inherent and unavoidable parts of the interpretation of this right.

• *The nature of property and the goods that it protects requires state assertion of redistributive claims.*

We have seen how property rights differ from other constitutional rights by virtue of their allocative nature. Where external, physical, finite resources are concerned, the allocative decisions that a property regime enforces cannot be separated from our interpretation of the meaning of the constitutional right to property protection. As Frank Michelman has observed, '[t]he question of distribution is endemic in the very idea of a constitutional scheme of proprietary liberty.'[32]

---

[29] See Constitution of the Republic of Hungary, Article 13(1) ('The Republic of Hungary shall guarantee the right to property').

[30] See László Sólyom, 'Introduction to the Decisions of the Constitutional Court of the Republic of Hungary', in László Sólyom and Georg Brunner (eds.), *Constitutional Judiciary in a New Democracy: The Hungarian Constitutional Court* (Ann Arbor, Mich.: University of Michigan Press, 2000), 1, 5–6. For cases that illustrate this approach, see, e.g., *On the Freedom of Enterprise and on the Licensing of Taxis*, Decision 21/1994 (16 April 1994) (Hung.), reprinted in Sólyom and Brunner (eds.), above, 292; *On Local Government Apartments*, Decision 64/1993 (22 December 1993) (Hung.), reprinted in *ibid.*, 284.

[31] *Ibid.*, 288.

[32] See Michelman, n. 18 above, 99. See also Frank I. Michelman, 'Socio-Political Functions of Constitutional Protection for Private Property Holdings (In Liberal Political Thought)', in G. E. van Maanen and A. J. van der Walt (eds.), *Property Law on the Threshold of the 21st Century* (Antwerp: Maklu, 1996) 433, 436–438.

Simple awareness of distributional outcomes does not, of course, *of itself* demand that the acquisitive goals of certain persons be protected or that particular distributional outcomes be achieved. We could—in theory, at least— decide that a property regime that protects the vast holdings of some and awards nothing to others is a regime which should be entrenched through constitutional guarantees. Societal recognition of the existence of distributional questions or even of distributional inequalities does not, of itself, compel the conclusion that action is needed. To compel the conclusion that a particular property regime is *unjust*—that the constitutional right to property protection requires (or toler- ates) the consideration of redistributive claims—we must rely upon another argument, another substantive guarantee.

Perhaps the principle of equality could provide this substance. Indeed, the idea that the state should undertake efforts to 'equalize' property holdings to some degree is reflected in our general acceptance of the idea that some claims for property protection are more worthy than others—and that worthiness depends, sometimes, upon the size of the individual's holdings. Property is not necessarily seen—by the lay person or the student of property—as a 'box' in which individual holdings are equally justified and equally protected. There is, instead, a common intuitive notion that claims may weaken as one moves from a limited core of personal wealth into the penumbra of larger and more wide- spread property claims. For instance, we recognize—through graduated income taxes, taxes on luxury goods, and similar schemes—that some claims to the pro- tection of property are more worthy than others, and that worthiness may depend (sometimes, at least) on the amount of an individual's wealth.

The use of equality as the reason to compel the assertion of redistributive claims is, however, notoriously difficult. The uttering of 'equality' and 'prop- erty' in the same breath is something with which we, as a society, feel distinctly uncomfortable.[33] The levelling of property entitlements which the principle of equality would truly require is something that a largely free-market society such as ours is scarcely prepared to implement. Although the idea of equality may serve a vital role, as a burr under our saddles of complaisance, it conflicts too profoundly with property's other goals to make it a broadly applicable prin- ciple. We may *choose* (in some circumstances) to recognize that the property of those who have more should, in fact, be protected less, but we do not want to feel bound by the principle of equality to do so.

Is there any other principle—less easy to deny—that compels the assertion of redistributive claims? Let us consider, for a moment, the nature of property and the needs that it assuages. Much has been written about what seems to be the

---

[33] See, e.g., Jean Baechler, 'Liberty, Property, and Equality', in J. Roland Pennock and John W. Chapman (eds.), *Nomos XXII: Property* (New York: New York University Press, 1980), 269, 287 (tracing our reluctance to redistribute property in accordance with notions of equality to our ident- ification of property 'with the private and with autonomous centers of decision and initiative', values which oppose the merger of equality and property).

deep, primaeval need of human beings to appropriate.[34] As one psychologist has observed, most animals recognize possessory claims, and in human beings such ideas must be considered an innate tendency.[35] As James Baldwin has written:

Psychologically, the 'acquisition impulse' (or 'instinct') . . . seems to be very deeply rooted and to require recognition. . . . Even among animals we find the recognition of a 'meum and tuum' not only towards other individuals, as for the young of the family, but also towards things. The bird claims the nest and even the whole tree as his own, and the dog guards his kennel with his life. . . . In children this impulse develops very early. It must be counted a native tendency, though no doubt it owes much of its strength, and also the direction its development takes, to social example and precept. Its utility, from the genetic point of view, is so great . . . that its survival and evolution would seem to be simply a great sociological fact.[36]

This deep impulse is undoubtedly rooted in a stark biological fact: that without the appropriation of food, water, and other resources—without consumption of the physical substances necessary for life—living beings die. The fact that property and the goods that it involves cannot be analytically or physically separated from the maintenance of life itself makes the substance of property, in a fundamental sense, far more important to human beings than the substance of other constitutional rights that we so cherish. Indeed, the ability to live—and the possession of the minimal property necessary to do so—*is assumed* by freedom of speech, freedom of religion, the assurance of due process of law, and other rights. As a South African commentator has written, '[c]ontemporary experience makes it clear that "without at least some modicum of such basic necessities as food, shelter and clothing, the enjoyment of other rights appears highly theoretical".'[37] As a developing country, South Africa 'may find it difficult to convince its millions of squatters and poverty-stricken people that the protection of civil and political rights is of value to them if they do not have the material, intellectual, and social ability and circumstances to make use of such rights'.[38]

We do not, in American society, like to think in these terms; we shrink from the recognition of a positive right to the possession of 'a modicum' of necessary

[34] See, e.g., Kevin Gray, 'Equitable Property' (1994) 47 (pt.2) *Current Legal Problems* 157, 157–159, and 158 n. 2 .

[35] Léon Litwinski, 'Is There an Instinct of Possession?' (1942) 33 *British Journal of Psychology* 28, 36.

[36] James Mark Baldwin (ed.), *Dictionary of Philosophy and Psychology* (New York: Macmillan Company, 1920), bk. ii, 360.

[37] De Villiers, n. 7 above, 604 (quoting Mitchell I. Ginsberg and Leonard Lesser, 'Current Developments in Economic and Social Rights: A United States Perspective' (1981) 2 *Human Rights Law Journal* 237, 241).

[38] *Ibid.* 621. See also Dion A. Basson, *South Africa's Interim Constitution: Text and Notes* (Kenwyn: Juta and Company, Ltd., 1994), p. xxvii ('[A] liberal state which is characterised by a representative government which is obliged to recognise the rights and freedoms of individuals . . . is merely one important dimension of the [constitutional state] . . . . The dignity of every person demands that he or she shall not merely be free from oppression, but also free from hunger, free from want and free from fear.').

property, or any other rights that impose affirmative duties on government. The heart of our objection is the belief that rights protect individuals, and it is undesirable to *require* the state—by constitutional interpretation or otherwise—to acknowledge material inequality and to take particular, positive steps toward its amelioration. As we have seen, however, this model of separation of individual and collective actions—while it may be possible for many liberal rights—is not possible for property. By the act of implementing a regime of protected holdings, we are necessarily and inevitably interlocking private and public spheres. By the act of implementing a regime of protected holdings, we choose those who will have the material resources necessary for the exercise of all rights, and those who will not. Our stock aversion to the idea of positive rights does not answer the challenge that property systems themselves present, or constitutional claims of the severely dispossessed.

The provision of the bare necessities for life for human beings in our midst is not a discretionary act which we choose to implement—or not implement—in accordance with notions of charity. It is a compelled response to the right to life that our system of individual constitutional guarantees assumes, and to property's role in sustaining that right.[39] When we consider what the protection of property means, as a constitutional right—when we consider the claim that existing property holdings should be considered sacrosanct, entrenched beyond the state's redistributive power—we must be aware that deprivation of 'the bare necessities of life' is 'deprivation pro tanto of . . . [the] right to live',[40] and that the rest is worth little without it.

---

[39] See, e.g., Amartya Sen, 'Property and Hunger', originally published in (1988) 4 *Economics and Philosophy* 57, reprinted in Elizabeth Mensch and Alan Freeman (eds.), *Property Law: International Library of Essays in Law and Legal Theory* (New York: New York University Press, 1992), bk. i, 203, 210 (freedom from hunger 'is . . . a moral claim[,] as to what should be valued'; '[s]ince property rights over food are derived from property rights over other goods and resources . . ., the entire system of rights of acquisition and transfer is implicated in the emergence and survival of hunger and starvation'). Cf. David Copp, 'The Right to an Adequate Standard of Living: Justice, Autonomy, and the Basic Needs', in Ellen Frankel Paul, Fred D. Miller, Jr., and Jeffrey Paul (eds.), *Economic Rights* (Cambridge: Cambridge University Press, 1992) 231 (arguing that individuals must have the ability to meet their basic needs in order to be fully autonomous).

[40] *Francis Coralie Mullin*, n. 21 above, 753.

13

Doctrinal Payoffs: New Approaches to Takings Law

In the earlier chapters of this book, we uncovered various insights about the nature of property claims and their conflicts with public interests, both as a general matter and in the particular setting of interpreting constitutional guarantees. In this chapter, I will suggest how—as a very practical matter—these insights would change the approach currently taken by the Supreme Court to the Takings Clause.

The insights of prior chapters can be briefly summarized as follows:

1. There are four dimensions involved in any legally cognizable conception of property: theory, space, stringency, and time. The content of these dimensions will determine what property means and its strength against competing public interests.

2. We find, in law, the use of two different conceptions of property (constructed through different choices of theory, space, stringency, and time): one that provides individuals with powerful protection against competing public interests, and one that does not. The use of the latter, 'operative' conception of property is particularly mysterious, since it contradicts the common assumption that property rights provide protection against competing public interests.

3. The use of two different conceptions of property can be explained by an examination of the nature of rights, public interests, and the conflicts between them. Rights and public interests, as those terms are used in legal discourse, are both content-specific and reason-dependent. In other words, rights and public interests involve particular content—they protect certain states of affairs—for particular reasons. In any particular case, we can articulate the 'core values' (content and reasons) that a claimed right or a competing public interest involves.

4. The idea of the *prima facie* or 'trumping' power of rights, under the traditional model of rights, is grounded in the assumed normative superiority of the core values that the claimed right involves. This assumption fails when such core values are shared, in fact, by the competing public interest. By examining the core values that claimed rights and competing public interests involve, we can determine when claimed rights will enjoy—and should enjoy—*prima facie* power, and when they will—and should—not.

5. When claimed rights and competing public interests involve different core values, they are truly different and distinct entities. When they involve the

same or similar core values, the situation is very different. In such cases, they are viewed, most accurately, as presenting different interpretations of the nature of a foundational right which both attempt, in different ways, to implement. The conflict between them in these cases is actually a struggle that is *internal to that right*, over that right's definition, scope, and meaning.

6. The principles just articulated apply to all legal rights and legally recognized public interests. They explain why claimed property rights enjoy presumptive power in some cases (for instance, in cases involving public-health challenges to patent claims, or to the taking of title to land for a highway project), and not in others (for instance, in cases involving the control of land use for environmental, zoning, or historic-preservation reasons).

7. Property is, in addition, of an often unique character that affects its recognition and treatment as an entrenched constitutional guarantee. When property rights to external, physical, finite resources are claimed, the *very existence* of a legally enforced property regime necessarily involves the state in critical allocational questions. In such cases, questions of social aspirations and social goals are raised not only by particular, claimed public interests (that conflict with claimed property rights)—they are raised by the very existence of a state-enforced property regime.

8. The right to the protection of property is unique among constitutional rights, in that it—and it alone—involves the allocation of resources necessary to sustain life. If we value the individual constitutional rights that we bestow, and the right to life on which their exercise is necessarily predicated, we must recognize the minimal resource claims of all citizens in establishing the meaning of property guarantees.[1]

What changes would these insights demand in the approach now taken to the Takings Clause? To answer this question, we will begin with a brief sketch of the Supreme Court's current treatment of takings cases.

Any coherent statement of the Court's approach to takings cases is notoriously difficult. The Court's opinion in *Mugler* v. *Kansas*[2] is generally considered to mark the beginning of modern takings law in the United States. Since that opinion, more than eighty decisions construing the Takings Clause have been issued by the Court, including at least fourteen important decisions in the last fifteen years.[3] Repeated attempts by the Court to articulate a workable

---

[1] This principle raises an important question. What about the claims of *non-citizens*? Do the citizens of other countries, in danger of starvation or other privation, have a claim to the physical resources that we—in this country—enjoy? Since this book deals with the protection of property as a legally enforced guarantee, this question is (strictly speaking) beyond its purview. However, the same moral issues are obviously involved in both contexts.

[2] 123 US 623 (1887).

[3] See *Tahoe-Sierra Preservation Council, Inc.* v. *Tahoe Regional Planning Agency*, 122 S Ct 1465 (2002) (U.S.); *Palazzolo* v. *Rhode Island*, 533 US 606 (2001); *City of Monterey* v. *Del Monte Dunes*, 526 US 687 (1999); *Eastern Enterprises* v. *Apfel*, 524 US 498 (1998); *Phillips* v. *Washington Legal Foundation*, 524 US 156 (1998); *Dolan* v. *City of Tigard*, 512 US 374 (1994); *Lucas* v. *South Carolina Coastal Council*, 505 US 1003 (1992); *Yee* v. *Escondido*, 503 US 519 (1992); *Duquesne Light*

approach to the Takings Clause have resulted in a body of law that has been criticized as largely incoherent.[4] Perhaps the dominant impression that lingers from these cases is the truth of Justice Brennan's observation that '[t]he question of what constitutes a "taking" [of property] for purposes of the Fifth Amendment has proved to be a problem of considerable difficulty.'[5]

If one stands back from this mass of cases, however, the following general principles emerge. When confronted with a takings claim, the Court's analysis logically begins with a determination of whether the challenged government action is substantively permissible—whether it is, in the words of the Clause, for a permissible 'public use'.[6] This inquiry has traditionally been a narrow one, with the Court accepting the governmental judgement unless '"it is shown to involve an impossibility"'[7] or is '"palpably without reasonable foundation"'.[8] It was extended in two recent cases to include the requirements that there be an 'essential nexus' between the stated government interest and its action[9] and that the government interest be 'roughly proportional' to the harm that the government action seeks to prevent.[10] Although these requirements may open the door to wide-ranging, substantive challenges to the validity of government actions,[11] the Court has indicated that the proportionality requirement, at least, does not extend beyond the special context of 'exactions', or cases in which land development permits are granted in exchange for the dedication of property for public use.[12]

Once the government action is found to be substantively permissible, the Court proceeds to determine whether its impairment of the claimant's property interest is such that compensation must be paid. In early cases, the Court assumed that 'the Takings Clause reached only a "direct appropriation" of property . . ., or the functional equivalent of "a practical ouster of [the owner's] possession"'.[13] This was later extended to include recognition of 'takings' by

---

Company v. Barasch, 488 US 299 (1989); *Nollan v. California Coastal Commission,* 483 US 825 (1987); *Bowen v. Gilliard,* 483 US 587 (1987); *First English Evangelical Lutheran Church v. County of Los Angeles,* 482 US 304 (1987); *Hodel v. Irving,* 481 US 704 (1987); *Keystone Bituminous Coal Association v. DeBenedictis,* 480 US 470 (1987).

[4] For classic critiques of the development and current state of the Supreme Court's takings doctrine, see Gregory S. Alexander, 'Takings, Narratives, and Power' (1988) 88 *Columbia Law Review* 1752; Richard A. Epstein, 'Takings: Descent and Resurrection' 1987 *Supreme Court Review* 1; Glynn S. Lunney, Jr., 'A Critical Reexamination of the Takings Jurisprudence' (1992) 90 *Michigan Law Review* 1892; Frank Michelman, 'Takings, 1987' (1988) 88 *Columbia Law Review* 1600; Jed Rubenfeld, 'Usings' (1993) 102 *Yale Law Journal* 1077.

[5] *Penn Central Transportation Company v. New York City,* 438 US 104, 123 (1978).

[6] See *Hawaii Housing Authority v. Midkiff,* 467 US 229 (1984).

[7] *Ibid.* 240 (quoting *Old Dominion Company v. United States,* 269 US 55, 66 (1925)).

[8] *Ibid.* (quoting *United States v. Gettysburg Electric Railway Company,* 160 US 668, 680 (1896)).

[9] See *Nollan,* n. 3 above, 837.   [10] See *Dolan,* n. 3 above, 391.

[11] See, e.g., Edward J. Sullivan, 'Substantive Due Process Resurrected Through the Takings Clause: *Nollan, Dolan,* and *Ehrlich*' (1995) 25 *Environmental Law* 155.

[12] *City of Monterey,* n. 3 above, 702–703.

[13] *Lucas,* n. 3 above, 1014 (quoting *Legal Tender Cases,* 12 Wall. 457, 551 (1871) (U.S.) and *Transportation Company v. Chicago,* 99 US 635, 642 (1879)).

government regulation.[14] The Court now refers to 'the oft-cited maxim that, "while property may be regulated to a certain extent, if regulation goes too far it will be recognized as a taking"'.[15]

The problem, of course, is determining 'when, and under what circumstances, a given regulation would be seen as going "too far" for purposes of the Fifth Amendment'.[16] The Court has established two discrete categories of regulatory action which are compensatable as a *per se* matter: those in which the government 'physically takes possession of an interest in property for some public purpose',[17] and those in which the regulation 'deprives an owner of "all economically beneficial uses" of his land'.[18] In all other cases, the Court engages in 'essentially ad hoc, factual inquiries'.[19] These have, as a practical matter, involved an examination of the degree to which the claimant's property interest is impaired, the importance of the interest advanced by the government action, and whether it is fair (under the circumstances) that the claimant rather than the public bears this burden.[20] In addition, the regulation's impact on the behaviour of others may provide sufficient benefit to the complaining party such that no further compensation need be paid.[21]

If the insights developed in this book were implemented in these cases, how would the existing approach change? The speculations that follow are an admittedly incomplete exploration of this subject. However, they begin to suggest the framework for a new doctrinal approach to the Takings Clause. First, recognition of the dimensions involved in the construction of any legally cognizable conception of property would bring a rigour to the Court's analysis that is currently missing from its decisions. Whether one's ultimate approach to the Takings Clause is based upon social, economic, or other theories,[22] it is apparent

---

[14] See *Pennsylvania Coal Company* v. *Mahon*, 260 US 393 (1922).

[15] *Lucas*, n. 3 above, 1014 (quoting *Pennsylvania Coal Company*, n. 14 above, 415).

[16] *Ibid*. 1015.

[17] *Tahoe-Sierra Preservation Council, Inc.*, n. 3 above, 1478. See also *Loretto* v. *Teleprompter Manhattan CATV Corporation*, 458 US 419 (1982) (government has a categorical duty to compensate when the owner suffers a permanent physical invasion of his land).

[18] *Tahoe-Sierra Preservation Council, Inc.*, n. 3 above, 1483 (quoting *Lucas*, n. 3 above, 1019) (emphasis deleted).

[19] *Penn Central Transportation Company*, n. 3 above, 124. The essential approach of *Penn Central* was recently reaffirmed in *Tahoe-Sierra Preservation Council, Inc.*, n. 3 above, 1478, 1481.

[20] See, e.g., *Tahoe-Sierra Preservation Council, Inc.*, n. 3 above, 1485–1486; *Palazzolo*, n. 3 above, 617–618; *Lucas*, n. 3 above, 1015.

[21] See, e.g., *Keystone Bituminous Coal Association*, n. 3 above, 491; *Plymouth Coal Company* v. *Pennsylvania*, 232 US 531 (1914).

[22] For differing approaches, see, e.g., Jules L. Coleman, 'Corrective Justice and Property Rights' (1994) 11 *Social Philosophy and Policy* 124, 136–137 (distinguishing systematic and non-systematic redistributive takings in determining when compensation is required); Daniel A. Farber, 'Public Choice and Just Compensation' (1992) 9 *Constitutional Commentary* 279 (advocating 'uniformity theory' for regulatory takings); William A. Fischel, 'Introduction: Utilitarian Balancing and Formalism in Takings' (1998) 88 *Columbia Law Review* 1581 (advocating an 'economic-utilitarian approach' to takings and land use); Frank I. Michelman, 'Property, Utility, and Fairness: Comments on the Ethical Foundations of "Just Compensation" Law' (1967) 80 *Harvard Law Review* 1165 (advocating consideration of the 'efficiency gains' of the governmental action, the 'settlement costs'

that the threshold question—what 'property' is, for constitutional purposes—is most crucial. There is little point in discussing whether a taking of property promotes efficiency, or creates demoralization costs, or is (truly) for 'public use', if we have no understanding of what property is in the first place. In fact, the answer to this question seems, in many cases, to be determinative of later ones. Until we know what the property at stake is, it is impossible to evaluate whether it has been taken or whether compensation for its loss should be paid.

Despite the importance of this question, finding any coherent, underlying analysis or understanding of constitutionally cognizable property in the Supreme Court's takings cases is a difficult task. In fact, in the mountains of Supreme Court takings jurisprudence in recent years, comparatively little attention has been devoted to this first, threshold question. The question of the 'property' involved has generally received superficial gloss, with the Court moving quickly to the issue of 'taking.' In *Dolan* v. *City of Tigard*,[23] for instance, the Court alternatively implied that the 'property interest' at stake was the right to exclude[24] (which was sometimes portrayed as absolute in nature[25] and sometimes not[26]); the right to use (which was apparently assumed to be contingent in nature);[27] the entire parcel owned;[28] or the strip of land subject to the public-use request.[29] In *Lucas* v. *South Carolina Coastal Council*,[30] another important recent decision, the Court suggested that constitutionally cognizable property in takings cases might be 'the owner's reasonable expectations' or possibly 'the [s]tate's law of property'—ending with the observation that, '[i]n any event, we avoid this difficulty in the present case, since the "interest in land" that Lucas has pleaded (a fee simple interest) . . . [has] a rich tradition of protection at common law'.[31] The Court has often, in a single case, denied that the definition of property is a federal or constitutional question, only to apply tests derived from federal law;[32] or assumed that a state has sweeping prerogative in determining

involved in evaluating injuries, and the 'demoralization costs' of uncompensated takings); Stephen R. Munzer, *A Theory of Property* (Cambridge: Cambridge University Press, 1990), 425–436 (takings questions should be considered in light of principles, of utility, efficiency, justice, equality, and 'desert'-based labour); Jeremy Paul, 'The Hidden Structure of Takings Law' (1991) 64 *Southern California Law Review* 1393, 1542–1548 (takings jurisprudence should recognize and more stringently protect 'a set of core human needs', such as the need for shelter and other necessities); Jed Rubenfeld, 'Usings' (1993) 102 *Yale Law Journal* 1077 (compensation should hinge upon whether there is actual 'public use' of the property by government); William Michael Treanor, 'The *Armstrong* Principle, the Narratives of Takings, and Compensation Statutes' (1997) 38 *William and Mary Law Review* 1151, 1170–1174 (compensation should be more readily extended to individuals and groups which lack political power).

[23] 512 US 374 (1994).   [24] *Ibid.* 384.   [25] *Ibid.*   [26] *Ibid.* 386–387.
[27] *Ibid.* 384–385.   [28] *Ibid.* 385 n.6.   [29] *Ibid.* 384.   [30] 505 US 1003 (1992).
[31] *Ibid.* 1016 n. 7. See also *Palazzolo*, n. 3 above, 629–630 (rejecting the assertion that a new regulation, once enacted, becomes a part of the 'property' and cannot be challenged by subsequent title holders. In addition, the precise circumstances under which a legislative enactment could be deemed a part of the property interest was something the Court had 'no [present] occasion to consider').
[32] Compare, e.g., *PruneYard Shopping Center* v. *Robins*, 447 US 74, 84 (1980) ('Nor as a general proposition is the United States, as opposed to the several States, possessed of residual authority that enables it to define "property" in the first instance') with *ibid.* 83 n. 6 ('The term "property" as used in the Takings Clause includes the entire "group of rights inhering in the citizen's [ownership]"',

property interests, only to deny—in the same case—the state's ability to change those interests.[33]

If the constituent dimensions of property that we have identified were recognized, this kind of incoherence and inconsistency would be impossible, or—at the very least—exposed for what it is. If courts were forced to reckon in each case with the *theory* of rights used, the conceptual *space* to which those rights apply, the *stringency* with which those rights are protected, and whether those rights can change in *time*, the failure to consider any aspect of what property involves would be obvious. How can a theory that defines property involve a right to exclude which is absolute, and not absolute? How can the space that defines property be both the complainant's land as legally described, and the smaller part of that land subject to state action? How can the rights that we have chosen for the property interest at stake be both frozen in time and changeable—later—without legal consequence? If courts were forced to recognize the constituent dimensions of the property interest involved in each case, they would be forced to confront such questions.

Awareness of the dimensions that property involves would also force an awareness of the choices that we—as a society—are making in these cases, either explicitly or by default. If we recognize the questions that construction of any legally cognizable interest in property involves, our analysis will be far more penetrating and far more honest than that which the Supreme Court's opinions currently offer. *What are* the theories of rights that we are using? *What are* a landowner's 'reasonable expectations' of development? *Why should* we protect them? *Why should* we discard the claims of others—the social or collective demands—that compete with these rights? *What values* does the content that we are choosing for our conception of property serve? Are there reasons why we, as a society, *should wish* to promote or preserve those values? Claimed entitlements—even those traditionally recognized—would no longer be of assumed and unquestioned validity. Instead, they would be seen for what they are: social choices that we, as a society, have intentionally (or unintentionally) made.

If the constituent dimensions of property were recognized takings cases, we would further realize that the choices made for property's dimensions predetermine—in crucial ways—the strength that claimed rights to property will have against competing public interests. The Takings Clause proscribes the taking of property for public use without just compensation. The question is what 'property', as used in that sentence, means. If, for instance, we choose a conception of property in which protected interests—once chosen—are frozen in time thereafter, there will be an impairment of 'property' if collective change of those interests is later attempted. If, on the other hand, we choose a conception of property in which—as a part of that interest—protected interests change as

quoting *United States* v. *General Motors Corporation*, 323 US 373, 378 (1945)), and *ibid.* 83 ('reasonable investment-backed expectations' establish property interests, citing *Kaiser Aetna* v. *United States*, 444 US 164, 175 (1979)).

[33] See, e.g., *Phillips*, n. 3 above.

social needs change, there will be no impairment of 'property' if individual interests must later yield to collective goals. By choosing particular constituent dimensions for property, we choose a particular conception of property, which—in turn—determines the applicability, or the non-applicability, of the Takings Clause guarantee.

Knowledge that property can be understood in ways that trigger takings guarantees, and in ways that do not, is important; however, it does not—of itself—give any guidance on when we should view property in one way, or the other. If, for instance, the city takes a strip of land for a highway project, or prohibits a use of land that was previously permitted, should the court see this change in previously existing individual prerogatives as something that 'impairs' previously defined rights (frozen in time), or as something that is 'a part' of the rights that property confers? Should we see such changes as presenting a *prima facie* case of the taking of property, or not?

We could make this decision on philosophical, policy, or other grounds: we could decide, for instance, that expecting the individual to absorb such losses would deter investment in land, and thus should be compensatable. Or we could decide that the social goals that these local actions represent are of such importance that we should not make them compensatable, lest they be—for sheer reasons of cost alone—deterred. Consideration of such issues is the way in which takings cases have been traditionally approached, and they will obviously remain an important part of the judicial analysis of any takings case.

There is, however, another phenomenon that is at work in these cases, an awareness of which explains many decisions for which an articulated rationale is otherwise missing. Indeed, although philosophical or policy issues of the type just described have been advanced—with great force—by academic commentators, one sees little explicit consideration of them in the Supreme Court's opinions. Those opinions seem often to be driven by some other, unarticulated rationale, one that (in the aggregate) often seems correct to us, even if we do not fully understand its operation.

This hidden rationale is exposed, and explained, by the insights that we developed in the previous chapters of this book. As we have previously seen, the conception of property as a 'right' which 'protects' is driven by the underlying assumption that the case involves the assertion of the highly prized values associated with property against those of an unrelated (and lesser-valued) public interest. We assume that the core values, which the individual interest asserts, are *presumptively superior* to the core values that the competing public interest involves. In this situation, we intuitively choose a conception of property that protects its holder, since the property interest, in this case, should have presumptive or *prima facie* power.

We must be aware, however, of the underlying reasons that drive this choice. For if the assumption that underlies this choice is *not* true—if the core values that the individual property interest asserts *are in fact shared* by the competing public interest—there is no reason to choose the 'protective' conception of property. In such a case, both competing interests are grounded in the values that we associate with property. We do not adjudicate, in such a case, the power of property values against unrelated values; rather, we adjudicate an internal dispute over what the right to property protection—as a fundamental matter—should be.

When these insights are applied to takings cases, we can see why a protective conception of property is used in some cases and not in others. In particular:

—If the case involves the assertion of a claimed property right against an *unrelated* public interest, the traditional idea of a presumptively powerful right opposing the public interest is triggered, and we envision property as a protective force. In 'takings' terms, we see this case as one in which a protective conception of property opposes a public interest, with the question whether that public interest—all things considered—should overcome the presumptive power of that right.

—If, on the other hand, the case involves the assertion of a claimed property right against a *related* public interest, the situation is quite different. In such a case, the traditional idea of the power of rights does not apply, and we do not envision property as a protective force. The reason for this is quite simple. This is not a 'takings' case in the traditional sense, in which a property interest with settled content and meaning is asserted against a public interest of an unrelated nature. Rather, it is a dispute over what 'property'—as used in the Takings Clause—*means*.

We understand—in short—that what may be seen as the arbitrary choices of particular protecting or non-protecting conceptions of property in takings cases are, in fact, *predictable outcomes that are driven by the nature of the competing private and public interests involved in each case*. Property rights (protected by the Takings Clause) do not, in all times and places, presumptively insulate owners from risk, change, and impairment of wealth. They perform that function only when the *actual* values that underlie the *actual* claims present a case that justifies that approach.

It is important to remember that our analysis determines only whether property should protect or not protect, as a *prima facie* matter; it does not necessarily dictate the ultimate outcome of the case. A property claim which enjoys protective, *prima facie* power may be trumped by a particularly compelling public interest, and a property claim which lacks that power may nonetheless prevail (on other grounds) against a presumptively equally matched public-interest claim. Understanding the power relations involved in these cases will, however, enable us to make all of the choices involved in them in a far more principled and intelligent way. Rather than seeing the protective or non-protective character of property as a seemingly random event, we will understand that the presumptive power of claimed property rights in takings cases—whether we use, in effect, a conception of property that protects or not—is a function of the values that the competing claims involve. If we deviate from those presumptive outcomes, we must do so for clearly articulated and persuasive reasons.

Finally, the insights that we have developed in this book compel recognition of the *inherently allocational* nature of property regimes, when the objects of those regimes are external, physical, finite resources. State attempts to change property allocations to meet the minimal property needs of citizens will often assert core values that match those asserted by the competing individual property claims. There are, as a result, very good and demonstrable reasons why welfare plans, Medicaid programmes, and other explicitly redistributive schemes are not—and should not—be the appropriate subjects for successful takings challenges. *If* our society asserts, through the political process, a decision to heed its citizens' needs for the resources necessary to sustain life, that social goal will be grounded in the same values as those that ground resisting property claims. And *if* our society values the individual rights that the Constitution bestows, that redistribution of property necessary to preserve life must be undertaken.

14

The Constitutionalization of Property: Some Final Thoughts

The idea that individual property rights should be included among constitutional guarantees is controversial. By constitutionalizing rights we attempt to enhance their power by placing them beyond the workings of ordinary majoritarian government. The attempt to place property rights in this category seems to be particularly inappropriate in view of the special need to question and change the physical resource allocations that property rights so often involve. It can be forcefully argued that property—not being, in truth, a negative right, but rather a positive right involving state distributional decisions—should not be placed, by deliberate design, beyond the questionings and revisions of ordinary political life.[1]

Indeed, for critics of the constitutionalization of property rights, the United States is often seen as the archetypical example of the blindness and excesses that are by-products of this approach.[2] With our strong tradition of 'negative' constitutional rights, and our firm inclusion of property among those rights, we seem to aspire toward a system characterized by 'free-market, minimalist-state libertarianism', with the erection of a sturdy barrier between public and private spheres.[3] Our inclusion of property as a constitutional right reinforces the notion that property is a pre-political institution, defined by private law and insulated (by constitutional guarantee) from otherwise legitimate public demands.

It is impossible, of course, for the constitutionalization of property to achieve this vision of government; in the United States, for example, the protection of property has been honoured as an historical matter more in the breach than in the practice. When one considers the scope of property claims—from land-use claims, to intellectual-property claims, to regulatory-status claims, to claims rooted in virtually any right or power conferred by existing law—and the myriad of interferences with those claims by state, local, and federal legislative and adjudicative bodies, the idea that property in the United States or elsewhere is a 'pre-political' institution is clearly a fanciful one. The critics' charge, however, is not that the constitutionalization of property will ensure the achievement of

---

[1] See, e.g., Jennifer Nedelsky, 'Should Property Be Constitutionalized? A Relational and Comparative Approach', in G. E. van Maanen and A. J. van der Walt (eds.), *Property Law on the Threshold of the 21st Century* (Antwerp: Maklu, 1996), 417.

[2] See, e.g., *ibid*. 422–423.

[3] See A. J. van der Walt, 'The Constitutional Property Clause: Striking a Balance Between Guarantee and Limitation', in Janet McLean (ed.), *Property and the Constitution* (Oxford: Hart Publishing, 1999), 109, 124 (discussing this view).

this vision of government, but rather that it will warp our consideration of property by reference to this ideal. Although such a charge could be made regarding the constitutionalization of any individual right, it is (one could argue) particularly troubling when we consider what must be—by their very nature—the *most compromised* of individual claims. In cases in which we should be most aware of the contingent nature of rights' presumptive power, the constitutionalization of property seems to distort this critical understanding.

There is no doubt but that the constitutionalization of property in the United States has, to some extent, reinforced notions of the 'pre-political' nature of property holdings and the existence of a public/private divide. The constitutionalization of property has (at the very least) important legal doctrinal consequences, and undoubtedly has other inhibitory influences as well. However, the role of the constitutionalization decision in the creation or perpetuation of these ideas must be kept in proper perspective. The constitutionalization of property rights is certainly not necessary to entrench ideas of the sanctity of property rights or the division between public and private spheres. As critics have acknowledged, such ideas flourish in England, Canada, New Zealand, India, and elsewhere without the benefit of property's constitutionalization.[4] These ideas are rooted in the fundamental tensions between individual security and collective control, a tension which runs far deeper than the constitutionalization question.

In addition, and perhaps paradoxically, the constitutionalization of property can present a powerful opportunity for a more direct and honest facing of the question of the meaning of property and its role in contemporary social and political life. Carol Rose has observed that takings questions in American law become particularly acute when previously settled understandings of property suffer transformative stress due to technological change, social unrest, increasing awareness of ecological or other physical limitations, or other upheavals in social and political life.[5] Through the continual reinterpretation of the takings guarantee, Americans have chosen (as a society) to provide a particular, nationally focused forum for the consideration of these questions.

Perhaps the issue is less the constitutionalization of property, and more how we, as a society, view the constitutional enterprise. In a series of provocative essays, André van der Walt has posed the question as whether we see a constitution—and the public sphere behind it—as simply a way to adjust or referee jockeying private interests, or as something that articulates a positive, substantive vision of societal goals and aspirations.[6] Indeed, he argues, the

---

[4] See, e.g., Nedelsky, n. 1 above, 423.

[5] See, e.g., Carol M. Rose, 'Property Rights and Responsibilties', in Marian R. Chertow and Daniel C. Esty (eds.), *Thinking Ecologically: The Next Generation of Environmental Policy* (New Haven, Conn.: Yale University Press, 1997), 49.

[6] See, e.g., A. J. van der Walt, 'Un-doing Things With Words: The Colonisation of the Public Sphere by Private-Property Discourse', in Graham Bradfield and Derek van der Merwe (eds.), *'Meaning' in Legal Interpretation* (Kenwyn: Juta and Company, Ltd.,1998), 235; A. J. van der Walt, 'Dancing With Codes—Protecting, Developing and Deconstructing Property Rights in a Constitutional State' (2001) 118 *South African Law Journal* 258.

constitutionalization of property may (at least in some cases) be the best way to initiate and focus public debate about the social and political character of property, with the hope that it may—through this process—be a 'catalyst for the transformation of [the] common law'.[7] The constitutionalization of property does not, of course, guarantee such debate or outcomes; but the chances of their happening, van der Walt argues, are (all things considered) much better with this focus than without it.[8]

The context in which van der Walt writes is that of South African politics and law—one in which the Constitution is, by widespread agreement, a socially and legally transformative document which works to create a new governmental regime on the ashes of apartheid. It is much easier to imagine a constitution as a locus for reflection, reconsideration, debate, and change when it is superimposed (as a revolutionary act) upon a now discredited social, political, and legal order. It is much more difficult to imagine this role, when the constitution is—as in the United States—simply an entrenched part of a stable and long-standing governmental regime.

The consideration and accommodation of change is, however, something that no government can avoid. When a regime is stable, it may be more difficult to perceive a constitution's role in facilitating change in individually guaranteed rights, as well as ensuring their preservation. However, the Constitution of the United States and those of other stable regimes are, in truth, as aspirational as others, with the declarations of their meanings a publicly influenced and publicly influencing process. The question is not whether our Constitution will in fact have this role, but whether we will engage its recognition.

---

[7] Van der Walt, n. 3 above, 145.   [8] *Ibid.* 145–146.

Conclusion

The power of property as an emotional, social, and legal idea is undeniable. Property rights in all of their various forms structure—for better or for worse—our daily lives, our human relationships, our horizons, and our fears. They dictate our ability to realize our dreams and our very physical survival.

The importance of property rights in individuals' lives has fuelled the popular outcry against many of the restrictions and deprivations affecting property that contemporary governmental regimes have imposed. Zoning ordinances, wetlands-preservation laws, endangered-species laws, cultural-property laws, welfare laws, and other collective measures have often outraged those affected and seemingly challenged traditional notions about what property is and the protection it provides. The brushing aside of property-rights claims by contemporary government is, however, far from uniform. For while the ability to fill and build on one's wetlands or to preserve money from redistributive taxation may be lost under current law, the monopolies conferred by patents or the title to land and chattels are consistently—and remarkably—secure. Indeed, the sanctity of these forms of wealth and power in the face of desperate poverty, land maldistribution, and public-health crises has bitterly frustrated those attempting to meet critical human needs in many places of the world.

This 'cognitive dissonance' in our treatment of property claims has perplexed theorists at both ends of the property-rights spectrum, and has contributed to the notion that property is neither a consistent nor a coherent idea in law. The traditional reasons for recognition of property rights—such as the encouragement of industry, the protection of expectations, the promotion of individual security, and so on—often fail to distinguish the claims that are recognized and those that are not. The ability to use one's land for a cherished project is not (for instance) obviously less grounded in traditional property values than the title to an incidental chattel. Nor does the simple nature of the public interests that oppose these claims obviously perform this function. It is difficult to see immediately why (for instance) the saving of lives is assumed to be subordinate to property (patent) claims, but the prevention of erosion or the preservation of historic structures is not.

We could see this variable power of property in law simply as a matter of *ad hoc* social judgements. Property rights are, after all—like all legal rights—merely socially constructed phenomena. We could conclude that we have, as a society, simply decided that property rights in the form of patent claims or title claims should (for whatever reason) be rigorously protected, while other property rights should not. However, for those whose expectations or critical needs have been thwarted, this answer is viscerally unsatisfactory. We need to know *why* property claims are respected or not—whether we view the question from an individual perspective or as a matter of broader social policy.

This book has argued that there are, in fact, deep and identifiable reasons why property claims sometimes deserve presumptive power and sometimes do not—reasons grounded in the nature of property, as an idea, and the conflicts of that idea with competing public interests. In many cases, the values that property claims assert stand unchallenged by the competing public interests—yielding, intuitively and in law, individual claims with clear presumptive power. In many other cases, however—*indeed, in a disproportionate number of cases*—the opposite is true. Because of the particular nature of property as an idea—because of its essential character as involving, so often, the allocation and control of external, physical, finite resources—the values that the individual property claim asserts are often matched by values of the same kind asserted (on behalf of others) by the competing public interest. Whether the case involves a physical interdependence or other interconnectedness (of an ecological, biological, economic, or other nature) between the interests that the duelling claims assert, or whether the case involves the simple allocation of a particular resource to the property-rights claimant to the derogation of the possessory claims of others, the foundational assumption that a right deserves presumptive power because of the uniquely worthy nature of the values that it asserts fails across a wide range of property cases.

The claims of property-rights advocates that individual property rights are unjustifiedly trammelled by land-use regulations, environmental controls, cultural-property laws, welfare laws, and other laws is, therefore, an overly simplistic one. By the same token, those who would solve the problem of property's cognitive dissonance by adopting a position at the other extreme—by rendering property claims of no special power across the board—are in similar, and equal, error. If we are to honour the value-driven basis of the presumptive power of rights, our analysis must be far more nuanced. An individual claim to property protection is neither invariably powerful nor invariably not—its power depends, in each conflicted case, upon far more complex factors.

The dynamics of power that this book exposes do not, of themselves, articulate a particular political or social vision. They do not determine what property rights *should* be, or what we—as a society—*should* assert as competing public interests. The claims and their values with which this book grapples are the products of independent social, political, and economic forces. However, the understanding of property that this book advances raises important issues of justice. It compels us to confront the demands that property, as an idea, inevitably makes—and the costs that it imposes upon others.

Bibliography

ACKERMAN, BRUCE A., *Private Property and the Constitution* (New Haven, Conn.: Yale University Press, 1977).

ALEINIKOFF, T. ALEXANDER, 'Constitutional Law in the Age of Balancing' (1987) 96 *Yale Law Journal* 943.

ALEXANDER, GREGORY S., 'Takings, Narratives, and Power' (1988) 88 *Columbia Law Review* 1752.

—— 'Takings and the Post-Modern Dialectic of Property' (1992) 9 *Constitutional Commentary* 259.

—— 'Civic Property' (1997) 6 *Social and Legal Studies* 217.

—— *Commodity & Propriety: Competing Visions of Property in American Legal Thought 1776–1970* (Chicago, Ill.: University of Chicago Press, 1997).

ALEXY, ROBERT, 'Individual Rights and Collective Goods', in Carlos Nino (ed.), *Rights: International Library of Essays in Law and Legal Theory* (New York: New York University Press, 1992).

ANDREWS, LORI B., 'My Body, My Property', originally published in (1986) 16 *Hastings Center Report* 28, reprinted in Elizabeth Mensch and Alan Freeman (eds.), *Property Law: International Library of Essays in Law and Legal Theory* (New York: New York University Press, 1992), bk. ii.

BAECHLER, JEAN, 'Liberty, Property, and Equality', in J. Roland Pennock and John W. Chapman (eds.), *Nomos XXII: Property* (New York: New York University Press, 1980).

BAKER, C. EDWIN, 'Property and Its Relation to Constitutionally Protected Liberty' (1986) 134 *University of Pennsylvania Law Review* 741.

BALDWIN, JAMES MARK (ed.), *Dictionary of Philosophy and Psychology* (New York: Macmillan Company, 1920), bk. ii.

BASSON, DION A., *South Africa's Interim Constitution: Text and Notes* (Kenwyn: Juta and Company, Ltd., 1994).

BECKER, LAWRENCE C., *Property Rights—Philosophic Foundations* (London: Routledge and Kegan Paul, 1977).

BENTHAM, JEREMY, 'Principles of the Civil Code', in C. K. Ogden (ed.), *The Theory of Legislation* (London: Kegan Paul, Trench, Trubner and Company, Ltd., 1931).

—— *An Introduction to the Principles of Morals and Legislation* (J. H. Burns and H. L. A. Hart (eds.), London: University of London—Athlone Press, 1970).

BERLIN, ISAIAH, 'Two Concepts of Liberty', in his *Four Essays on Liberty* (New York: Oxford University Press, 1970).

BERMAN, HAROLD J., *Law and Revolution: The Formation of the Western Legal Tradition* (Cambridge, Mass.: Harvard University Press, 1983).

BODENHEIMER, EDGAR, 'Prolegomena to a Theory of the Public Interest', in Carl J. Friedrich (ed.), *Nomos V: The Public Interest* (New York: Atherton Press, 1962).

BONYHADY, TIM, 'Property Rights', in Tim Bonyhady (ed.), *Environmental Protection and Legal Change* (Sydney: The Federation Press, 1992).

BOULIER, WILLIAM, 'Sperm, Spleens, and Other Valuables: The Need to Recognize Property Rights in Human Body Parts' (1995) 23 *Hofstra Law Review* 693.

BRANSCOMB, ANNE WELLS, *Who Owns Information?* (New York: Basic Books, 1994).

CALABRESI, GUIDO, and MELAMED, A. DOUGLAS, 'Property Rules, Liability Rules, and Inalienability: One View of the Cathedral' (1972) 85 *Harvard Law Review* 1089.

CALDWELL, LYNTON K., 'Rights of Ownership or Rights of Use?—The Need for a New Conceptual Basis for Land Use Policy' (1974) 15 *William and Mary Law Review* 759.

CASSINELLI, C. W., 'Some Reflections on the Concept of the Public Interest' (1958) 69 *Ethics* 48.

CAVARELLO, DANIEL T., 'From Penn Central to United Artists' I & II: The Rise to Immunity of Historic Preservation Designation from Successful Takings Challenges' (1995) 22 *Boston College Environmental Affairs Law Review* 593.

CHRISTMAN, JOHN (ed.), *The Inner Citadel: Essays on Individual Autonomy* (New York: Oxford University Press, 1989).

—— *The Myth of Property: Toward an Egalitarian Theory of Ownership* (New York: Oxford University Press, 1994).

COHEN, FELIX S., 'Dialogue on Private Property', originally published in (1954) IX *Rutgers Law Review* 357, reprinted in Elizabeth Mensch and Alan Freeman (eds.), *Property Law: International Library of Essays in Law and Legal Theory* (New York: New York University Press, 1992), bk. i.

COHEN, G. A., *Self-Ownership, Freedom, and Equality* (Cambridge: Cambridge University Press, 1995).

COLEMAN, JULES L., 'Corrective Justice and Property Rights' (1994) 11 *Social Philosophy and Policy* 124.

COLM, GERHARD, 'The Public Interest: Essential Key to Public Policy', in Carl J. Friedrich (ed.), *Nomos V: The Public Interest* (New York: Atherton Press, 1962).

COOMBE, ROSEMARY J., 'The Properties of Culture and the Politics of Possessing Identity: Native Claims in the Cultural Appropriation Controversy', in Dan Danielsen and Karen Engle (eds.), *After Identity: A Reader in Law and Culture* (New York: Routledge, 1995).

—— *The Cultural Life of Intellectual Properties: Authorship, Appropriation, and the Law* (Durham, N.C.: Duke University Press, 1998).

COPP, DAVID, 'The Right to an Adequate Standard of Living: Justice, Autonomy, and the Basic Needs', in Ellen Frankel Paul, Fred D. Miller, Jr., and Jeffrey Paul (eds.), *Economic Rights* (Cambridge: Cambridge University Press, 1992).

CORDES, MARK W., 'Leapfrogging the Constitution: The Rise of State Takings Legislation' (1997) 24 *Ecology Law Quarterly* 187.

COSTONIS, JOHN J., 'Presumptive and Per Se Takings: A Decisional Model for the Taking Issue' (1983) 58 *New York University Law Review* 465.

COVER, ROBERT M., *Justice Accused: Antislavery and the Judicial Process* (New Haven, Conn.: Yale University Press, 1975).

CZAJKOWSKI, CASIMIR, *The Theory of Private Property in John Locke's Political Philosophy* (Notre Dame, Ind.: University of Notre Dame Press, 1941).

DAGAN, HANOCH, 'Takings and Distributive Justice' (1999) 85 *University of Virginia Law Review* 741.

DAVIS, DENNIS, CHASKALSON, MATTHEW, and DE WAAL, JOHAN, 'Democracy and Constitutionalism: The Role of Constitutional Interpretation', in Dawid van Wyk, John Dugard, Bertus de Villiers, and Dennis Davis (eds.), *Rights and Constitutionalism: The New South African Legal Order* (Oxford: Clarendon Press, 1996).

DELONG, JAMES V., *Property Matters: How Property Rights Are Under Assault—And Why You Should Care* (New York: The Free Press, 1997).

DEMSETZ, HAROLD, 'Toward a Theory of Property Rights' (1967) 57 *American Economic Review* (Papers and Proceedings) 347.

DE VILLIERS, BERTUS, 'Social and Economic Rights', in Dawid van Wyk, John Dugard, Bertus de Villiers, and Dennis Davis (eds.), *Rights and Constitutionalism: The New South African Legal Order* (Oxford: Clarendon Press, 1996).

DRIMMER, JONATHAN, 'Hate Property: A Substantive Limitation for America's Cultural Property Laws' (1998) 65 *Tennessee Law Review* 691.

DU PLESSIS, LOURENS, and CORDER, HUGH, *Understanding South Africa's Transitional Bill of Rights* (Kenwyn: Juta and Company, Ltd., 1994).

DWORKIN, RONALD, *Taking Rights Seriously* (Cambridge, Mass.: Harvard University Press, 1977).

EISGRUBER, CHRISTOPHER L., and SAGER, LAWRENCE G., 'The Vulnerability of Conscience: The Constitutional Basis for Protecting Religious Conduct' (1994) 61 *University of Chicago Law Review* 1245.

ELLICKSON, ROBERT C., *Order Without Law: How Neighbors Settle Disputes* (Cambridge, Mass.: Harvard University Press, 1991).

ELY, JAMES W., JR., *The Guardian of Every Other Right: A Constitutional History of Property Rights* (New York: Oxford University Press, 1992).

EMERSON, THOMAS I., *The System of Freedom of Expression* (New York: Random House, 1970).

EPSTEIN, RICHARD A., 'A Theory of Strict Liability' (1973) 2 *Journal of Legal Studies* 151.

—— *Takings: Private Property and the Power of Eminent Domain* (Cambridge, Mass.: Harvard University Press, 1985).

—— 'Takings: Descent and Resurrection' 1987 *Supreme Court Review* 1.

—— 'Property, Speech, and the Politics of Distrust' (1992) 59 *University of Chicago Law Review* 41.

—— 'Life in No Trump: Property and Speech Under the Constitution' (2001) 53 *Maine Law Review* 23.

FARBER, DANIEL A., 'Public Choice and Just Compensation' (1992) 9 *Constitutional Commentary* 279.

FINNIS, JOHN M., '"Reason and Passion": The Constitutional Dialectic of Free Speech and Obscenity' (1967) 116 *University of Pennsylvania Law Review* 222.

FISCHEL, WILLIAM A., 'Introduction: Utilitarian Balancing and Formalism in Takings' (1998) 88 *Columbia Law Review* 1581.

FREYFOGLE, ERIC, 'Context and Accommodation in Modern Property Law' (1989) 41 *Stanford Law Review* 1529.

—— 'The Construction of Ownership' 1996 *University of Illinois Law Review* 173.

—— 'Ethics, Community, and Private Land' (1996) 23 *Ecology Law Quarterly* 631.

GERSTENBLITH, PATTY, 'Identity and Cultural Property: The Protection of Cultural Property in the United States' (1995) 75 *Boston University Law Review* 559.

GEWIRTH, ALAN, 'Human Rights and Conceptions of the Self' (1998) 18 *Philosophia* 129.

GEY, STEVEN G., 'The Case Against Postmodern Censorship Theory' (1996) 145 *University of Pennsylvania Law Review* 193.

GOODIN, ROBERT E., *Reasons for Welfare: The Political Theory of the Welfare State* (Princeton, N.J.: Princeton University Press, 1988).

GORDON, ROBERT W., 'Paradoxical Property', in John Brewer and Susan Staves (eds.), *Early Modern Conceptions of Property* (London: Routledge, 1996).

GOSTIN, LAWRENCE O., 'Health Information Privacy' (1995) 80 *Cornell Law Review* 451.

GRAY, KEVIN, 'Property in Thin Air' (1991) 50 *Cambridge Law Journal* 252.

—— 'Equitable Property' (1994) 47 (pt.2) *Current Legal Problems* 157.

—— and GRAY, SUSAN FRANCIS, 'The Idea of Property in Land', in Susan Bright and John Dewar (eds.), *Land Law: Themes and Perspectives* (Oxford: Oxford University Press, 1998).

—— and —— 'Private Property and Public Propriety', in Janet McLean (ed.), *Property and the Constitution* (Oxford: Hart Publishing, 1999).

GREENAWALT, KENT, *Fighting Words: Individuals, Communities, and Liberties of Speech* (Princeton, N. J.: Princeton University Press, 1995).

GREY, THOMAS C., 'The Disintegration of Property', in J. Roland Pennock and John W. Chapman (eds.), *Nomos XXII: Property* (New York: New York University Press, 1980).

HALPIN, ANDREW, *Rights and Law Analysis and Theory* (Oxford: Hart Publishing, 1997).

HAREL, ALON, 'What Demands are Rights? An Investigation into the Relation between Rights and Reasons' (1977) 17 *Oxford Journal of Legal Studies* 101.

—— 'The Boundaries of Justifiable Tolerance: A Liberal Perspective', in David Heyd (ed.), *Toleration: An Elusive Virtue* (Princeton, N. J.: Princeton University Press, 1996).

—— 'Revisionist Theories of Rights: An Unwelcome Defense' (1998) XI *Canadian Journal of Law and Jurisprudence* 227.

HARRIS, J. W., *Property and Justice* (Oxford: Clarendon Press, 1996).

—— 'Is Property a Human Right?', in Janet McLean (ed.), *Property and the Constitution* (Oxford: Hart Publishing, 1999).

—— 'Inheritance and the Justice Tribunal', in Stephen R. Munzer (ed.), *New Essays in the Legal and Political Theory of Property* (Cambridge: Cambridge University Press, 2001).

HART, H. L. A., 'Bentham on Legal Rights', in A. W. B. Simpson (ed.), *Oxford Essays in Jurisprudence 2nd Series* (Oxford: Clarendon Press, 1973).

HOHFELD, WESLEY NEWCOMB, *Fundamental Legal Conceptions as Applied in Judicial Reasoning and Other Legal Essays* (New Haven, Conn.: Yale University Press, 1923).

HONORÉ, A. M., 'Ownership', in A. G. Guest (ed.), *Oxford Essays in Jurisprudence* (Oxford: Clarendon Press, 1961).

HORWITZ, MORTON J., *The Transformation of American Law 1780–1860* (Cambridge, Mass.: Harvard University Press, 1977).

HUTT, SHERRY, and McKEOWN, C. TIMOTHY, 'Control of Cultural Property as Human Rights Law' (1999) 31 *Arizona State Law Journal* 363.

JONES, PAUL, 'Freedom and the Redistribution of Resources' (1982) 11 *Journal of Social Policy* 217.

KANG, JERRY, 'Information Privacy in Cyberspace Transactions' (1998) 50 *Stanford Law Review* 1193.

KAPLOW, LOUIS, and SHAVELL, STEVEN, 'Property Rules Versus Liability Rules: An Economic Analysis' (1996) 109 *Harvard Law Review* 713.

KENNET, WAYLAND, *Preservation* (London: Maurice Temple Smith Ltd., 1972).

KNETSCH, JACK L., 'The Endowment Effect and Evidence of Nonreversible Indifference Curves' (1989) 79 *American Economic Review* 1277.

KOMMERS, DONALD P., 'The Jurisprudence of Free Speech in the United States and the Federal Republic of Germany' (1980) 53 *Southern California Law Review* 657.

—— 'German Constitutionalism: A Prolegomenon' (1991) 40 *Emory Law Journal* 837.

KRETZMER, DAVID, 'Freedom of Speech and Racism' (1987) 8 *Cardozo Law Review* 445.

LANGTON, RAE, 'Speech Acts and Unspeakable Acts' (1993) 22 *Philosophy and Public Affairs* 293.

LARKIN, PASCHAL, *Property in the Eighteenth Century* (Dublin: Cork University Press, 1930).

LAZARUS, RICHARD J., 'Changing Conceptions of Property and Sovereignty in Natural Resources: Questioning the Public Trust Doctrine' (1986) 71 *Iowa Law Review* 631.

LEWIS, CAROLE, 'The Right to Private Property in a New Political Dispensation in South Africa' (1992) 8 *South African Journal on Human Rights* 389.

LITWINSKI, LÉON, 'Is There an Instinct of Possession?' (1942) 33 *British Journal of Psychology* 28.

LOCKE, JOHN, 'Second Treatise of Government', in his *Two Treatises of Government* (Peter Laslett (ed.), 2nd edn., Cambridge: Cambridge University Press, 1960 (1698)).

LOOPER-FRIEDMAN, SUSAN E., ' "Keep Your Laws Off My Body": Abortion Regulation and the Takings Clause' (1995) 29 *New England Law Review* 253.

LUCY, WILLIAM N. R., and BARKER, FRANÇOIS R., 'Justifying Property and Justifying Access' (1993) VI *Canadian Journal of Law and Jurisprudence* 287.

LUNNEY, GLYNN S., JR., 'A Critical Reexamination of the Takings Jurisprudence' (1992) 90 *Michigan Law Review* 1892.

MACKINNON, CATHARINE A., 'Pornography, Civil Rights, and Speech' (1985) 20 *Harvard Civil Rights—Civil Liberties Law Review* 1.

—— 'Pornography as Defamation and Discrimination' (1991) 71 *Boston University Law Review* 793.

—— *Only Words* (Cambridge, Mass.: Harvard University Press, 1993).

MACPHERSON, C. B., 'Human Rights as Property Rights' (1977) 24 *Dissent* 72.

—— 'The Meaning of Property', in C. B. MacPherson (ed.), *Property: Mainstream and Critical Positions* (Toronto: University of Toronto Press, 1978).

MARSALA, NANCY G., 'State Private Property Rights Initiatives as a Response to "Environmental Takings"' (1995) 46 *South Carolina Law Review* 613.

—— and MARSALA, ROGER J., *Property Rights: Understanding Government Takings and Environmental Regulation* (Rockville, Md.: Government Institutes, 1997).

MASSEY, CALVIN R., 'Hate Speech, Cultural Diversity, and the Foundational Paradigm of Free Expression' (1992) 40 *University of California at Los Angeles Law Review* 103.

MASTALIR, ROGER W., 'A Proposal for Protecting the "Cultural" and "Property" Aspects of Cultural Property Under International Law' (1992–1993) 16 *Fordham International Law Journal* 1033.

MATSUDA, MARI J., 'Public Response to Racist Speech: Consider the Victim's Story', in Mari J. Matsuda, Charles R. Lawrence III, Richard Delgado, and Kimberlé Williams Crenshaw (eds.), *Words That Wound: Critical Race Theory, Assaultive Speech, and the First Amendment* (Boulder, Colo.: Westview Press, 1993).

McCAFFERY, EDWARD J., 'Must We Have the Right to Waste?', in Stephen R. Munzer, *New Essays in the Legal and Political Theory of Property* (Cambridge: Cambridge University Press, 2001).

McEWEN, JEAN E., 'DNA Sampling and Banking: Practices and Procedures in the United States', in Barth Maria Knoppers (ed.), *Human DNA: Law and Policy—International and Comparative Perspectives* (The Hague: Kluwer Law International, 1997).

McLEAN, JANET, 'Property as Power and Resistance', in Janet McLean (ed.), *Property and the Constitution* (Oxford: Hart Publishing, 1999).

MERRILL, THOMAS W., 'The Landscape of Constitutional Property' (2000) 86 *Virginia Law Review* 885.

MERRYMAN, J. H., 'The Public Interest in Cultural Property' (1989) 77 *California Law Review* 339.

MICHELMAN, FRANK I., 'Property, Utility and Fairness: Comments on the Ethical Foundations of "Just Compensation" Law' (1967) 80 *Harvard Law Review* 1165.

—— 'Possession vs. Distribution in the Constitutional Idea of Property' (1987) 72 *Iowa Law Review* 1319.

—— 'Takings, 1987' (1988) 88 *Columbia Law Review* 1600.

—— 'Liberties, Fair Values, and Constitutional Method' (1992) 59 *University of Chicago Law Review* 91.

—— 'Property, Federalism, and Jurisprudence: A Comment on Lucas and Judicial Conservatism' (1993) 35 *William and Mary Law Review* 301.

—— 'Socio-Political Functions of Constitutional Protection for Private Property Holdings (In Liberal Political Thought)', in G. E. van Maanen and A. J. van der Walt (eds.), *Property Law on the Threshold of the 21st Century* (Antwerp: Maklu, 1996).

MINOGUE, KENNETH R., 'The Concept of Property and Its Contemporary Significance', in J. Roland Pennock and John W. Chapman (eds.), *Nomos XXII: Property* (New York: New York University Press, 1980).

MUELLER, DENNIS C., *Public Choice II* (Cambridge: Cambridge University Press, 1989).

MUNZER, STEPHEN R., *A Theory of Property* (Cambridge: Cambridge University Press, 1990).

—— 'Property as Social Relations', in Stephen R. Munzer (ed.), *New Essays in the Legal and Political Theory of Property* (Cambridge: Cambridge University Press, 2001).

NAFZIGER, JAMES A. R., 'The Underlying Constitutionalism of the Law Governing Archeological and Other Cultural Heritage' (1994) 30 *Willamette Law Review* 581.

NARVESON, JAN, *The Libertarian Idea* (Philadelphia, Pa.: Temple University Press, 1988).

NEDELSKY, JENNIFER, 'American Constitutionalism and the Paradox of Private Property', in Jon Elster and Rune Slagstad (eds.), *Constitutionalism and Democracy* (Cambridge: Cambridge University Press, 1988).

—— 'Reconceiving Autonomy: Sources, Thoughts, and Possibilities' (1989) 1 *Yale Journal of Law and Feminism* 7.

—— *Private Property and the Limits of American Constitutionalism: The Madisonian Framework and Its Legacy* (Chicago, Ill.: University of Chicago Press, 1990).

—— 'Should Property Be Constitutionalized? A Relational and Comparative Approach', in G. E. van Maanen and A. J. van der Walt (eds.), *Property Law on the Threshold of the 21st Century* (Antwerp: Maklu, 1996).

NEUHAUS, RICHARD JOHN, 'Renting Women, Buying Babies and Class Struggles', originally published in *Society*, March/April 1988, 8, reprinted in Elizabeth Mensch and Alan Freeman (eds.), *Property Law: International Library of Essays in Law and Legal Theory* (New York: New York University Press, 1992), bk. ii.

NIEMEYER, GERHART, 'Public Interest and Private Utility', in Carl J. Friedrich (ed.), *Nomos V: The Public Interest* (New York: Atherton Press, 1962).

NINO, CARLOS, 'Introduction', in Carlos Nino (ed.), *Rights: International Library of Essays in Law and Legal Theory* (New York: New York University Press, 1992).

NOZICK, ROBERT, *Anarchy, State, and Utopia* (New York: Basic Books, Inc., 1974).

PAUL, JEREMY, 'The Hidden Structure of Takings Law' (1991) 64 *Southern California Law Review* 1393.

PENNER, J. E., *The Idea of Property in Law* (Oxford: Clarendon Press, 1997).

PENNOCK, J ROLAND, 'The One and the Many: A Note on the Concept', in Carl J. Friedrich (ed.), *Nomos V: The Public Interest* (New York: Atherton Press, 1962).

—— 'Thoughts on the Right to Private Property', in J. Roland Pennock and John W. Chapman (eds.), *Nomos XXII: Property* (New York: New York University Press, 1980).

PERRY, STEPHEN R., 'Libertarianism, Entitlement, and Responsibility' (1997) 26 *Philosophy and Public Affairs* 351.

PETERSON, ANDREA L., 'The Takings Clause: In Search of Underlying Principles (pt. 2)' (1990) 78 *California Law Review* 55.

PHILBRICK, FRANCIS S., 'Changing Conceptions of Property in Law' (1938) 86 *University of Pennsylvania Law Review* 691.

PILDES, RICHARD H., 'Why Rights Are Not Trumps: Social Meanings, Expressive Harms, and Constitutionalism' (1988) 27 *Journal of Legal Studies* 725.

POSNER, RICHARD A., *Economic Analysis of Law* (4th edn., Boston, Mass.: Little, Brown and Company, 1992).

RADIN, MARGARET JANE, 'Property and Personhood' (1982) 34 *Stanford Law Review* 957.

—— 'Market-Inalienability' (1987) 100 *Harvard Law Review* 1849.

—— 'The Liberal Conception of Property: Cross-Currents in the Jurisprudence of Takings' (1988) 88 *Columbia Law Review* 1667.

—— *Reinterpreting Property* (Chicago, Ill.: University of Chicago Press, 1993).

RAES, KOEN, 'Individualist Subjectivism and the World as Property: On the Interrelations Between Concepts of Value and Concepts of Ownership', in G. E. van Maanen and A. J. van der Walt (eds.), *Property Law on the Threshold of the 21st Century* (Antwerp: Maklu, 1996).

RAZ, JOSEPH, 'On the Nature of Rights' (1984) 93 *Mind* 194.

—— *The Morality of Freedom* (Oxford: Clarendon Press, 1986).

—— 'Rights and Individual Well-Being', in his *Ethics in the Public Domain: Essays in the Morality of Law and Politics* (Oxford: Clarendon Press, 1994).

REEVE, ANDREW, *Property* (Atlantic Highlands, N. J.: Humanities Press International, Inc., 1986).

REICH, CHARLES A., 'The New Property' (1964) 73 *Yale Law Journal* 733.

RIVARD, MICHAEL D., 'Toward a General Theory of Constitutional Personhood: A Theory of Constitutional Personhood for Transgenic Humanoid Species' (1992) 39 *University of California Los Angeles Law Review* 1425.

ROBERTSON, MICHAEL, 'Liberal, Democratic, and Socialist Approaches to the Public Dimensions of Private Property', in Janet McLean (ed.), *Property and the Constitution* (Oxford: Hart Publishing, 1999).

ROCHE, PATRICIA, '*Caveat Venditor*: Protecting Privacy and Ownership Interests in DNA', in Barth Maria Knoppers (ed.), *Human DNA: Law and Policy—International and Comparative Perspectives* (The Hague: Kluwer Law International, 1997).

ROSE, CAROL M., 'Preservation and Community: New Directions in the Law of Historic Preservation' (1981) 33 *Stanford Law Review* 473.

—— 'Possession as the Origin of Property' (1985) 52 *University of Chicago Law Review* 73.

—— 'Property as Wealth, Property as Propriety', in John W. Chapman (ed.), *Nomos XXXIII: Compensatory Justice* (New York: New York University Press, 1991).

—— 'Environmental Lessons' (1994) 27 *Loyola Los Angeles Law Review* 1023.

—— *Property and Persuasion: Essays on the History, Theory, and Rhetoric of Ownership* (Boulder, Colo.: Westview Press, 1994).

ROSE, CAROL M., 'A Dozen Propositions on Private Property, Public Rights, and the New Takings Legislation' (1996) 53 *Washington and Lee Law Review* 265.

—— 'Property Rights and Responsibilities', in Marian R. Chertow and Daniel C. Esty (eds.), *Thinking Ecologically: The Next Generation of Environmental Policy* (New Haven, Conn.: Yale University Press, 1997).

—— 'What Government Can Do for Property (and Vice Versa)', in Nicholas Mercuro and Warren J. Samuels (eds.), *The Fundamental Interrelationships Between Government and Property* (Stamford, Conn.: JAI Press, 1999).

RUBENFELD, JED, 'Usings' (1993) 102 *Yale Law Journal* 1077.

—— 'Affirmative Action' (1997) 107 *Yale Law Journal* 427.

SAMUEL, GEOFFREY, 'The Many Dimensions of Property', in Janet McLean (ed.), *Property and the Constitution* (Oxford: Hart Publishing, 1999).

SAX, JOSEPH L., 'Takings and the Police Power' (1964) 74 *Yale Law Journal* 36.

—— 'Takings, Private Property and Public Rights' (1971) *Yale Law Journal* 149.

—— 'Liberating the Public Trust Doctrine from Its Historical Shackles' (1980) 14 *University of California Davis Law Review* 185.

—— 'Some Thoughts on the Decline of Private Property' (1983) 58 *Washington Law Review* 481.

—— 'Heritage Preservation as a Public Duty: The Abbe Gregoire and the Origins of an Idea' (1990) 88 *Michigan Law Review* 1142.

—— *Playing Darts with a Rembrandt: Public and Private Rights in Cultural Treasures* (Ann Arbor, Mich.: University of Michigan Press, 1999).

SCANLON, T. M., 'Rights, Goods, and Fairness', in Stuart Hampshire (ed.), *Public and Private Morality* (Cambridge: Cambridge University Press, 1978).

SCHAUER, FREDERICK, 'A Comment on the Structure of Rights' (1993) 27 *Georgia Law Review* 415.

SEN, AMARTYA, 'Property and Hunger', originally published in (1988) 4 *Economics and Philosophy* 57, reprinted in Elizabeth Mensch and Alan Freeman (eds.), *Property Law: International Library of Essays in Law and Legal Theory* (New York: New York University Press, 1992), bk. i.

SIEGAN, BERNARD H., *Property and Freedom: The Constitution, the Courts, and Land-Use Regulation* (New Brunswick, N.J.: Transaction Publishers, 1997).

SINGER, JOSEPH WILLIAM, 'Sovereignty and Property' (1991) 86 *Northwestern Law Review* 1.

—— 'The Reliance Interest in Property', originally published in (1988) 40 *Stanford Law Review* 611, reprinted in Elizabeth Mensch and Alan Freeman (eds.), *Property Law: International Library of Essays in Law and Legal Theory* (New York: New York University Press, 1992), bk. i.

—— *The Edges of the Field: Lessons on the Obligations of Ownership* (Boston, Mass.: Beacon Press, 2000).

—— *Entitlement: The Paradoxes of Property* (New Haven, Conn.: Yale University Press, 2000).

—— and BEERMANN, JACK M., 'The Social Origins of Property' (1993) VI *Canadian Journal of Law and Jurisprudence* 217.

SÓLYOM, LÁSZLÓ, 'Introduction to the Decisions of the Constitutional Court of the Republic of Hungary', in László Sólyom and Georg Brunner (eds.), *Constitutional Judiciary in a New Democracy: The Hungarian Constitutional Court* (Ann Arbor, Mich.: University of Michigan Press, 2000).

SORAUF, FRANK J., 'The Conceptual Muddle', in Carl J. Friedrich (ed.), *Nomos V: The Public Interest* (New York: Atherton Press, 1962).

STEVENS, JAN S., 'The Public Trust: A Sovereign's Ancient Prerogative Becomes the People's Environmental Right' (1980) 14 *University of California Davis Law Review* 195.

SULLIVAN, EDWARD J., 'Substantive Due Process Resurrected Through the Takings Clause: *Nollan, Dolan,* and *Ehrlich*' (1995) 25 *Environmental Law* 155.

SUNSTEIN, CASS R., 'On Property and Constitutionalism' (1993) 14 *Cardozo Law Review* 907.

TREANOR, WILLIAM MICHAEL, 'The Origins and Original Significance of the Just Compensation Clause of the Fifth Amendment' (1985) 94 *Yale Law Journal* 694.

—— 'The *Armstrong* Principle, the Narratives of Takings, and Compensation Statutes' (1997) 38 *William and Mary Law Review* 1151.

UNDERKUFFLER, LAURA S., 'On Property: An Essay', originally published in (1990) 100 *Yale Law Journal* 127, reprinted in Elizabeth Mensch and Alan Freeman (eds.), *Property Law: International Library of Essays in Law and Legal Theory* (New York: New York University Press, 1992), bk. i.

—— 'The Perfidy of Property' (1991) 70 *Texas Law Review* 293.

VAN DER WALT, A. J., 'Subject and Society in Property Theory—A Review of Property Theories and Debates in Recent Literature: Part I', 1995–2 *Journal of South African Law* 322.

—— 'Property Rights, Land Rights, and Environmental Rights', in Dawid van Wyk, John Dugard, Bertus de Villiers, and Dennis Davis (eds.), *Rights and Constitutionalism: The New South African Legal Order* (Oxford: Clarendon Press, 1996).

—— *The Constitutional Property Clause: A Comparative Analysis of Section 25 of the South African Constitution of 1996* (Kenwyn: Juta and Company, Ltd., 1997).

—— 'Un-doing Things With Words: The Colonisation of the Public Sphere by Private-Property Discourse', in Graham Bradfield and Derek van der Merwe (eds.), *'Meaning' in Legal Interpretation* (Kenwyn: Juta and Company, Ltd., 1998).

—— 'The Constitutional Property Clause: Striking a Balance Between Guarantee and Limitation', in Janet McLean (ed.), *Property and the Constitution* (Oxford: Hart Publishing, 1999).

—— *Constitutional Property Clauses: A Comparative Analysis* (Cape Town: Juta and Company, Ltd., 1999).

—— 'Dancing With Codes—Protecting, Developing and Deconstructing Property Rights in a Constitutional State' (2001) 118 *South African Law Journal* 258.

WALDRON, JEREMY, 'Can Communal Goods Be Human Rights?' (1987) 28 *Archives Européennes de Sociologie* 296.

—— *The Right to Private Property* (Oxford: Clarendon Press, 1988).

—— 'Property Law', in Dennis Patterson (ed.), *A Companion to Philosophy of Law and Legal Theory* (Cambridge, Mass.: Blackwell Publishers, 1996).

—— 'Property, Honesty, and Normative Resilience', in Stephen R. Munzer (ed.), *New Essays in the Legal and Political Theory of Property* (Cambridge: Cambridge University Press, 2001).

WELLMAN, CARL, 'Upholding Legal Rights', originally published in (1975) 86 *Ethics* 49, reprinted in Carlos Nino (ed.), *Rights: International Library of Essays in Law and Legal Theory* (New York: New York University Press, 1992).

WILLIAMS, JOAN, 'The Rhetoric of Property' (1998) 83 *Iowa Law Review* 277.

WILLIAMS, PATRICIA, 'Spirit-Murdering the Messenger: The Discourse of Fingerpointing as the Law's Response to Racism' (1987) 42 *University of Miami Law Review* 127.
WOODWARD, BEVERLY, 'The Computer-Based Patient Record and Confidentiality' (1995) 333 *New England Journal of Medicine* 1419.

Index